Palgrave Macmillan Studies in Banking and Financial Institutions

Series Editor

Philip Molyneux
Bangor University, UK

Aim of the Series

The Palgrave Macmillan Studies in Banking and Financial Institutions series is international in orientation and includes studies of banking systems in particular countries or regions as well as contemporary themes such as Islamic Banking, Financial Exclusion, Mergers and Acquisitions, Risk Management, and IT in Banking. The books focus on research and practice and include up to date and innovative studies that cover issues which impact banking systems globally.

More information about this series at
http://www.springer.com/series/14678

Santiago Carbó Valverde • Pedro Jesús Cuadros Solas •
Francisco Rodríguez Fernández
Editors

Bank Funding, Financial Instruments and Decision-Making in the Banking Industry

palgrave
macmillan

Editors
Santiago Carbó Valverde
Bangor University, UK

Pedro Jesús Cuadros Solas
University of Granada, Spain

Francisco Rodríguez Fernández
University of Granada, Spain

Palgrave Macmillan Studies in Banking and Financial Institutions
ISBN 978-3-319-80869-7 ISBN 978-3-319-30701-5 (eBook)
DOI 10.1007/978-3-319-30701-5

Softcover reprint of the hardcover 1st edition 2016

Printed on acid-free paper

This Palgrave Macmillan imprint is published by Springer Nature
The registered company is Springer International Publishing AG Switzerland

Acknowledgements

First and foremost we would like to thank all our contributors, whose biographies are provided in this volume, without which this edited book would not have been possible.

Also we want to express our gratitude to all the participants of the 2015 Wolpertinger Conference organized by the European Association of University Teachers of Banking and Finance in September 2015 for their insightful comments about all the papers included in this volume.

We would also like to show our gratitude to Professor Philip Molyneux (Professor of Banking and Finance and Dean of the College of Business, Law, Education and Social Sciences), Editor-in-Chief for the Palgrave Macmillan Studies in Banking and Financial Institution Series, for approving our book proposal and for his support during the process.

Also many thanks to the Palgrave Macmillan team, Aimee Dibbens and Alexandra Morton, for their support during the publishing process.

Contents

Notes on Contributors

Editors and ContributorsFederico Beltrame is Lecturer in Banking and Finance at the Department of Economics and Statistics, University of Udine, where he teaches corporate finance. He graduated in Economics at the University of Udine and received his PhD in Business Science from the same University. His main research interests are related to SMEs' cost of capital, banks capital structure, and mutual guarantee credit institutions.

Gianni Brighetti is an Associate Professor of Cognitive Psychology at the Department of Psychology, University of Bologna, Italy. His research interests are in the field of assessment, diagnosis and cognitive-behavioural therapy of anxiety-related and cognitive-emotional disturbances in personality disorders, and drug-addiction. Recently his research interests have turned also to the psychological aspects of decision-making in the field of financial investments with reference to economic choices and savings (gianni.brighetti@unibo.it).

Santiago Carbó-Valverde is Professor of Economics and Finance at the Bangor University (United Kingdom). He holds a Bsc in Economics from the University of Valencia. He holds a PhD in Economics and an Msc in Banking and Finance from the University of Wales, Bangor, (United Kingdom). He was Professor of Economics at the University of Granada (Spain). He is Director of the Financial Services Studies of Spanish Savings Banks Association (FUNCAS). He is researcher at the Institute of Economics Research of Valencia (Ivie). He is President of the Rating Committee of Axexor. He is an independent advisor of Cecabank. He is President of Game Stores Iberia. He has been a collaborator and advisor of the European Central Bank, the Federal Reserve Bank of Chicago, some financial institutions such as BMN, and internationally prestigious firms. He has published in internationally prestigious journals in economics and finance such as the *European Economic Review*, the *Review of Finance*, the *Journal of Money, Credit and Banking*, *Review of Economics and Statistics*, the *Journal of International Money and Finance*, and the *Journal of Banking and Finance*. He has been a speaker in International Conferences and Seminars at the G-20 forum, as well as in several Central Banks Conferences.

Cristiana Cardi is a PhD Candidate in Management at Università Politecnica delle Marche, Ancona, Italy. She teaches financial intermediation at Università Niccolò Cusano, Rome, Italy. Her research interests involve initial public offerings and behavioral finance, with a focus on the effects of psychological biases on investment choices.

Giusy Chesini is Associate Professor of Banking and Finance at the University of Verona, Italy, where she specializes in the structure and regulation of international financial markets. Her main research topics include the stock exchange industry, the evolution of financial systems, banking and risk management. She often participates in Italian and international conferences and she has written numerous paper and books on the above subjects.

Helen Chiappini is a Ph.D. Candidate with grant research in Management, Banking and Commodity Sciences, curricula Banking and Finance, at Sapienza University of Rome. She is a member of different research and consulting teams both in national and international contexts. Her main research interests relates to social impact investing, microfinance and measurability of social impact.

Pedro Jesús Cuadros-Solas is Lecturer in Economics and researcher in Banking and Finance at the University of Granada (Spain). He holds a Bsc in Business Management and Law from the University of Jaén (Spain) as well as an Msc in Economics from the University of Granada (Spain). He is member of the Department of Economic Theory and History at the University of Granada. He has been visiting scholar at the Bangor Business School (Wales, United Kingdom) and also the University of St. Andrews (Scotland, United Kingdom). His main researches interests lie in the area of Banking and Finance, especially in corporate finance, securitization, underwriting and the role of reputation for banks, and non-financial firms in the capital markets.

Alberto Dreassi is Associate Professor in Banking and Finance at the University of Trieste. His main research areas include regulation and supervision of financial intermediaries, and insurance and bank accounting.

Giulia Giansiracusa studied cognitive psychology at Bologna University, where she graduated in 2014. Her masters' dissertation, in partnership with Heidelberg University under the supervision of Professor Joachim Funke, investigated the relationship between perspective memory and intertemporal-choices and the related cultural differences. Her research area focuses on mental time traveling and decision-making (giuliagiansi@yahoo.it).

Elisa Giaretta is a research fellow at the University of Verona, Italy, where she received a PhD degree. She works in the "Polo Scientifico e Didattico di Studi sull'Impresa", an academic center focused on the analyses of Italian enterprises. Research topics include asset management companies, private equity, firm networks, and bank risks. She has participated in Italian and international conferences on these subjects.

Krzysztof Kil is Assistant Professor of Banking and Finance at the Cracow University of Economics, Faculty of Finance, Poland. His research concentrates on the issues of bank stability and bank efficiency in Central and Eastern Europe.

Mario La Torre is Full Professor in Banking and Finance at the University of Rome "La Sapienza". His main research areas are banking and financial innovation, ethical finance, impact finance and microfinance, audiovisual and art financing. He is editor of the series "*Studies in Impact Finance*" published by Palgrave Macmillan. His main international publications include: *Microcredit Securitization*, in "Bank Stability, Sovereign Debt and Derivatives", *Social Lending in Europe: Structures, Regulation and Pricing Models*, in "Crisis, Risk and Stability in Financial Markets", *Asset-Backed Securitization and Financial Stability: the Downgrading Delay Effect*, in "Banks Performance Risk and *Firm Financing, Banks in the Microfinance Market*, in "Frontiers of Banks in a Global Economy". He is currently member of the taskforce on Social Impact Investments established by the G8 countries, member of the Board of the Italian National Body for Microcredit, and member of the Audiovisual Working Party at the European Commission. He has been member of the Board of Directors of Cinecittà Holding and Counsellor of the Minister of Culture. He has been member of the consultative group for the definition of the Italian Microcredit Law and lawmaker of the Italian Tax Credit Law for the film industry.

Caterina Lucarelli is an Associate Professor of Banking and Financial Markets at the Department of Management, University Politecnica Marche- Italy. Her research interests are in the fields of market microstructure and investors behaviour. Since 2007, as National Coordinator of a Research Project supported by the Italian Ministry of University and Research, she has studied issues relating to individual risk tolerance. As part of this work she has developed several research streams focusing on behavior under uncertainty, moving from financial topics (portfolio theory and risk tolerance assessments) to insurance and consumers' behavior (c.lucarelli@univpm.it).

Nicoletta Marinelli is an Assistant Professor of Banking and Financial Markets at the Department of Economics and Law, University of Macerata,Italy. Her main academic interests are in the area of investors' behavior, from both the perspectives of individual and institutional investors. Individual investors have been studied with a specific focus on their risk tolerance assessment and the related impact upon financial choices as well as insurance decisions. Institutional investors have been investigated as a broad category or individually defined types (for example, sovereign wealth funds) with a specific attention to their effect upon firm value (nicoletta.marinelli@unimc.it).

Camilla Mazzoli is an Assistant Professor of Financial Intermediation at the Department of Management, Università Politecnica delle Marche, Ancona, Italy. She teaches financial intermediation, trading, and insurance. Her research interests involve behavioral finance issues, such as financial risk tolerance and investors' behavior, initial public offerings, and market microstructure.

Stefano Miani is Full Professor of Banking and Insurance at the Department of Economics and Statistics, University of Udine. Recent research topics include pension funds and pension systems, the regulation and monitoring of insurance companies, and the regulation of financial markets and intermediaries.

Ewa Miklaszewska is Professor in Banking and Finance at the Cracow University of Economics, Faculty of Finance, where she chairs the Banking Division. She is the Associate Professor of Economics at the Jagiellonian University in Cracow, Department of Management and Public Communication. She has held several visiting positions in foreign universities and Polish financial regulatory institutions. Her research interests focus on bank regulation and bank strategies.

Andrea Paltrinieri is Assistant Professor of Banking and Finance Insurance at the Department of Economics and Statistics, University of Udine. Research topics include, Islamic Finance, financial markets in emerging countries, asset management and institutional investors, with a particular focus on sovereign wealth funds.

Daniele Previtali is post-doc fellow and lecturer at Luiss Guido Carli University (Rome, Italy). He holds a Ph.D. in banking and finance from the University of

Rome "Tor Vergata". In 2012 he has been visiting PhD at Stern School of Business (New York, USA). His main research interests concern banks valuation and banks capital structure. He also works as a consultant for a professional studio which is involved in strategy advice for banks and other financial intermediaries.

Francisco Rodríguez-Fernández is Professor of Economics at the University of Granada (Spain). He holds a Bsc in Business and Economics from the University of Granada. He holds a PhD in Economics from the University of Granada. He is Senior Economist at the Spanish Savings Banks Foundation (FUNCAS). He has spent time as visiting scholar at the University of Modena, the Bangor Business School, and the Federal Reserve Bank of Chicago. He is the consultant of several prestigious institutions namely the European Commission, the European Research Framework Programme, the Spanish Ministry of Labour, KPMG or Euro 6000. His research work has been published in internationally prestigious journals in economics and finance such as the *European Economic Review*, the *Review of Finance*, the *Journal of Money, Credit and Banking*, *Review of Economics and Statistics*, the *Journal of International Money and Finance*, and the *Journal of Banking and Finance*. His main research interests lie in the economics of banking, banking regulation, finance and economic growth, industrial organization, and payment instruments.

Alex Sclip is Ph.D. student in Banking and Finance at the Department of Economics and Statistics, University of Udine. His main research topics include insurance and asset management.

Sabrina Severini is a PhD Student in Economics at Università Politecnica delle Marche, Ancona, Italy. She is interested in financial economics, with a particular focus on the effects of initial public offerings on the cost of capital.

List of Figures

List of Tables

1

Introduction

Santiago Carbó-Valverde, Pedro J. Cuadros-Solas, and Francisco Rodríguez-Fernández

With this book, we aim to enrich the banking and finance literature, providing insight into new research topics which are being undertaken in the aftermath of the financial crisis. In this sense, the main purpose of the researches included in this volume is to span all the major research fields in finance and banking.

This book is divided into different chapters that cover a selection of some of the most recent research studies on banking and finance. These studies are carried out by a selection of academics from a range of prestigious European universities and research institutions. All these investigations have benefited from being discussed during the 2015 Wolpertinger

---

S. Carbó-Valverde
Bangor University, Bangor, UK

P.J. Cuadros-Solas (✉) • F. Rodríguez-Fernández
Universidad de Granada, Granada, Spain
e-mail: pjcuadros@ugr.es

S. Carbó Valverde et al. (eds.), *Bank Funding, Financial Instruments and Decision-Making in the Banking Industry*, Palgrave Macmillan Studies in Banking and Financial Institutions,
DOI 10.1007/978-3-319-30701-5_1

Conference organized by the European Association of University Teachers of Banking and Finance, held in September 2015.

Nowadays, the finance literature is specially focused on the implications of post- banking crisis developments. However, after the financial crisis, the current research lines in banking and finance are quite broad. In this volume we have aimed to reflect some of these lines, including outstanding papers dealing with interesting issues. According to our selected title the research topics covered in this volume can be structured into different blocks:

- **Bank funding**
- Banks needs to finance their activity, and the cost of funding affects a range of economic variables with important implications for both monetary and financial stability. Several aspects of bank funding are covered in this volume. In particular we look at how issuers are matched with reputable underwriters in debt markets and whether earnings management are likely to affect banks' cost of funding. Furthermore, bank enterprise lending is studied using bank-specific, macroeconomics and structural variables
- **Financial instruments**
- The greater use of financial instruments and the development of sophisticated financial techniques during the pre-crisis period are also covered in this volume. In this sense, together with IPOs financial instruments like sukuks and corporate bonds are studied from different perspectives. Beside this, microfinance investment vehicles (MIVs), listed on the market and identified as "impact investments-oriented", are also examined analyzing if they are compliant with the recent definition of social impact investment suggested by OECD.
- The relationship between new financial instruments and the importance of the funding gap is also addressed. The situation in which companies, because of market imperfections, do not get the amount of capital that they would get in an efficient market has important implications for their financial stability.

- **Decision-Making in the Banking Industry**
- Acknowledging that intertemporal people decisions are not rational and that irrationality interferes with long-range financial decision-making; our study possesses an examination about the role of episodic prospection in long-range financial decisions.
- Furthermore, the rationality behind the different characteristics of dividend policies is also investigated using as sample data the policies of listed companies in the main European markets during the last 15 years.

The second chapter, "Does earnings management affect banks' cost of funding? An empirical investigation across an European sample", by Federico Beltrame, Daniele Previtali and Alex Slip investigates how loan loss provisions are used discretionally to smooth earnings, manage capital requirements, and increase the stock market valuation. As managers' discretionary behavior might have a negative effect, they study its impact on the cost of funding. Their findings suggest that the discretionary usage of provisioning affects the cost of funding, due to the increase of the overall risk of the bank.

Chapter 3, "Volatility linkages and co-movements between international stocks and the sukuk market" by Alberto Dreassi, Stefano Miani, Andrea Paltrinieri and Alex Sclip examines the volatility behavior and the co-movements between *sukuk* and international stock indexes. They provide evidence of lower correlations between *sukuk* and US and EU stock markets as well as strong volatility linkages between *sukuk* and regional market indexes during financial crisis. These higher volatility linkages and dynamic correlations during financial crises show that *sukuks* are hybrid instruments positioned between bonds and equity.

In Chap. 4, "Bank-specific, macroeconomic or structural variables: which explains bank enterprise lending? The evidence from transition countries" by Ewa Miklaszewska and Krzysztof Kil analyze trends in lending policies in Central and Eastern Europe (CEE). They argue in favor of a greater importance for the macroeconomic environment, an increasing scale, and the universal profile of banks in the structure of banks' loan portfolios.

Chapter 5, "The reputable underwriting matching in corporate bond issuances: Evidence for non-financial bonds", by the editors Santiago Carbó-Valverde, Pedro J. Cuadros-Solas and Francisco Rodríguez-Fernández provides an insight into the role of the underwriter's reputation in debt markets, analyzing the bonds features by underwriter reputation. We present an overview of the corporate bonds markets in Europe during 2007–2013 which argues in favour of the existence of differences in bond terms (bond size, maturity, callability and collateralization) by underwriters' reputation. Our findings confirm that firms and underwriters are not randomly matched in debt markets; underwriters' reputation plays a role in the bond design.

In Chap. 6, "New financing instruments to bridge the funding gap: The lesson from Italy", by Elisa Giaretta and Giusy Chesini analyzes the funding gap evaluating mini-bonds and companies' networks as two alternative funding instruments to bank debt. Using the data of Italian companies they suggest that mini-bonds' issuers present better financial structures compared with networked companies to the detriment of the cost of financing on companies' revenues.

The next chapter, "Microfinance investment vehicles: How far are they from OECD social impact investment definition?" by Mario La Torre and Helen Chiappini studies Microfinance impact investments from the OECD social impact investment definition. Applying a content analysis they are able to demonstrate that there is still much to do in order to "mind the gap" between MIVs management approach and the OECD definition.

Chapter 8, "Intellectual capital disclosure and IPO results: Is it a matter of classification?" by Cristiana Cardi, Camilla Mazzoli and Sabrina Severini, analyzes the effects produced by Intellectual Capital (IC) disclosure on the IPO results. Applying two different IC classifications they argue that the effects of IC disclosure on the IPO results are comprehensively consistent across the different IC classifications, although some differences emerge. This study makes clear, for listing firms, the great benefits deriving from the proper disclosure of their non-financial assets, to investors.

Chapter 9, "The drivers of dividend policies in Europe", also by Giusy Chesini and Elisa Giaretta, study which dividend policies theories drive the distribution of dividends for listed companies traded on the main European markets. Many drivers of companies' dividend policies are still present while the agency cost theory does not explain European dividend policy. In this chapter, they provide evidence that pecking order theory, signaling theory and bird-in-the-hand theory complementarily explain dividends' payments.

The final chapter, "Long-range financial decision-making: the role of episodic prospection", by Gianni Brighetti, Caterina Lucarelli, Nicoletta Marinelli and Giulia Giansiracusa, analyzes time-inconsistent preferences when making intertemporal choices for monetary rewards. The authors argue that temporal discounting is sensitive to the type of prospection involved. Their results suggest that episodic prospection might attenuate intertemporal choice inefficiencies, when in the form of hyperbolic discounting. This was found to be particularly true if the solicited scenario referred to a primary need (a first priority).

2

Does Earnings Management Affect Banks' Cost of Funding? An Empirical Investigation Across an European Sample

Federico Beltrame, Daniele Previtali, and Alex Sclip

1 Introduction

Banks' managers use accruals such as loan loss provisioning (Anandarajan et al. 2003, 2007; Curcio e Hasan 2015; DeBoskey and Jiang 2012; Dong et al. 2012; Kanagaretnam et al. 2003; Liu and Wahlen 1997; Ma 1988; Pérez et al. 2008; Wahlen 1994) and the timing of securities' gains and losses (Cornett et al. 2009), to adjust earnings to meet stakeholders' and analysts' expectations. But managers' discretionary behavior through accruals—in particular loan loss provisions (LLPs)—might have considerable effects on a bank's level of risk as well Bhat (1996). As a matter of

F. Beltrame • A. Sclip
University of Udine, Udine, Italy

D. Previtali (✉)
Luiss Guido Carli University, Rome, Italy
e-mail: dprevitali@luiss.it

S. Carbó Valverde et al. (eds.), *Bank Funding, Financial Instruments and Decision-Making in the Banking Industry*, Palgrave Macmillan Studies in Banking and Financial Institutions,
DOI 10.1007/978-3-319-30701-5_2

fact, accruals might hide on the one hand, latent profits generally used to smooth earnings over time, but on the other hand, relevant potential losses.

The extant literature has widely investigated how earnings management are used by banks as an incentive for income smoothing (among others: Ma 1988; Greenwalt et al. 1988), capital management (among others: Anandarajan et al. 2003; Pérez et al. 2008; Curcio and Hasan 2015) and stock market valuation (among others: Beaver et al. 1989; Wahlen 1994). However the literature has just focused on incentives of earnings management, but has not still investigated whether there might be a "disincentive effect" on managers' discretionary behavior.

In this paper, we test whether the discretionary behavior of banks' managers might have a negative effect on banks' cost of funding (that is our "disincentive effect") and, therefore, on their future earnings.

We argue that the discretionary usage of accruals, instead of having a general positive effect on earnings, might conversely, in the medium and long-term period, have a negative impact on interest expenses reducing future net interest margins. This might happen because markets might be able to read the implicit level of hidden profits or losses of loan portfolio and securities through the managers' disclosure and company's financial statements, making costly an over-discretionary usage of accruals (Francis et al. 2005). However debt and equity markets might be very different in terms of the reaction-time to earnings management.

Existing literature has already shown that equity investors react positively to unexpected higher provisions (Beaver et al. 1989; Wahlen 1994). And such an effect is even stronger for the discretionary component of accruals (Beaver and Engel 1996) and for those banks characterized by a lower financial solidity (Liu and Wahlen 1997). Therefore, positive reaction towards an unexpected higher provision might mean that equity investors consider as good news the reduction of the hidden risks in the credit portfolio. They might feel that they are not able to discount the discretionary component of earnings management before it is communicated to the markets.

Conversely, in the Debt capital market, Rating agencies (in the primary market) and Credit Default Swap (CDS) spread, immediately transfer potential higher risks in the pricing. Consequently, *ceteris paribus*, it is likely that the higher the level of the discretionary component of earnings management, the higher should be the cost of funding. The aim of our paper is to extend the literature on banks' earnings management testing whether banks' manager behavior might have a negative effect on earnings due to the increase of the cost of funding.

Following prior researches which highlighted the scarce explanatory power of realized security gains and losses as accruals (Beatty et al. 1995, 2002; Cornett et al. 2009), we calculated the discretionary component of LLPs as a proxy of earnings management and we analyze the relationship between funding cost—that we measured as the yearly average CDS—and earnings management. We ran our panel regression model on 369 observations taken from a sample of European banks in a time range from 2005 (that is the IAS/IFRS introduction) to 2013.

We found that, after having made adjustments for specific financial statements' variables and macroeconomic effects, discretionary behavior of banks' managers has a positive, statistically significant, influence on the cost of funding. Therefore, earnings management have a negative impact on interest expenses, reducing the expected net interest margin, and the overall value of the company. This suggests that the earnings management incentives to meet stakeholders' expectations can actually transfer economic margins from shareholders to debtholders increasing the overall risk of the bank.

The paper is organized as follows: Sect. 2 provides the conceptual development, Sect. 3 defines our research methods, Sect. 4 describes our data and sample period, Sects. 5 and 6 provide results and concluding remarks respectively.

2 Conceptual Development

2.1 Earnings Management: A Definition

Earnings management can be generally defined as an action to alter financial reports and mislead stakeholders on economic performance fundamentals that managers put in place, using their own judgment in reporting financial data and composite transactions (Schipper 1989; Prencipe 2006).

From an accounting point of view, earnings management is defined as the strategic exploitation of discretion spaces inherent in the preparation of financial statements, in order to obtain personal benefits or other special purposes (Healy and Wahlem 1999). Generally, the magnitude of earnings management actions is measured by analyzing the portion of the discretionary accruals, which can be defined as the proportion of income that is not turned into cash flow (Dechow and Dichev 2002).

The extant literature has highlighted that earnings management basically occurs by manipulating specific accruals. Several papers investigated how banks' managers handle earnings through loan loss provisioning (Anandarajan et al. 2003, 2007; Curcio e Hasan 2015; DeBoskey and Jiang 2012; Dong et al. 2012; Kanagaretnam et al. 2003; Liu and Wahlen 1997; Ma 1988; Pérez et al. 2008; Wahlen 1994) and the timing of securities' gains and losses (Cornett et al. 2009).

2.2 Incentives to Earnings Manipulation

Previous findings suggest a list of three main incentives to earnings manipulation in the banking industry: income smoothing, capital management, and signaling effect.

With regard to income smoothing, preliminary results provided by Ma (1988) and Greenwalt et al. (1988), claim that bank managers are inclined to manage earnings in relation to both the trend of the economic cycle and the general performance of the company. In this way, managers' smooth reported earnings over time making them compliant to stakeholders' expectations independently from the specific condition (Anandarajan et al. 2003, 2007; Liu and Ryan 1995, Liu and Wahlen 1997; Pérez et al. 2008). Hence, the executives have an incentive to maintain and convey shareholders' approval on their management, reinforcing their relationship with the owners and thus, reducing the probability of being fired from the company. In addition, since executive pay is, for the most part, linked to the economic results and stock market performance, managing earnings contributes to stabilizing managers' income even during periods of downturn.

The second incentive to earnings management in banking is represented by capital management. In particular, discretionary provisioning—

basically realized through LLPs—leads to mitigation of regulation costs with the aim of increasing the capital adequacy ratio (Beatty et al. 1995; Moyer 1990). More specifically, managers have been using accruals in LLPs, in order to prevent the falling of the capital adequacy ratio below the minimum desired (and required) level. As a matter of fact, LLPs were totally (before the Basel regulation) taken into consideration as a source of capital. However, at the time when the Basel accord came into play, LLPs could no longer be included in Tier 1 capital, but only for a small portion of Tier 2. Thus, after the Basel accord, LLPs management no longer has a significant effect on the capital adequacy ratio adjustment both in the U.S. (Ahmed et al. 1999; Kim and Kross 1998), and in the EU banking sector (among others: Anandarajan et al. 2003; Curcio and Hasan 2015; Pérez et al. 2008).

The third incentive of earnings management is represented by the signaling hypothesis that happens when managers disclose to equity markets unexpected adjustments on provisioning. Findings show that banks with higher LLPs are associated with higher market to book ratios (Beaver et al. 1989) and higher abnormal returns (Wahlen 1994). Both studies conclude that investors view positively unexpected increases in LLPs, independently of the bank's financial condition. In these terms, Liu and Ryan (1995) concluded that an increase in LLP is good news, only for banks that the market perceives to have considerable loan default problems; if a bank possesses virtuous loan portfolio quality, no significant stock market reaction occurs. In conflict to these previous results, Ahmed et al. (1999) asserts that LLPs were not used as a tool for signaling, due to the specific period examined in the study.

By dividing the LLP into the discretionary and non-discretionary component, Beaver and Engel (1996) found that the market assigned different prices to each component; the upturn of the discretionary component is viewed as good news. Moreover Liu and Wahlen (1997) claims that the good news signaled through the discretionary LLPs are more prominent for banks with low regulatory capital requirements and loan default problems.

Finally, according to Kanagaretnam et al. (2005) the propensity to signal through LLPs varies negatively with bank size, and positively with earnings variability and investment opportunity. The propensity is also greater when banks are undervalued by the market. Managers in this case attempt to raise their banks' market value by communicating their favorable inside information to market participants (Kanagaretnam and Lobo 2004).

On the whole, the empirical evidence on the signaling effect has highlighted that investors price positively unexpected higher provisions and therefore, react positively when banks disclose and reduce the risk of their credit portfolio. Thus the market incentive of earnings management is due to the positive stock market reaction for unexpected provisioning.

2.3 Earnings Manipulation and Banks' Risks

The empirical evidence about the incentives of earnings management in banking show that while it is aimed at meeting stakeholders' expectations, it might also increase the level of outstanding risk of a bank. As a matter of fact, Bhat (1996) discovered that banks managing earnings through LLPs are characterized by lower growth; lower book to assets ratios, higher loans to deposit ratios, higher leverage, and lower return on assets.

With regards to the income smoothing effect, which is aimed at stabilizing earnings over time, it might raise risks for investors, depending on the managers' risk propensity (Fonseca and González 2008; Kanagaretnam et al. 2003). In particular, the outstanding risk will be proportional to the strategy of unrealized earnings accumulation or distribution in relation to the economic cycle. Other things being equal, managers that distribute unrealized earnings during periods of downturns expose the bank to higher risks, while those accumulating reserves will show lower earnings, but will be much safer. On the whole, the income smoothing effect can help managers to meet expectations, but expose banks to higher future risks.

With regard to the capital management incentive, empirical evidence has shown that provisions are no longer considered as a means to raising capital adequacy after the Basel regulation came into play (Ahmed et al. 1999; Anandarajan et al. 2003; Curcio and Hasan 2015; Kim and Kross 1998; Pérez et al. 2008). Under Basel II, LLPs can be included in the Tier 2 capital according to the bank usage of standard or internal ratings based approach. If the bank employs a standard approach, the regulatory framework foresees that LLPs can be included up to the limit of 1.25% of the RWAs. For those which have an internal rating model, banks must compare the expected credit losses with the total provisions. When expected credit losses are higher than total provisions, banks deduct the difference (50% from Tier 1 capital and 50% from Tier 2 capital). On the contrary, when total provisions are greater than expected losses, the difference can be computed as Tier 2 capital, up to the maximum of 0.6% of credit risk weighted assets (RWAs). Such limitations in computing provisions as a source of capital have had an important effect on the capital management incentive for earnings management. What was firstly an incentive to earnings management in the banking sector; has now become a disincentive. In fact, higher provisioning considerably affects earnings reduction, without contributing to the enhancement of the stakeholders' view on bank management. In other words, this suggests that the limitations on computing provisions as regulatory capital introduced within the Basel framework have had resulted in increasing the risk of the credit portfolio.

2.4 Research Question

From the literature already discussed, we can argue that researchers have been concerned with analyzing the incentive effects of earnings management, but it have not yet investigated the "disincentive effect" that might be linked to discretionary accruals management in the banking sector. In particular, this "disincentive effect" might be linked to the negative aspects related to hidden risks in the income smoothing and capital management strategy.

In order to capture the negative effects of banks' accruals management, we use the corporate bond market, where rating agencies and CDS spread incorporate the value of potential risks. We anticipate that the higher the level of the discretionary component of earnings management, the higher should be the cost of funding.

Following prior researches which highlighted the limited explanatory power of using realized security gains and losses as accruals (Beatty et al. 1995, 2002; Cornett et al. 2009), we calculated the discretionary component of

LLPs as a proxy of earnings management and we analyzed the relationship between funding cost—that we measured as the yearly average CDS—and earnings management. Therefore the research question we answered in this paper is: *does earnings management affect the cost of funding of banks?*

3 Research Methods

3.1 Discretionary Component of LLPs

To formally test the earnings management effect on the cost of funding, we first start our analysis by measuring the discretionary component of the LLPs and, then run a regression that presents the cost of funding as the dependent variable and discretionary LLPs as one among the explanatory variables.

Following prior studies (Ahmed et al. 1999; Balboa et al. 2013; Leaven and Majnoni 2003), in the first regression, we tested the relationship of LLPs and a set of banks characteristics and macroeconomic variables. More precisely, we assumed that the relative level of LLPs obeys the following regression model:

$$\begin{aligned} LLP_{i,t} = {} & \alpha_t + \beta_1 \text{size}_{i,t} + \beta_2 NPL_{i,t} + \beta_3 LLR_{i,t} + \beta_4 \text{Tier 1}_{i,t} \\ & + \beta_5 GDPgrowth_t + \varepsilon_{it} \end{aligned} \tag{2.1}$$

Where:

- i represents the bank identifier;
- t is the year (from 2005 to 2013);
- α_i represents bank-specific effects that are constant over time but vary across banks;
- *LLP* measures total loan loss provision scaled by the bank's assets;
- *Size* the natural log of total assets to control for potential size effects;
- *NPL* gauges Non-Performing Loans to total assets, as a proxy for credit risk exposure;
- *LLR* represent the total loan loss allowance as a percentage of total assets;

- *Tier 1* is Tier 1 capital ratio of the bank, and proxies for the level of solvency of banks;
- *GDP* growth measures change in GDP per capita, as a proxy for the general economic condition and business cycle dynamics;
- ε_{it} stands for the error term.

The LLPs discretionary component is the error term from the previous regression formula.

We make the following comments for Eq. (2.1). Notwithstanding that our sample is composed of the major European banks, we take account of potential size effects by including the logarithm of total assets. We have no prior expectations about the relationship between size and LLPs. According to Hakanes and Schnabel (2011), larger banks may be able to provide better credit risk diversification (negative relationship) and, on the other hand, the larger size would require additional provisions and capital buffers due to the major outstanding risks.

The variables NPL, LLR are bank- specific controls that proxy the credit quality conditions, which have a relevancy to the non-discretionary component of the LLPs. Provisions, can be viewed as a capital buffer against credit losses, so we expected a positive sign from these credit quality variables and the LLPs. As a matter of fact, usually banks' managers increase provisions when credit risk worsens and reduce them when credit quality improves.

The level of Tier 1 ratio controls for the level of regulatory capital: Recent findings (among others Anandarajan et al. 2003; Curcio and Hasan 2015; Pérez et al. 2008) do not highlight a significant relationship between Tier 1 ratio and earnings management via LLPs. We expect a negative sign due to the fact that banks that need Tier 1 capital do not have incentives to retain earnings through the LLPs.

Finally we add a macroeconomic variable as a proxy to economic conditions and the business cycle dynamics, in order to take into account the pro-cyclical effect of the LLPs asserted by Bikker and Metzemakers (2005).

3.2 The Cost of Funding

According to Babihuga and Spaltro (2014), a bank cost of funding can be quantified as the marginal cost of the unsecured funds, and therefore we can refer to the credit default premium, that is the CDS spread. In particular, we measured the cost of funding as a combination of the sum of the five years CDS premium and the three-month Euribor/Libor rate.

On this basis, several studies tried to check whether CDS spread reflected the effect of the most common variables used to measure the default risk of the financial intermediaries. In general, all the empirical models using the CDS premium separated the pre-crises and crisis period highlighting the higher explanatory power of accounting-created variables in the financial crisis (Annaert et al. 2013; Casu and Chiaramonte 2013; Samaniego-Medina et al. 2013). Following the previous studies, the explanatory variables most-used, can be classified as: country-specific market variables (e.g. equity returns), macroeconomic variables (e.g. market returns), liquidity variables (e.g. bid-ask and bid-off spread) and accounting variables (e.g. leverage). Empirical results showed that market variables, both those country-specific and macroeconomic, have a great impact on CDS spread. Equity returns and market returns are negatively related and equity volatility is positively related to CDS (Samaniego-Medina et al. 2013). Conversely, the liquidity position is negative correlated to CDS spread both before and after the crisis (Annaert et al. 2013). The only significant accounting variables in the pre-crisis period are the asset quality measures, and in particular, loan loss reserves to gross loans, while in the post-crisis period, both loan loss reserve to gross loans and liquidity were significant (Casu and Chiaramonte 2013). Despite the evidence of these previous studies about the limited explanatory power of leverage, Tier 1, and operations ratios, a recent research by De Vincentiis (2014) highlighted a significant negative relationship of CDS with tangible equity capital on RWAs and return on assets (ROA). Finally, size is in general negatively related to CDS due to "Too big to fail" effect whereby, in order to preserve the integrity of the financial system, big banks cannot be left to fail.

3.3 The Model

According to Casu and Chiaramonte (2013), we built a model that uses solely accounting data, because the fluctuation of market data could bias the relation with accounting variables on which earning management measures are based.

Since the cost of funding varies across banks, owing to specific business models and financial statement soundness, in the regression we used a set of financial ratios to capture cross-sectional differences. Furthermore, we also add a macroeconomic variable explaining the effect of the monetary policy on banks' funding cost. More precisely we adopted the following regression model:

$$\begin{aligned} Funding\ cost_{i,t} = {} & \alpha_t + \beta_1 Size_{i,t} + \beta_2 Interest\ rates_t + \beta_3 Tier_{i,t} \\ & + \beta_4 Loa\_dep_{i,t} + \beta_5 NPL_{i,t} + \beta_6 Roa_{i,t} + \beta_7 CIR_{i,t} \\ & + \beta_8 DLLP_{i,t} + \varepsilon_{i,t} \end{aligned} \tag{2.2}$$

Where:

- *Funding cost* identifies the bank i's marginal cost of funding (the sum of five-year CDS premia and the three-month Euribor/Libor rate);
- α_t represents bank-specific effects that are constant over time but vary across banks;
- *Size* the natural log of total assets, to take into account the relation between size and cost of funding;
- *Interest rates* refer to short-term policy interest rates set by ECB or BOE at time t;
- *Tier* is Tier 1 capital ratio of the bank, and proxies for the level of solvency of banks;
- *Loa_dep* is the ratio of loans to deposits, as a proxy for liquidity risk;
- *NPL* represent Non-Performing Loans to total loans, as a proxy for credit risk exposure;
- *Roa* indicate returns of assets, as a measure of bank i's profitability;
- *CIR* is the cost to income ratio, as a measure of bank i's efficiency;
- *DLLP* is our proxy of discretionary loan loss provision.

Some comments follow Eq. (2.2). Even in this regression we recognize size effects. We predict a negative correlation between banks' size and cost of funding, given that larger banks are typically associated with lower levels of risk and therefore exhibit lower CDS premium (Demirgüç-Kunt and Huizinga 2013). To account for the effect of the monetary policy on the banks' cost of funding, we added into the regression formula the level of short-term policy rates set by the European Central Bank and by the Bank of England. We expect a negative relationship between policy short-term rates and funding cost, due to the fact that central banks set lower policy rates during crisis periods in order to reduce the effects of crisis.

According to Chiaramonte and Casu (2013), the determinants of bank CDS spread could be explained by a set of bank balance sheet ratios; expressive of credit and liquidity risk, solvency, and profitability. The relationship between solvency and cost of funding is addressed by using the Tier 1 capital ratio. In these terms, we predict a negative correlation with the funding cost, given that a lower level of capital increases the bank solvency risk.

Credit and liquidity risk have a strong impact on the bank's asset-liability and financial equilibrium. Credit risk has a positive correlation with funding cost, the reduction of cash flow, and profitability due to loan defaults increasing the market perception of risk and therefore the cost of funding. So we predict a positive relationship between non-performing loans and the cost of funding. As regards to liquidity risk, we use the loan to deposit ratio. The relationship could be seen negatively when high loans for the same level of deposits is perceived as safer by the market, since loans represent the core banking business, which are safer than the trading business activity (Demirgüç-Kunt and Huizinga 2010). On the other hand, higher values may be perceived as risky because they represent lower liquidity and a strong reliance on the wholesale funding market, which is a type of funding that is less stable than deposits.

In our regression, we also consider whether profitability (ROA) and efficiency (cost-income ratio) might affect the cost of funding. The link between ROA and the cost of funding is still uncertain. More precisely, the market may perceive a bank with higher levels of profitability as more risky, but, on the other hand, may react positively if it assumes that lower profitability leads to higher banks' risk (Fiordelisi et al. 2011). As a measure of efficiency we include the cost-to-income ratio. The greater this ratio, the lower the bank efficiency, and thus the higher the funding costs.

Finally, we predict a positive sign for discretionary provisioning. Such a relationship is expected to be positive due to the fact that manipulating earnings could increase the market perception of risk. It is important to recognize that, the primary effect of earnings management practices is to reduce bank transparency and inhibit monitoring by outsiders that inevitably increases investors' perception of risk.

4 Data and Sample

The data analyzed in this paper are obtained from the Bankscope-Bureau Van Dijk database. We collected year-end information of 41 banks listed in EU countries during the years 2005–2013. We collected data on LLPs, measured as the reported amount of loan loss provisions. In addition, we collected data on the main bank specific characteristics that the previous literature identified as potential explanations of the discretionary and non-discretionary portion of LLPs. Data for CDS, Libor and Euribor are taken from the Bloomberg professional services, while macroeconomic data is gathered from the World Developed indicators (World Bank database).

The decision to use the sum of five-year CDS premia and the three-month Euribor/Libor rate had reduced our sample size to 41 banks, due to the limited number of banks with listed CDS. This restriction biases our sample to banks that are larger than the European banks population.

Table 2.1 reports the means, quartiles and standard deviations of the variables used in the regression analyses, reported in Sect. 4.

The sample of banks is large (median market value of equity is about 270 million €), profitable (median return of assets is about 0.0023) and exhibits, on average, 2.32% of non-performing loans to total assets. We compared this sample's attributes to those of the European banks' population for the same time period. Consistent with the selection bias noted above, our sample is larger, less profitable and presents less non-performing loans than the average European population (the median European banks over our sample period has a market value of equity of 12 million €, ROA of 0.67% and non-performing loans 2.77%).

Table 2.1 Summary of financial information about the sample, 2005–2013

	Mean	1° Quartiles	Median	3° Quartiles	Std. Dev.
LLP	0.0042	0.003	0.0016	0.0057	0.0046
Size	8.561	8.6366	8.1714	9.0605	0.5296
NPL	0.0232	0.0153	0.0067	0.0294	0.0237
LLR	0.0143	0.012	0.0057	0.0183	0.0121
Tier 1	0.0924	0.086	0.074	0.1073	0.0241
GDP growth	0.0106	0.016	0.0101	0.028	0.0261
Funding cost	0.0402	0.0291	0.015	0.0537	0.0352
Policy rates	0.0237	0.0225	0.0125	0.0325	0.0129
Liquidity	0.4083	0.3286	0.2125	0.494	0.2924
Roa	0.005	0.0053	0.0023	0.0084	0.0049
CIR	0.6227	0.605	0.5291	0.6807	0.1634
DLLP	0.0001	−0.0018	−0.0003	0.0012	0.037

Sample description and variable definitions: The sample contains 41 bank-year observations over t = 2005–2013. LLP = total loan loss provision scaled by the bank's assets, Size = the natural log of total assets, LLR = total loan loss allowance as a percentage of total assets, Tier 1 = Tier 1 capital ratio, GDP growth = change in GDP per capita, Funding cost = the sum of five-year CDS premia and the three-month Euribor/Libor rate, Policy rates = short-term policy interest rates set by ECB or BOE at time t, Liquidity = liquid assets to short term liabilities, Roa = returns of assets, DLLP = discretionary loan loss provision, CIR = the cost of income ratio

5 Results

Equation 2.1 is estimated through a random effects regression taking each bank LLPs scaled by total assets as a dependent variable. The choice of the random effect rather than the fixed model has been tested through the Hausman (Hausman and Taylor 1981) and the Baltagi Li test (Baltagi and Li 1995). The value obtained by the Hausman test rejects the null hypothesis, suggesting that the fixed effects estimator is a more appropriate choice. However, due to the limitations of the Hausman test, we employed the Baltagi and Li test as well. The results of the latter test asserted the presence of random effects and serial correlation in the idiosyncratic error. According to the test, the estimators of the fixed effects model may be inefficient. We also compared the R^2 obtained by the two different models and we found that the random effects model provided a better R^2.

Table 2.2 Panel data—Random effect—LLP (Regression 1)

Variables	Coefficients	Std. Error	t-value	Significance
Intercept	0.01007	0.0031	3.28	**
Size	−0.0009	0.0003	−2.486	*
NPL	0.0276	0.0106	2.617	**
LLR	0.2064	0.0218	9.445	***
TIER	−0.0178	0.006	−2.944	**
GDP	−0.0579	0.008	−7.159	***
R^2	49.60%			
R^2 Adjusted	49.25%			

Signif. Codes: ***0.001; **0.01; **0.05; *0.1

The regression model is finally estimated by using the White's transformation in order to control for cross-section heteroskedasticity of the variables. Table 2.2 displays the empirical estimation of Eq. (2.1).

Our findings show that size has a negative effect on provisioning. According to Hakanes and Schnabel (2011), size is negatively correlated because large institutions are able to take lower credit risk due to the IRB approaches and, in addition, large portfolios may provide better credit risk diversification.

Moving to the variables connected to asset quality, we found a statistically significant correlation with provisioning. More precisely, the portions of NPLs on total assets and the loan loss rate have a strongly positive relationship with LLPs. As expected, a higher level of outstanding credit risk positively affects the level of provisioning. Similarly, the present degree of loan losses is directly connected to higher provisions, since the purpose of the loan loss reserve is to account for anticipated loan default. Basically these two effects capture the most important components of the cost of credit risk and thus, of provisioning.

In addition, we found that the higher the capital adequacy, the lower the level of provisioning. Notwithstanding, as evidenced in the literature, the capital management should not affect the manipulation of provisioning after Basel accords came into play, however provisions also affect the amount of net income and consequently, the level of the primary quality capital. In our model, we found that the incremental level of Tier 1 ratio is negatively correlated to LLPs. This might indicate that usually the most capitalized banks are those with lower riskiness in terms of RWAs. Our findings are supported by several empirical analyses such as Berger and

Young (1997), Fiordelisi et al. (2011) and Williams (2004), who claimed that banks with higher capital ratios, on average, tend to hold riskless portfolios and therefore lower credit losses and provisions.

Besides, in accordance with Bikker and Metzemakers (2005), Fonseca and González (2008), Leaeven and Majnoni (2003), we found a significant negative correlation between provisions and changes in GDP per capita. Such a relationship can be justified by the fact that, in the case of economic growth, usually credit losses and provisions tend to be lower and the rating of the counterparts tend to be better than the one during a period of downturn.

In the second regression, we aim to test the statistical significance of the discretionary component of provisioning on cost of funding. As a matter of fact, when banks manipulate earnings to meet stakeholders' expectations, it is likely that the level of hidden risks, or rather of the future expected losses, might raise the cost of funding for financing such riskier assets. In other words, earnings management can affect the perceived risk to existing or new debt-holders, who will require higher returns to finance riskier counterparties. We also tested our model for the financial crisis effect, since the credit portfolio of banks has been a very relevant variable for determining earnings. Hence, we added a dummy variable which took the value of 1 for the years after 2008, and 0 before.

In order to choose the appropriate model we performed the same tests as in the first regression. Results suggested using the fixed effect model. Therefore, we estimated the relationship between funding cost and the discretionary component of provisioning through the fixed effect estimator.

The model (2), as (1), is also finally estimated using the White's transformation. Table 2.3 reports the empirical estimations of model (2).

Our empirical results clearly show a strong and significant relationship between the cost of funding and earnings management. This finding is notably important for the aim and the research questions that this paper tries to address. As a matter of fact, such result highlight that, after having controlled a wide set of variables, earnings management (DLLP) affected the cost of funding. Thus it can be claimed that the way managers handle and manipulate earnings, have a significant impact on the cost of the debt issued. The results provided evidence that the transparency reached through clear and unmanaged financial statements slightly reduced funding costs, as markets perceived banks as less risky.

Table 2.3 Panel data—Fixed effects (Regression 2)

	Model 2 (a)				Model 2 (b)			
Variables	Coefficients	Std. Error	t-value	Signif.	Coefficients	Std. Error	t-value	Significance
Size	7.196	1.978	3.638	***	6.95	2.605	2.667	**
Rates	−112.07	19.675	−5.696	***	−111.46	19.699	−5.657	***
Tier	−27.64	11.552	−2.392	*	−28.35	11.224	−2.526	*
Loa_dep	2.326	0.724	3.211	**	2.302	0.545	4.224	***
NPL	21.939	10.847	2.022	*	21.456	7.381	2.907	**
Roa	−57.761	71.487	−0.808		−58.752	65.729	−0.893	
CIR	−2.996	1.166	−2.569	*	−3.044	1.757	−1.833	*
DLLP	203.517	69.265	2.938	**	200.932	84.089	2.389	*
CR					0.1056	0.3797	0.278	
R^2	51.79%				R^2	52.17%		
R^2 Adj	41.35%				R^2 Adj	41.43%		

Signif. Codes: ***0.001; **0.01; **0.05; *0.1

Among the other explanatory variables, the size variable exhibits a positive sign, in contrast to findings that postulated that large banks have a funding cost benefit associated with implicit government support (Araten and Turner 2013; Demirgüç-Kunt and Huizinga 2013). The different sign could be related to the fact that during periods of turmoil , due to the sovereign debt crisis, larger banks from peripheral European countries had no implicit government support; therefore CDS spreads became higher even for systemically important banks.

As regard the monetary policy control variable, we found, as expected, a negative relationship between interest rates level and the cost of funding. Generally, during crisis periods, it is reasonable to expect a slight increase in both CDS spreads and interbank spreads, even if the monetary authorities set interest rates at levels close to zero.

Among banks' risk variables, we found a positively significant relationship of the cost of funding with liquidity risk, which can be justified by the fact that distressed banks present higher loan to deposit ratios that have increased during the financial crisis as a result of reduced access to deposits. Furthermore, many empirical studies (Demirgüç-Kunt and Huizinga 2010; Goldsmith-Pinkham and Yorulmazer 2010; Vazquez and Federico 2012) showed that the reliance on wholesale funding (higher loan to deposit ratios), instead of deposits, was a major source of bank vulnerability during the financial crisis.

As regards the credit risk variable, we found a strong positive relationship between the cost of funding and credit risk (NPL), consistent with the literature that supported the idea that the CDS market is notably efficient in capturing credit risk (Di Cesare and Guazzarotti 2010).

In terms of capital adequacy, as expected, we found a negative sign, as higher capital ratios should signal more solid banks, although, as suggested by Chiaramonte and Casu (2013), Tier 1 ratio is not seen as a sufficiently useful indicator to safeguard banks from potential risks.

In terms of profitability, we found a not-significant relationship between return on assets and funding cost. With regard to efficiency, surprisingly the cost to income ratio is found negative and statistically significant in the regression model, possibly reflecting the diseconomies of scale related to higher banks' size (Demirgüç-Kunt and Huizinga 2013).

Finally, the control for the financial crisis showed that the effect is not significant related to the cost of funding, leaving all the other explanatory variables significant.

6 Implications and Further Research

This paper investigates whether earnings management can affect the cost of funding of banks. Our results show that banks' cost of funding is affected by earnings management and consequently, managers' ability to manipulate earnings has a significant impact on the marginal cost of debt.

The first implication of our findings is that earnings management do not only have positive effects in meeting stakeholders' expectations, but over-discretionary behavior of managers might reduce the expected positive impact. Therefore, this suggests that the literature should also take into account the "disincentive effect" correlated to earnings management which directly affects economic margins. In particular, the disincentive might be represented by the correlated costs of a high discretionary usage of accruals, which practically raises the level of risk and transfers the negative effects on the cost of funding. Hence, managers should pay attention to the equilibrium between present benefits and future costs, for the bank and its shareholders.

The second important implication is that banks' managers, following the income smoothing effect and the meeting of stakeholders expectations, might lead to an opposite effect from that expected. As long as managers increase the level of risk due to accruals, the rise of the cost of funding, transfers economic margins from shareholders to bondholders. This might be happening because while managers increase the level of accruals, other thing remaining equal, the higher risk makes the cost of funding more costly and thus, it becomes more profitable being a bondholder rather than a shareholder.

The future developments of the paper consist of adding other robustness checks, in particular in terms of the crisis. We will make a separation of the effects before and after the financial crisis in order to understand whether there can be significant variation between the sub-periods. Finally we will add the auto-regressive component of provisioning in order to detect a more precise measure of the discretionary component of LLPs and thus, of our earnings management variable.

Appendix A

Table 2.4 Reports sample correlations of the variables involved in our analysis

	LLP	Size	NPL	Tier 1	LLR	GDP growth	Funding cost	Policy rates	Liquidity	Roa	CIR
LLP	1	−0.08	0.6	0.01	0.35	−0.14	0.29	−0.1	−0.01	−0.16	0.09
Size		1	−0.21	−0.37	−0.25	−0.05	−0.31	0	−0.05	−0.08	−0.13
NPL			1	0.15	0.82	−0.26	0.28	−0.39	−0.03	−0.34	0.23
Tier 1				1	0.17	−0.04	0.21	−0.24	0.19	0.23	0.02
LLR					1	−0.1	0.29	0.27	−0.03	−0.25	0.17
GDP growth						1	−0.12	0.44	0.01	0.12	−0.1
Funding cost							1	−0.1	−0.01	−0.01	0
Policy rates								1	0.02	0.13	−0.11
Liquidity									1	0.14	−0.08
Roa										1	−0.26
CIR											1

Appendix B

Given the characteristics of the variables used in our empirical analysis, we decided to run the Variance Inflation Factor test (VIF).

Table 2.5 VIF test results

Model 1		Model 2	
Variable	Result	Variable	Result
Size	1.179	Size	1.367
NPL	2.944	RATES	1.547
LLR	2.932	TIER	2.105
TIER	1.149	Loan/deposits	1.117
GDP	1.111	NPL	2.221
		ROA	2.361
		CIR	1.444
		DLLP	1.171

References

Ahmed, A., Takeda, C., & Thomas, S. (1999). Bank loan loss provisions: A re-examination of capital management, earnings management and signalling effects. *Journal of Accounting and Economics, 28*, 1–25.

Anandarajan, A., Hasan, I., & Lozano-Vivas, A. (2003). The role of loan loss provisions in earnings management, capital management, and signalling: The Spanish experience. *Advances in International Accounting, 16*, 45–65.

Anandarajan, A., Hasan, I., & McCarthy, C. (2007). Use of loan loss provisions for capital, earnings management and signalling by Australian banks. *Accounting and Finance, 47*(3), 357–379.

Annaert, J., De Ceuster, M., Van Roy, P., & Vespro, C. (2013). What determines euro area bank CDS spreads? *Journal of International Money and Finance, 32*, 444–461.

Araten, M., & Turner, C. (2013). Understanding the funding cost differences between global systemically important banks (GSIBs) and non GSIBs in the USA. *Journal of Risk Management in Financial Institutions, 6*(4), 387–410.

Babihuga, R., & Spaltro, M. (2014). *Bank funding costs for international banks* (No. 14–71). International Monetary Fund.

Balboa, M., Lòpez-Espinosa, G., & Rubia, A. (2013). Nonlinear dynamics in discretionary accruals: An analysis of bank loan-loss provisions. *Journal of Banking & Finance, 37*, 5186–5207.

Baltagi, B. H., & Li, Q. (1995). Testing AR (1) against MA (1) disturbance in an error component model. *Journal of Econometrics, 68*, 135–151.

Beatty, A., Chamberlain, S. L., & Magliolo, J. (1995). Managing financial reports of commercial banks: The influence of taxes, regulatory capital, and earnings. *Journal of Accounting Research, 33*, 231–261.

Beatty, A. L., Ke, B., & Petroni, K. R. (2002). Earnings management to avoid earnings declines across publicly and privately held banks. *The Accounting Review, 77*(3), 547–570.

Beaver, W., & Engel, E. (1996). Discretionary behaviour with respect to allowances for loan losses and the behavior of security prices. *Journal of Accounting and Economics, 22*, 177–206.

Beaver, W., Eger, C., Ryan, S., & Wolfson, M. (1989). Financial reporting and the structure of bank share prices. *Journal of Accounting Research, 27*, 157–178.

Berger, A. N., & De Young, R. (1997). Problem loans and cost efficiency in commercial banking. *Journal of Banking & Finance, 21*, 849–870.

Bhat, V. N. (1996). Banks and income smoothing: An empirical analysis. *Applied Financial Economics, 6*(6), 505–510.

Bikker, J. A., & Metzemakers, P. A. J. (2005). Bank provisioning behaviour and procyclicality. *Journal of International Financial Markets, Institutions and Money, 15*, 141–157.

Chiaramonte, L., & Casu, B. (2013). The determinants of bank CDS spreads: Evidence form the financial crisis. *The European Journal of Finance, 19*, 861–887.

Cornett, M. M., McNutt, J. J., & Tehranian, H. (2009). Corporate governance and earnings management at large US bank holding companies. *Journal of Corporate Finance, 15*(4), 412–430.

Curcio, D., & Hasan, I. (2015). Earnings and capital management and signalling: The use of loan-loss provisions by European banks. *The European Journal of Finance, 21*(1), 26–50.

De Vincentiis, P. (2014). Lo status di banca sistemica gioca un ruolo significativo? Una verifica empirica sui Cds delle maggiori banche europee. *Bancaria Special Issue, 12*, 12–27.

DeBoskey, D. G., & Jiang, W. (2012). Earnings management and auditor specialization in the post-sox era: An examination of the banking industry. *Journal of Banking & Finance, 36*(2), 613–623.

Dechow, P. M., & Dichev, I. D. (2002). The quality of accruals and earnings: The role of accrual estimation errors. *The Accounting Review, 77*(s-1), 35–59.

Demirgüç-Kunt, A., & Huizinga, H. (2010). Bank activity and funding strategies: The impact on risk and returns. *Journal of Financial Economics, 98*, 626–650.

Demirgüç-Kunt, A., & Huizinga, H. (2013). Are banks too big to fail or to big to save? International evidence from equity prices and CDS spreads. *Journal of Banking & Finance, 37*, 875–894.

Di Cesare, A., & Guazzarotti, G. (2010, March). *An analysis of the determinants of credit default swap spread changes before and during the subprime financial turmoil.* Working Papers Banca d'Italia No. 749, Banca d'Italia, Rome.

Dong, X., Liu, J., & Hu, B. (2012). Research on the relationship of commercial bank's loan loss provision and earning management and capital management. *Journal of Service Science and Management, 5*(2), 171.

Fiordelisi, F., Marques-Ibanez, D., & Molyneux, P. (2011). Efficiency and risk in European banking. *Journal of Banking & Finance, 35*(5), 1315–1326.

Fonseca, A. R., & González, F. (2008). Cross-country determinants of bank income smoothing by managing loan-loss provisions. *Journal of Banking & Finance, 32*(2), 217–228.

Francis, J., LaFond, R., Olsson, P., & Schipper, K. (2005). The market pricing of accruals quality. *Journal of Accounting and Economics, 39*(2), 295–327.

Goldsmith-Pinkham, P., & Yorulmazer, T. (2010). Liquidity, bank runs, and bailouts: Spillover effects during the Northern Rock episode. *Journal of Financial Services Research, 37*(2–3), 83–98.

Greenawalt, M. B., & Sinkey, J. F. (1988). Bank loan loss provision and the income smoothing hypothesis: An empirical analysis, 1976–1984. *Journal of Financial Services Research, 1*, 301–318.

Hakanes, H., & Schnabel, I. (2011). Bank size and risk-taking under Basel II. *Journal of Banking & Finance, 35*, 1436–1449.

Hausman, J. A., & Taylor, W. E. (1981). Panel data and unobservable individual effects. *Econometrica, 49*(6), 1377–1398.

Healy, P. M., & Wahlen, J. M. (1999). A review of the earnings management literature and its implications for standard setting. *Accounting Horizons, 13*(4), 365–383.

Kanagaretnam, K., & Lobo, G. (2004). Joint tests of signalling and income smoothing through bank loan loss provisions. *Contemporary Accounting Reseach, 21*(4), 843–884.

Kanagaretnam, K., Lobo, G., & Mathieu, R. (2003). Managerial incentives for income smoothing through bank loan loss provisions. *Review of Quantitative Finance and Accounting, 20*, 63–80.

Kanagaretnam, K., Lobo, G., & Yank, D. H. (2005). Determinants of signalling by banks through loan loss provisions. *Journal of Business Research, 58*(3), 312–320.

Kim, M., & Kross, W. (1998). The impact of the 1989 change in bank capital standards on loan loss provisions and loans write-offs. *Journal of Accounting and Economics, 25*, 69–100.

Laeven, L., & Majnoni, G. (2003). Loan loss provisioning and economic slowdowns: Too much, too late? *Journal of Financial Intermediation, 12*(2), 178–197.

Liu, C., & Ryan, S. (1995). The effect of bank loan portfolio composition on the market reaction to and anticipation of loan loss provisions. *Journal of Accounting Research, 33*, 77–94.

Liu, C., & Wahlen, J. (1997). Differential valuation implications of loan loss provisions across banks and fiscal quarters. *The Accounting Review, 72*, 133–146.

Ma, C. (1988). Loan loss reserves and income smoothing: The experience in the US banking industry. *Journal of Business Finance and Accounting, 15*, 487–497.

Moyer, S. (1990). Capital adequacy ratio regulations and accounting choices in commercial banks. *Journal of Accounting and Economics, 13*, 123–154.

Pérez, D., Salas-Fumas, V., & Saurina, J. (2008). Earnings and capital management in alternative loan loss provision regulatory regimes. *The European Accounting Review, 17*(3), 423–445.

Prencipe, A. (2006). *Earnings Quality, principi e metodi di analisi della qualità degli earnings in una prospettiva internazionale.* Milano: Pearson Education.

Samaniego-Medina, R., Trujillo-Ponce, A., Cardone-Riportella, C., & Parrado-Martínez, P. (2013). Determinants of European Bank CDS spreads in times of crisis. *WP Funcas*, (736).

Schipper, K. (1989). Commentary on earnings management. *Accounting Horizons, 3*(4), 91–102.

Vazquez, F., & Federico, P. (2012). *Bank funding structures and risk: Evidence from the global financial crisis* (IMF working paper no. 12/29). Washington: International Monetary Fund.

Wahlen, J. M. (1994). The nature of information in commercial bank loan loss disclosures. *The Accounting Review, 69*, 455–478.

Williams, J. (2004). Determining management behaviour in European banking. *Journal of Banking & Finance, 28*, 2427–2460.

3

Volatility Linkages and Co-movements Between International Stocks and the Sukuk Market

Alberto Dreassi, Stefano Miani, Andrea Paltrinieri, and Alex Sclip

1 Introduction

The recent US and European financial crises have affected both real economies and financial markets all around the world, causing a global contagion due to the closer relationship and integration across countries. This behavior has been more pronounced in financial markets, where globalization, technology improvements, and international diversified portfolios held by investors are important factors to consider. Since the pioneer works of Markowitz (1952, 1959), portfolio diversification has been an important issue for academic researcher and practitioner.

A. Dreassi • A. Sclip
University of Trieste, Trieste, Italy

S. Miani • A. Paltrinieri (✉)
University of Udine, Udine, Italy
e-mail: andrea.paltrinieri@univr.it

S. Carbó Valverde et al. (eds.), *Bank Funding, Financial Instruments and Decision-Making in the Banking Industry*, Palgrave Macmillan Studies in Banking and Financial Institutions,
DOI 10.1007/978-3-319-30701-5_3

Recently, this issue has received much more attention, due to the contagion effects and the financial crisis that hit the markets in the last years.

During the subprime financial crisis, for example, from mid-2007 to the first months of 2009, the plunge of US stock markets led to a collapse of both Asian and European stock markets, with other asset classes also affected by the propagation. We could cite the case of the plunge of WTI crude oil in 2008 from $120 a barrel to reach a bottom around $30 barrel. On the bond market instead, we had a slight increase of safer bond prices, due to the collapse of the 10 year yields. US 10 year yield for example plunged from more than 5% to 2.20% in less than a couple of years and the German 10 year yield had the same behavior. This phenomenon is known as *flight to quality*. Also during the 2011–2012 Euro area crisis, we had a huge sell-off of all European peripheral bonds with a massive spike in yields, causing a concurrent buying of worldwide core bonds.

We could conclude, therefore, that it's getting important for institutional investors and risk managers to examine intra-and cross-class correlations and volatilities, considering the potentially heavy losses they could afford in a short period of time. Moreover, there is a continuous research by academics and practitioners of an asset class that can ensure a low correlation and high portfolio diversification, in particular during financial crisis, when systemic risk could lead to a global contagion. Hence there is growing attention on Islamic finance and *sukuk*.

Sukuk, or "Islamic bonds", can be defined as "certificates [...] representing a proportional undivided ownership right in tangible assets, or a pool of predominantly tangible assets, or a business venture" (IFSB 2009), with a structure compliant to *Shari'ah* principles. They differ from conventional bonds because, in principle, they are required to be free from *riba* (interest rate). *Sukuk* are structured through an identification of the specific asset underlying the transaction and the temporary transfer of ownership to holders. These features present similarities to the conventional asset-backed securities (ABS).

In this paper we investigate volatility linkages and co-movements between *sukuk* and international conventional stock markets in the aftermath of the global crisis. By building a comprehensive cross-country market capitalization weighted index of high quality *sukuk*, listed in developed and developing countries, we explore the dynamic correlations and volatility linkages with ten global and emerging market stock indexes during the period 2010–2014.

To the best of our knowledge this is the first paper assessing co-movements between Islamic bonds and conventional stocks. Although co-movements and volatility linkages have been investigated in portfolio diversification literature by the end of last century (Keim and Stambaugh 1986; Campbell and Ammer 1993; Kwan 1996), among all, little attention has been so far devoted to cross-asset comparison between Islamic and conventional financial products.

Several papers explore co-movements between different Islamic assets such as *sukuk* and *Sharia* compliant stocks (Aloui et al. 2015a, 2015b), others analyze the degree of co-integration among Islamic countries' stock markets (Marashdeh 2005; Majid et al. 2007). Another strand of literature investigates the diversification benefits in including *Shariah* compliant stock indexes or securities in an international portfolio by analyzing the interdependencies between Islamic and conventional stock indexes (Achsani et al. 2007; Majid et al. 2009; Karim et al. 2010; Saiti 2013). Only Akhtar et al. (2012), through a comprehensive analysis, examines the volatility linkages between Islamic and conventional stocks, bonds and money markets as well, for the period 2007–2010.

Our paper differs from the previous ones because it investigates volatility linkages and co-movements between *sukuk* conventional stock indexes covering a wider period including European financial crisis (2010–2014). We focus on *sukuk* because they are increasingly included in institutional investors' portfolios, not only Islamic ones. In fact, they represent the fastest growing sector of Islamic finance. Moody's (2014) shows that *sukuk* grew from 8 to 300 billion USD in the period 2003–2014, expressing a CAGR of almost 20% in the period 2008–2013 and leading to an expected doubling of their current asset value (1 trillion USD) over the next few years. According to the Global Islamic Finance Report (GIFR 2012), in the early 2000s Islamic banks have issued about $150 billion of *sukuk* but, recently, also non-Islamic countries have raised funds through this kind of bond. In mid-2014, the UK became the first Western country to host such assets, attracting more than 10 times the size of the new issue (over 3 billion USD); Luxembourg and Honk Kong followed (Bloomberg 2015).

Considering this increase in importance, have *sukuk* exhibited a low correlation with conventional stocks similar to investment grade bonds? Have they experienced a *flight to quality* phenomenon during the European debt crisis? Is there any volatility linkage between them and emerging market stock indexes? Those are the main topics we try to address by using an advanced model, the Dynamic Conditional Correlation (DCC) GARCH.

Among several multivariate models, we decided to use the DCC GARCH model of Engle (2002), following Engle and Sheppard (2008) methodology, due to its better performance in terms of portfolio allocation among the families applicable to large panel models. Our results suggest that, during the periods of high market volatility, *sukuk* exhibit high correlations with US and EU stock indexes, without experiencing the well-known *flight to quality* phenomenon. Moreover we find that volatility linkages between *sukuk* and regional market indexes are stronger during turmoil periods.

Overall, we argue that investors could obtain portfolios' benefits including *sukuk* in a well-diversified equity portfolio, given their lower volatility compared to equity. But higher volatility linkages and dynamic correlations during financial crises show that the Islamic bonds are specific financial instruments, hybrid between bonds and equity. This behavior is consistent with their structure, based on *profit and loss sharing* and on a real underlying asset. We therefore prefer to classify *sukuk* as an alternative asset class, with price movements sometimes linked to emerging market bonds, other time to equities.

Our findings are relevant for institutional investors and asset managers, especially if they consider including and holding *sukuk* in a well-diversified portfolio. They have to be careful to evaluate *sukuk* similarly to conventional bonds, since during crisis they seem unaffected by a flight to quality. Moreover, considering their low liquidity and higher bid-ask spread, they are interesting instruments for investors with long term horizons such as pension funds and hedge funds. However, during crisis *sukuk* may also cause an increase of the overall portfolio's risk.

The remainder of the paper is organized as follows. Section 2 summarizes our literature review and the development of our hypothesis. Section 3 describes our data and the sample period. Section 4 analyzes the econometric methodology. Section 5 presents and discusses our findings, whereas Sect. 6 concludes with our final remarks and suggestions for future research.

2 Literature Review

2.1 Literature on Conventional Portfolio Diversification

The interrelationship between markets is a key feature of investor asset allocation because it is instrumental in determining the risk. Estimating the correlation structure and using this to select superior portfolios is a central key point for portfolio and risk managers. Furthermore, monetary policy authorities use information contained in assets prices with the aim of developing better expectations in terms of inflation and business cycle conditions. So understanding the co-movements between stocks and bonds may be useful for their purposes.

Several papers have analyzed the cross-linkage between conventional stock and bond markets. Earlier studies assume a constant relationship between stock and bonds over time. Shiller and Beltratti (1992) find a lower correlation between the two asset classes caused by discount rates. In accordance with the previously mentioned authors, Campbell and Ammer (1993) provide evidence of a similar lower positive correlation, explained by news about future excess stock returns and inflation. Further studies gave a refinement by analyzing the time-varying correlations (Li 2004; Cappiello et al. 2006; Andersson et al. 2008, among others). They show that stock and bond prices tend to move in the same direction, even if there are periods of negative correlations.

Despite the large body of literature, academic researchers have not reached a consensus about the driving forces behind correlations. Connolly et al. (2005) claim that stock–bond market correlation decreases with the increase of stock market uncertainty, suggesting that bonds may be a better hedge against stock market downturns. Kim et al. (2006), by analyzing the stock–bond market integration in EMU countries, confirm the negative relationship between stock market uncertainty and stock–bond market correlations. Also another strand of literature, investigating the flight-to-quality phenomenon from bonds to stocks, shows negative correlations between those asset classes. Baur and Lucey (2009) reveal that flights occur across countries, enhancing the diversification benefits when they are needed most.

Focusing on macroeconomic driving forces, Li (2004) demonstrates that the uncertainty about expected inflation rates is the primary driver of co-movements between stocks and bonds; while unexpected inflation and real interest rates are less influential. Also Andersson et al. (2008) confirm that stock and bond prices tend to move together during periods of high inflation expectations; while a lower level of inflation seems to move prices in the opposite direction. Moreover, the authors provide further evidence of a negative relationship between stock market volatility and correlations. Finally, Yang et al. (2009), by using a large time span that covers 150 years of data at a monthly frequency, recognize that higher stock–bond correlations tend to follow higher short rates or higher inflation rates.

2.2 Literature Review on Islamic Finance Portfolio Diversification

Despite the exponential growth of *Sharia* compliant debt instruments, literature has not yet documented the interdependence between *sukuk* and conventional stocks and the diversification benefits provided by this type of instrument during stock market downturns.

A significant number of studies focus on *sukuk* (Abdulkader and Nathif 2004; Iqbal and Mirakhor 2007; Vishwanath and Sabahuddin 2009), analyzing their structure, features, and their different exposure to risks. Rusgianto and Ahmadb (2013) examine their volatility through the *Dow Jones Citigroup Sukuk Index* and their relationship with subprime financial crisis shock. They find that pre and during-crisis volatility is more sensitive to market events than later. Other authors compare the risk/return profile of *sukuk* with conventional bonds (Fathurahman and Fitriati 2013; Zin et al. 2011; Mosaid and Boutti 2014), also through a case study analysis (Cakir and Raei 2007). Najeeb et al. (2014) analyze the portfolio diversification opportunities, including *sukuk* in a well-diversified portfolio. They find that returns of local (GCC and Malaysian) currency *sukuk* have low levels of long-term correlations, allowing gains in portfolio diversification; but international currency *sukuk* exhibit a high level of long-term correlations.

Recently, several papers have explored the interdependencies between *sukuk* and *Sharia* compliant stocks. Aloui et al. (2015a) assess co-movements between *Sharia stocks* and *sukuk* in the Gulf Cooperation Council countries, finding a strong dependence between them. They also show that Islamic assets don't seem to have a different behavior when compared to conventional stock and bond counterparts, with overall portfolio diversification varying across frequencies and time. In a subsequent paper the same authors (Aloui et al. 2015b), investigating the global factors driving the co-movement, show that oil prices and credit event information had a positive relationship during the period 2008–2013. Kim and Kang (2012), using a multivariate GARCH model, document the existence of uni-directional volatility spillovers from *Shariah* stocks to *sukuk* during subprime financial crisis. These studies are important because they analyze co-movements and dynamic correlations between two different asset classes within Islamic capital markets.

Previous literature only investigates the degree of inter asset-class co-integration, among Islamic country stock markets, showing mixed results. Marashdeh (2005) finds no co-integration between selected MENA stock markets during the period 1994–2004, implying potential diversification benefits. Bley and Chen (2006) show that there's some diversification opportunities investing in Middle-East stock markets, but they tend to be more integrated as time goes due to economic union and single currency area. Majid et al. (2007), analyzing the period 2002–2006, documented that Islamic markets in Asian region are integrated, while those in Mena region are not, providing some portfolio diversification benefits.

Widening the perspective, a few papers investigate the diversification benefits in including *Shariah* compliant stock indexes in an international portfolio by analyzing the interdependencies between Islamic and conventional stock indexes. Achsani et al. (2007) show that there are strong correlations between Malaysia, Indonesia Islamic indexes, and the US and Canada. There's also a strong relationship between Islamic stocks listed in US and other Islamic indexes. Majid et al. (2009) provide evidence of a strong co-integration between ASEAN stock markets with US and Japan, implying no benefits in portfolios' diversification. Karim et al. (2010) and Rahman and Sidek (2011), analyzing US subprime crisis effects on stock markets, come to opposite results, with the former showing no co-integration among Islamic and US, UK and Japan ones, while the latter finding co-integration between US and ASEAN-5. Saiti (2013), using a DCC GARCH approach, shows that Islamic countries provide better diversification benefits to US investors compared to Far East conventional stock markets.

Finally Aktar et al. (2015), argue that Islamic assets provide substantial diversification benefits during financial crises. In particular, for the period 2007–2010, volatility linkages between Islamic stocks and bonds are lower than volatility linkages between conventional stocks and bonds. Moreover the characteristics of Islamic financial markets also reduce volatility linkages between Islamic stocks and conventional bills.

Based on the literature, our hypothesis is that *sukuk* have high volatility linkages and high dynamic correlations with conventional stocks, especially during financial crisis, considering their special structure. In fact they are quite different from conventional bonds, given their close relationship with a real underlying asset (in a similar way to asset- backed securities) and their basement on profit and loss principle in several contracts (such as *al mudarabah* and *al musharakah*). We consider them as an hybrid financial instrument between conventional bonds and stocks. They shouldn't therefore experience the *flight to quality* phenomenon, considering their diversity compared to investment grade conventional bonds, and they could have higher co-movements with equity indexes than conventional bonds. But we also expect that dynamic correlations between *sukuk* and conventional stocks are lower than those among stocks, with Islamic bonds providing some diversification benefits.

3 Sample Characteristics and Statistical Properties

We collected daily data for the most liquid 68 *sukuk* listed in the major Islamic bond markets, such as Bursa Malaysia, Nasdaq Dubai and London Stock Exchange, from the Bloomberg Professional Service.

In order to test our hypothesis we decide to build a market-capitalization weighted index by using the same construction methodology and multiple criteria provided by MSCI (2012). We considered only highly-liquid *sukuk* with an outstanding amount in excess of 200 million USD, that in terms of credit risk received at least one credit rating from Moody's, S&P, RAM or MARC. We focus only on dollar-denominated *sukuk*, the majority within this market, excluding those with less than 12 months before maturity. Re-balancing of the index took place every three months, with new issues satisfying the selection criteria included while those with less than one year of maturity are automatically removed. Our *sukuk* index is composed of four contractual forms, well recognized by the literature (Abdulkader and Nathif 2004; Iqbal and Mirakhor 2007; Islamic Financial Services Board 2009): (1) *al mudarabah*, the capital provider and the manager share profits, whereas the former bears all losses except those attributable to misconduct, negligence, or breach of contract from the latter; (2) *al ijara*, involving the lease of a specific asset; (3) *al musharakah*, the capital provider and manager share profits as established in the contract and losses in proportion to the quota held; (4) *al wakala*, similar to an agency agreement, where the manager acts on behalf of the capital provider. Table 3.1 summarizes our sample.

Regarding the equity indexes, we gather daily prices of a list of 5 global and 5 emerging MSCI indexes (Table 3.2), from the Bloomberg professional service.

The daily returns y_t of both equity indexes and the *sukuk* index are computed using logarithmic price changes:

$$y_t = \left(\ln P_t - \ln P_{t-1}\right) \tag{3.1}$$

Table 3.1 Sample description

Features	2010	2011	2012	2013	2014
Issue type:					
– *al mudarabah*	3	4	4	4	4
– *al ijiara*	7	8	16	20	19
– *al musharakah*	3	2	1	1	1
– *al wakala*	1	3	5	6	4
Total	**14**	**17**	**26**	**31**	**28**
Mean values:					
Issue size ('000 USD)	880	825	750	750	750
Market value ('000 USD)	101.617	138.855	185.562	252.943	201.587
Rating	A+	A+	A	A+	A+
Coupon	5.13	5.02	4.78	4.15	3.88
Time-to-maturity	3.74	3.63	4.05	3.91	3.76
Effective duration	3.1	3.09	3.28	3.5	3.62
Yield-to-maturity	7.17	4.59	2.97	2.54	2.34
Option-adjusted spread	253.21	236.51	252.95	184.38	134.81

Source: Bloomberg professional services

Table 3.2 List of MSCI stock indexes in our sample

Index	Code
Global stock indexes	
MSCI Europe	MXEU
MSCI United States	MXUS
MSCI Emerging Markets	MXEF
MSCI Frontier Markets	MXFEM
MSCI Asia Pacific	MXAP
Emerging markets stock indexes	
MSCI Turkey	MXTR
MSCI Qatar	MXQA
MSCI United Arab Emirates	MXAE
MSCI Malaysia	MXMY
MSCI Indonesia	MXID

Source: Bloomberg professional services

The sample period is from January 1, 2010 to December 31, 2014. By using daily returns data we are able to capture all the possible interactions; weekly or monthly data block out interactions that last for only a few days. Table 3.3 provides the time series properties in terms of mean, standard deviation, skewness, and kurtosis of the price changes in the indexes selected.

Table 3.3 Descriptive statistics of daily price changes in sukuk and stock indexes

	Mean (%)	St. Dev. (%)	Skewness	Kurtosis	Normality-test	LM-test
SUKUK	0.036	0.165	1401	18,040	2.2e-16***	28.60***
Global						
MSCI Europe	0.040	1028	−0.063	3751	2.2e-16***	30.56***
MSCI United States	0.059	0.986	−0.407	4891	2.2e-16***	63.70***
MSCI Emerging Markets	0.013	1017	−0.324	2914	2.2e-16***	104.90***
MSCI Frontier Markets	0.029	0.577	−0.677	3235	2.2e-16***	121.87***
MSCI Asia Pacific	0.025	0.957	−0.362	1858	2.2e-16***	30.36***
Emerging markets						
MSCI Turkey	0.054	1522	−0.346	3387	2.2e-16***	30.14***
MSCI Qatar	0.061	0.912	0.724	15,038	2.2e-16***	42.28***
MSCI United Arab Emirates	0.076	1477	0.118	8815	2.2e-16***	41.35***
MSCI Malaysia	0.034	0.572	−0.249	3922	2.2e-16***	53.55***
MSCI Indonesia	0.059	1378	−0.381	5473	2.2e-16***	71.98***

Significance codes: '***' express significance at the 0.999 level, '**' at 0.99, '*' at 0.95

Source: Our own elaboration on Bloomberg professional service data

From the reported statistics, we can see that the mean daily returns are positive for all indexes. Stock indexes exhibit higher volatility than the *sukuk* index. Furthermore, the latter is skewed to the right, while eight of ten stock indexes are skewed to the left. All price changes exhibit high values of kurtosis, suggesting that the behavior of selected indexes presents some extreme values. Indeed, as the results in Table 3.3 show, the *Jarque-Bera* test rejects the null hypothesis of normality for all series. In an undisplayed figure daily returns are plotted. From the graphs, we see evidence of volatility clustering. The *Ljung-Box* auto-correlation test on the first twenty-five lag of the sample auto-correlation function (LM-Test) for all the daily price changes show significant auto-correlation at the 1% level.

The unconditional correlations between the asset series are given in the following Table 3.4. The *sukuk* index and all the stock indexes are

Table 3.4 Unconditional correlations between indexes

Unconditional correlations at the global level						
	SUKUK	MXEU	MXUS	MXEF	MXFEM	MXAP
SUKUK	1	22.07%	10.06%	34.33%	33.44%	34.81%
MXEU		1	69.76%	68.18%	54.62%	41.99%
MXUS			1	50.95%	49.22%	23.84%
MXEF				1	74.82%	81.01%
MXFEM					1	60.61%
MXAP						1
Unconditional correlations at the regional level						
	SUKUK	MXTR	MXQA	MXAE	MXMY	MXID
SUKUK	1	21.14%	23.36%	30.94%	29.89%	29.60%
MXTR		1	12.83%	17.61%	19.83%	30.78%
MXQA			1	53.24%	27.46%	28.19%
MXAE				1	26.73%	31.07%
MXMY					1	54.13%
MXID						1

Source: Our own elaboration on Bloomberg professional service data

positively correlated. Preliminary analysis suggest (unconditionally) correlations higher between the *sukuk* index and the emerging market stock indexes, which could be an indication that bonds in emerging markets are more equity alike than in developed countries.

4 Econometric Methodology

Multivariate GARCH models are designed with the aim of studying volatilities and correlations co-movements between markets, in order to provide better decision-making tools in portfolio selection, asset pricing and risk management techniques. Literature has provided several multivariate GARCH models, such as the VECH, BEKK, CCC, and DCC models. Among the several multivariate models, we decided to use the DCC model of Engle (2002), the choice of methodology follows Engle and Sheppard (2008): even using standard univariate GARCH specifications, DCC offers the best performance in terms of portfolio allocation among the families applicable to large panel models and is therefore more powerful than the constant correlation estimator developed by Bollerslev (1990).

We implement our DCC model in three steps. First, univariate volatilities are selected by using the Bayesian information criterion (BIC) from a class of GARCH models capable of capturing the common features of financial asset returns variances. We include the following models, all with one lag of innovation and one lag of volatility: (1) GARCH (Bollerslev 1986); (2) EGARCH (Nelson 1991); (3) GJR-GARCH (Glosten et al. 1993).

Once the univariate models are estimated, the standardized residuals are used to estimate the correlation parameters and the persistence parameters α and β. We implement the asymmetric DCC model; in order to take into account the asymmetric return volatility of equity time series (Cappiello et al. 2006).

4.1 The Univariate GARCH Model and Asymmetric Extensions

The GARCH model introduced by Bollerslev (1986) expressed conditional variance as a linear function of the square past values of the series. A generic GARCH (p,q) model can be described as follows:

$$h_t = \omega + \sum_{i=1}^{q} \alpha_i \varepsilon_{t-i}^2 + \sum_{j=1}^{p} \beta_j \sigma_{t-j}^2 \tag{3.2}$$

Where the α_i and β_j are non-negative constants and ω is a positive constant.

Since the conditional variance in Eq. (3.2) is a function of the lagged residuals and not their signs, the model enforces a symmetrical response of volatility to positive and negative shocks.

The Exponential GARCH model is the first that investigates the leverage effects; which refers to the fact that downward movements are more influential for predicting volatility than the upward movements. Nelson's (1991) EGARCH attempts to model fat tails in stock indexes returns by using a generalized exponential distribution; in formula the model can be represented as follows:

$$\log(h_t) = \omega + \sum_{i=1}^{q} \alpha_i \frac{|\varepsilon_{t-i}|}{\sigma_{t-i}} + \sum_{i=1}^{q} \gamma_i \frac{\varepsilon_{t-i}}{\sigma_{t-i}} + \sum_{j=1}^{q} \beta_j \log \sigma_{t-j}^2 \tag{3.3}$$

Equation (3.3) allows negative values of ε_t to have different impacts on volatility. Since the coefficient γ_i is typically negative, the model claims for an asymmetric behavior in volatility.

The GJR model of Glosten et al. (1993) introduces asymmetry as a function of the positive and negative parts of the past innovations; and can be defined as:

$$h_t = \omega + \sum_{i=1}^{q} \alpha_i \varepsilon_{t-i}^2 + \gamma_i \varepsilon_{t-i}^2 \mathbb{I}_{\{\varepsilon_{t-i}>0\}} + c\sum_{j=1}^{p} \beta_j \sigma_j^2 \tag{3.4}$$

In this model good news $(\varepsilon_t^2 > 0)$ and bad news $(\varepsilon_t^2 < 0)$ have a different impact on the conditional variance. More specifically, good news as an impact of α, while bad news as an impact of $(\alpha + \gamma)$. Hence the leverage effect is present when $\gamma > 0$.

The univariate GARCH models were estimated through the maximum likelihood approach of Bollorslev and Wooldridge (1992), where the log-likelihood function from the Gaussian normal distribution.

4.2 The Multivariate GARCH Model

The Dynamic Conditional Correlation (DCC) model of Engle (2002) is a generalization of the CCC model, which allows the correlation matrix to vary over time rather than requiring them to be constant. The DCC model of Engle is defined as:

$$H_t = D_t R_t D_t \tag{3.5}$$

Where:

H_t is a $n \times n$ matrix of conditional variances;

D_t is a $n \times n$ diagonal matrix of time varying standard deviations from univariate GARCH models (h_t), in formula:

$$D_t = diag\left(h_{11t}^{\frac{1}{2}} \ldots\ldots h_{NNt}^{\frac{1}{2}} \right) \tag{3.6}$$

R_t is the correlation matrix, defined as:

$$R_t = diag\left[Q_t\right]^{-1} Q_t diag\left[Q_t\right]^{-1} \quad (3.7)$$

Where the n × n symmetric positive definite matrix $Q_t = (q_{ij,t})$ is given by:

$$Q_t = \left(1-\alpha-\beta\right)\bar{Q} + \alpha u_{t-1}u'_{t-1} + \beta Q_{t-1} + \gamma\left(g_t g'_t\right) \quad (3.8)$$

with the standardized residuals $u_t = \varepsilon_{it} / \sqrt{h_{iit}}$, α and β are non-negative scalar parameters satisfying $\alpha + \beta < 1$, and the vectors g_t are defined as the negative parts of u_t as follows:

$$g_{i,t} \equiv \begin{cases} u_{i,t} \text{ if } u_{i,t} < 0 \\ 0 \text{ if } u_{i,t} \geq 0 \end{cases}, i = 1,\ldots,N.$$

DCC parameters are estimated by quasi-maximum likelihood by construction: because the model is implemented in three different steps, even though in each of these stages a log-likelihood function is estimated. In the third step, given the results of the Jarque-Bera test of normality, we relax the normality assumption and we adopt a student-t multivariate distribution for the time series returns, which is more suitable and gives better estimation results.

We use a three stage approach, rather than estimating all the volatility models and correlation model simultaneously, because in practice it is more feasible for large portfolios even if the estimator is less efficient.

5 Empirical Results

5.1 The Univariate Models

The first step of the DCC model consists of fitting univariate GARCH specifications to each of the time series and selecting the best one according to the BIC criterion. Table 3.5 summarizes information of the GARCH process selected and the estimated parameters. In accordance with Cappiello et al. (2006), which claims that equity returns show

Table 3.5 Univariate GARCH models

Assets	Model selected	w	a	d or g	b
Sukuk	GARCH	0.000007**	0.0721***		0.9275***
Global indexes					
MSCI Europe	GARCH	0.000002**	0.0914***		0.8287***
MSCI United States	GARCH	0.000003*	0.1351***		0.8307***
MSCI Emerging Markets	EGARCH	−0.1137***	−0.0866***	0.0659***	0.9877***
MSCI Frontier Markets	EGARCH	−0.4205	−0.0967*	0.1242***	0.9596***
MSCI Asia Pacific	EGARCH	−0.1784***	−0.0923***	0.1044***	0.9811***
Emerging markets indexes					
MSCI Turkey	GJR-GARCH	0.00001***	0.0242***	0.1242***	0.8614***
MSCI Qatar	GJR-GARCH	0.000001*	0.0411**	0.0454***	0.9151***
MSCI United Arab Emirates	GARCH	0.000004**	0.0604***		0.9221***
MSCI Malaysia	EGARCH	0.000002**	−0.1218***	0.1967***	0.9351***
MSCI Indonesia	GARCH	0.000009***	0.1595***		0.8028***

Source: Our own elaboration
Significance codes: '***' express significance at the 0.999 level, '**' at 0.99, '*' at 0.95

strong evidence of asymmetries in conditional volatility, we find that six of the 10 GARCH models selected contain an asymmetric term. More precisely, the symmetric GARCH model is more suited to capturing volatility dynamics of the *sukuk* market, Europe, United States, United Arab Emirates, and Indonesia indexes; while the asymmetric counterparts (EGARCH and GJR-GARCH) perform better in capturing volatilities of the MSCI Emerging Markets, Frontiers, Asia Pacific, Turkey, Qatar, and Malaysia indexes.

As shown from the table, for the case of the USA and the European indexes, the α parameter is relatively large suggesting that volatility is very sensitive to market events. Regarding the other three global indexes, we find a large leverage effect. Moving on to emerging market indexes, we find that the parameter γ measuring the leverage effect is highly significant in Turkey, Qatar and Malaysia. The α parameters, measuring the reaction of conditional volatility to market shocks, are significant in emerging market stock indexes.

On comparing the results and its implication for the *sukuk* market, we find that the *sukuk* index exhibits a lower α value and an higher β value than the stock indexes; suggesting a lower reaction to market shocks and an higher persistence in conditional volatility. Furthermore, there is no leverage effect in the *sukuk* market.

Concerning the goodness of fit tests the weighted *Ljung-Box* test on standardized residuals, computed with 10 lags; show for all the univariate specifications no serial correlation and no remaining ARCH test. Thus, the different models are correctly set for all the time series, since there is no evidence of statistical misspecification.

5.2 DCC Specifications

We ran two asymmetric DCC models, the first for all the global indexes and the *sukuk* index, in order to analyze volatilities and dynamic correlations at the global level. The second between the *sukuk* index and the emerging market stock indexes selected, with the aim of analyzing linkages at the regional level. Table 3.6 summarizes the results. According to the information criteria, and likelihood ratio test, we set a multivariate student-t distribution, which is more appropriate than the Gaussian counterpart.

Focusing on global indexes, as in the univariate models, in all cases coefficients are highly significant. For the six indexes the β parameter is highly significant, suggesting a high degree of persistence in volatility. Moreover the asymmetric terms γ are highly significant, suggesting the presence of leverage effects.

Table 3.6 DCC GARCH models

Assets	ω	α	δ or γ	β
Global indexes				
Sukuk	0.000001*	0.0708**		0.9212***
MSCI Europe	0.000003*	0.0933*		0.8804***
MSCI United States	0.000003*	0.1353***		0.8302***
MSCI Emerging Markets	−0.000066***	−0.1147***	−0.0891***	0.9876***
MSCI Frontier Markets	0.00019**	−0.0945***	−0.0415***	0.9600***
MSCI Asia Pacific	−0.0001***	−0.0891***	0.1066***	0.9813***
Log-Likelihood	31030.87			
Emerging markets				
Sukuk	0.000001*	0.0708**		0.9212***
MSCI Turkey	0.000011***	0.0237**	0.1207***	0.8654***
MSCI Qatar	0.000001*	0.0441*	0.0406*	0.9345***
MSCI United Arab Emirates	0.000004***	0.0592***		0.9231***
MSCI Malaysia	0.00019***	−0.1185***	0.1932***	0.9347***
MSCI Indonesia	0.000008**	0.1422***		0.8223***
Log-Likelihood	28733.2			

Source: Our own elaboration
Significance codes: '***' express significance at the 0.999 level, '**' at 0.99, '*' at 0.95

Results of the univariate models were confirmed also for emerging markets indexes. In particular, all the parameters are significant. The beta parameter is highly significant only in Qatar, UAE, and Malaysia; on the contrary in all the other countries volatilities are not persistent. The model confirms the higher significance of the leverage effect in emerging and frontiers stock indexes. Regarding the goodness-of-fit tests for the two DCC models, we run the Ljung-Box computed with 20 lags and we do not find serial correlation and remaining ARCH effect; suggesting no evidence of statistical mis-specification.

5.3 Volatility Linkages

A simple criterion to analyze volatility linkages across indexes is the unconditional correlation between the estimated variances. The conditional variances between the equity indexes and the *sukuk* index are moderately correlated at a global level; however the volatility linkages are much stronger at the regional level (see Table 3.7).

Figure 3.1 plots the univariate conditional volatility series. In absolute terms, the *sukuk* index volatility is nearly ten times lower than that observed in all of the stock indexes. Volatility tends to be lower in Islamic market debt due to the rules of Islamic finance, such as the prohibition of speculation and short selling. A further reason for the lower volatility can be the weak secondary market in most of the Islamic Countries (Tariq et al. 2007) and the subsequent higher *bid-ask spread* in the Islamic debt market. Hence the prevailing behavior of *sukuk* investors, is to hold these instruments until the maturity, without selling them to third counterparts.

However, as expected, the volatility of emerging markets stock indexes is usually higher in absolute terms than that observed at the global level. In particular, volatility in Turkey and UAE stock indexes is twice the average observed in global stock indexes.

Table 3.7 Unconditional correlations between estimated variances

Assets	All	2010	2011	2012	2013	2014
Global						
Sukuk-Europe	0.373	0.118	0.406	0.131	0.385	0.485
Sukuk-United States	0.360	−0.097	0.434	−0.057	0.148	0.372
Sukuk-Emerging Markets	0.396	0.200	0.311	0.342	0.740	0.434
Sukuk-Frontiers	0.358	0.052	0.387	0.347	0.696	0.650
Sukuk-Asia Pacific	0.401	0.136	0.353	0.380	0.650	0.267
Regional						
Sukuk-Turkey	0.250	0.307	0.439	0.520	0.463	0.426
Sukuk-Qatar	0.084	0.251	0.043	0.673	0.488	0.332
Sukuk-U.A.E.	0.199	0.464	0.240	0.476	0.621	0.633
Sukuk-Malaysia	0.246	0.153	0.410	0.313	0.276	0.536
Sukuk-Indonesia	0.307	0.335	0.528	0.230	0.752	0.014

Source: Our own elaboration

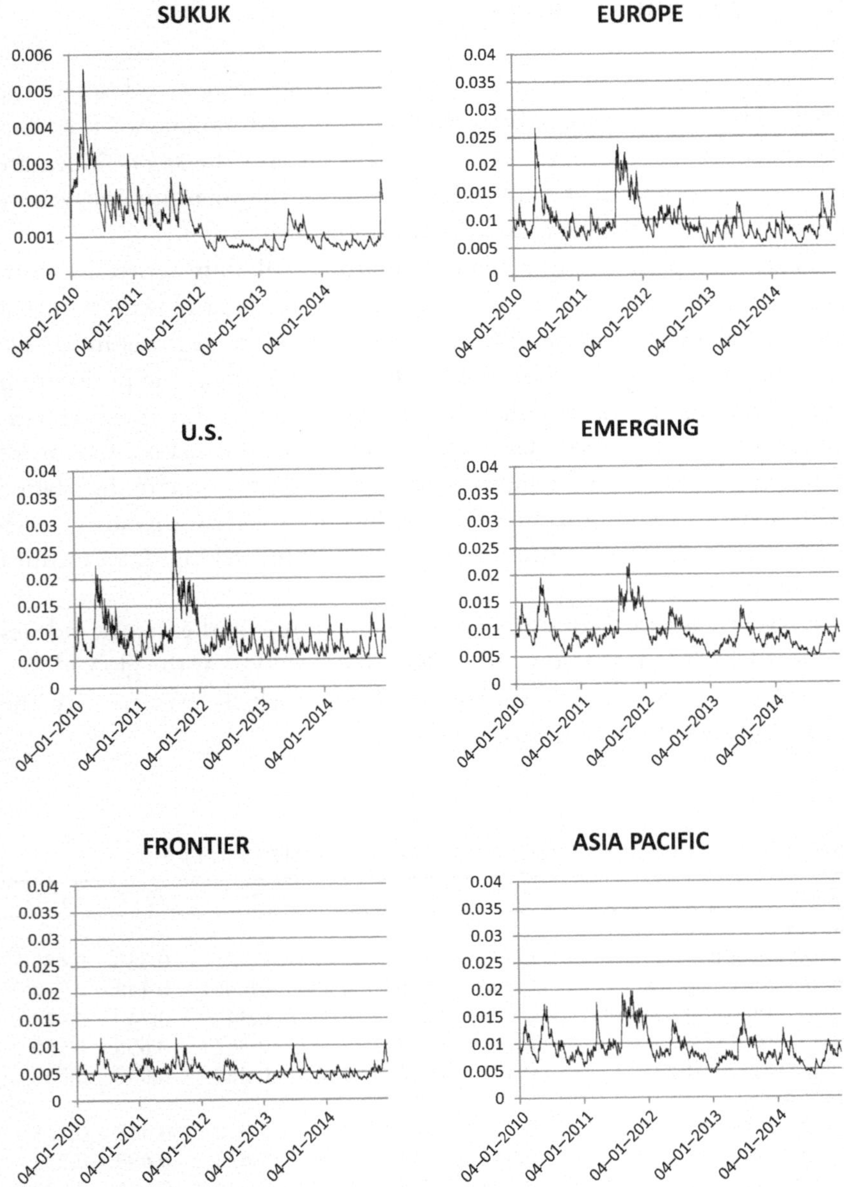

Fig. 3.1 Sukuk and global index volatility (*Source*: Our own elaboration)

As shown from the plots, at the global level the volatility linkage between the *sukuk* index and both the European and US stocks is most evident during certain tumultuous periods, such as the sovereign European debt crisis in the second half of the 2011; while in periods of bull stock markets volatility linkages are less strong. Moreover by comparing the volatility behavior of the *sukuk* index with the other three global stock indexes, we find a much more similar behavior than that observed previously. In particular, the convergence of volatilities during the year 2013 could reflect the downturn and the increase in volatility sparked by speculation that the Federal Reserve was looking to reduce stimulus efforts. The first tapering *rumors* during mid-2013 caused an increase in volatility in *sukuk*, emerging and frontier markets equity, considering that investors were ready to draw financial resources from emerging markets to invest in US dollar assets, expecting an appreciation of the US currency.

Looking at a regional level (Fig. 3.2), as mentioned above, the volatility linkage is much more pronounced, especially in those countries more sensitive to financial crisis and capital flows such as Turkey and UAE. In particular we find a strong linkage between the *sukuk* index and the UAE stock index, more evident during the last two years. This is consistent with the literature findings and it's related to the fact that volatility linkages in Islamic countries, and especially in Mena region, are stronger than in non-Islamic countries (Bley and Chen 2006; Akhtar et al. 2012).

5.4 Dynamic Conditional Correlations

Figures 3.3 and 3.4 plot the estimated DCCs between the global MSCI indexes and the *sukuk* index during the sample period. Conditional correlations between *sukuk* and global stock indexes are time varying and have remained positive and relatively low during the time span.

First of all, we compare the correlation between US and EU stock indexes and the *sukuk* index. As Fig. 3.3 show, conditional correlations increase during periods of high stock market volatility, such as in the second half of the year 2011. We notice the same behavior in the first half of both 2012 and 2013, although volatility linkages experienced a downturn during those years. This result is in contrast with the *flight-to*

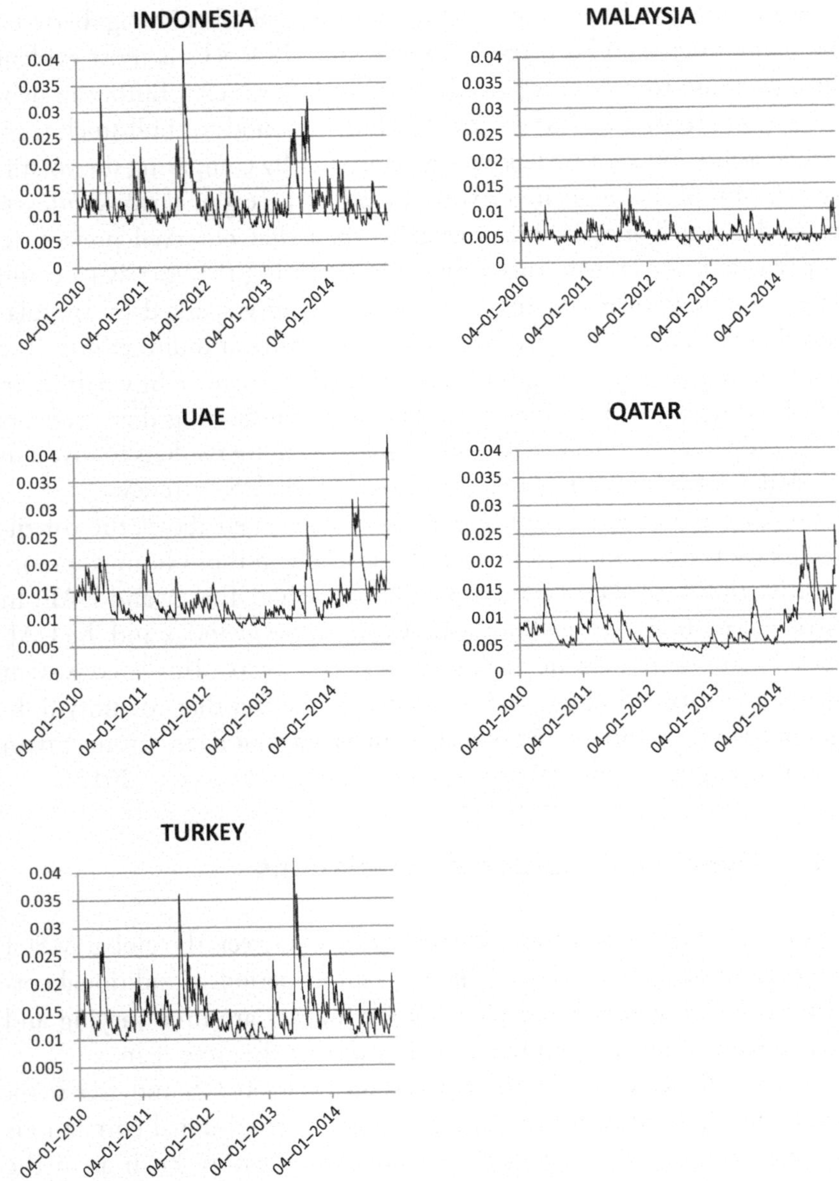

Fig. 3.2 Regional index volatility (*Source*: Our own elaboration)

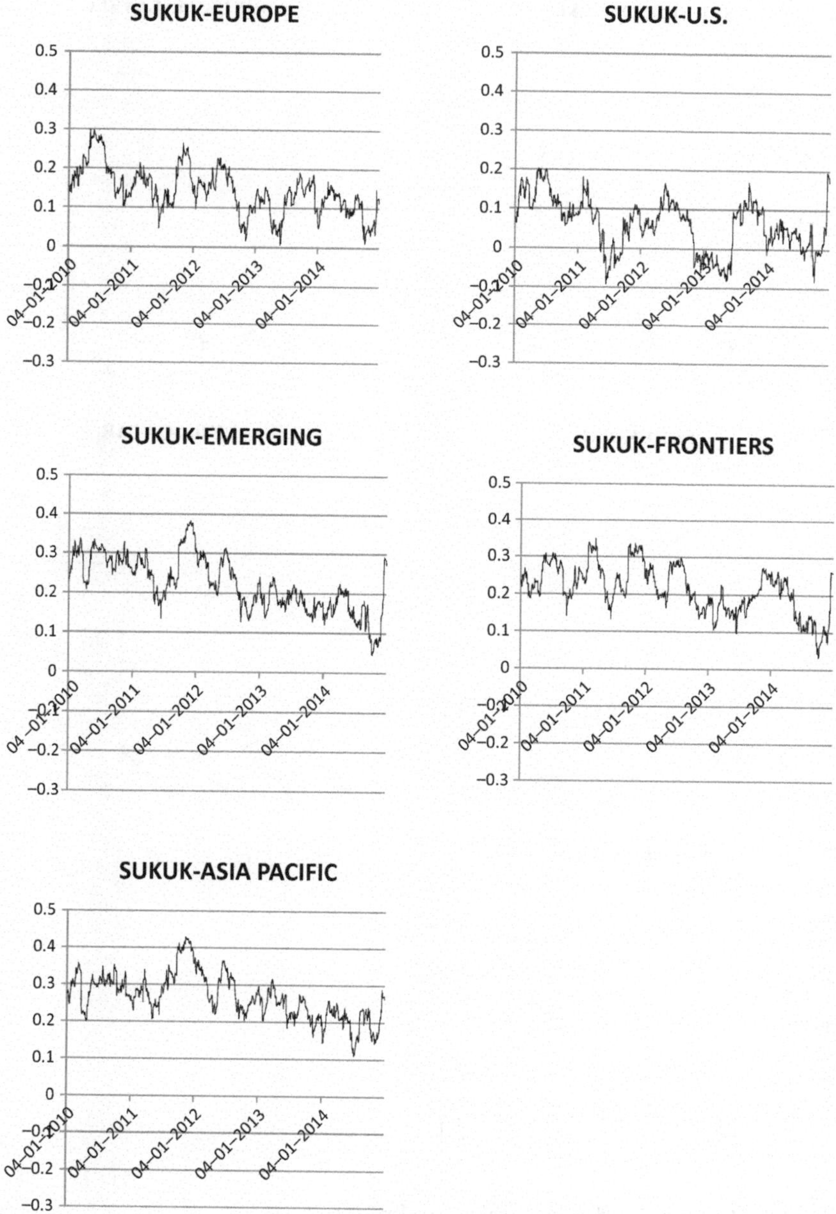

Fig. 3.3 Global index dynamic correlations (*Source*: Our own elaboration)

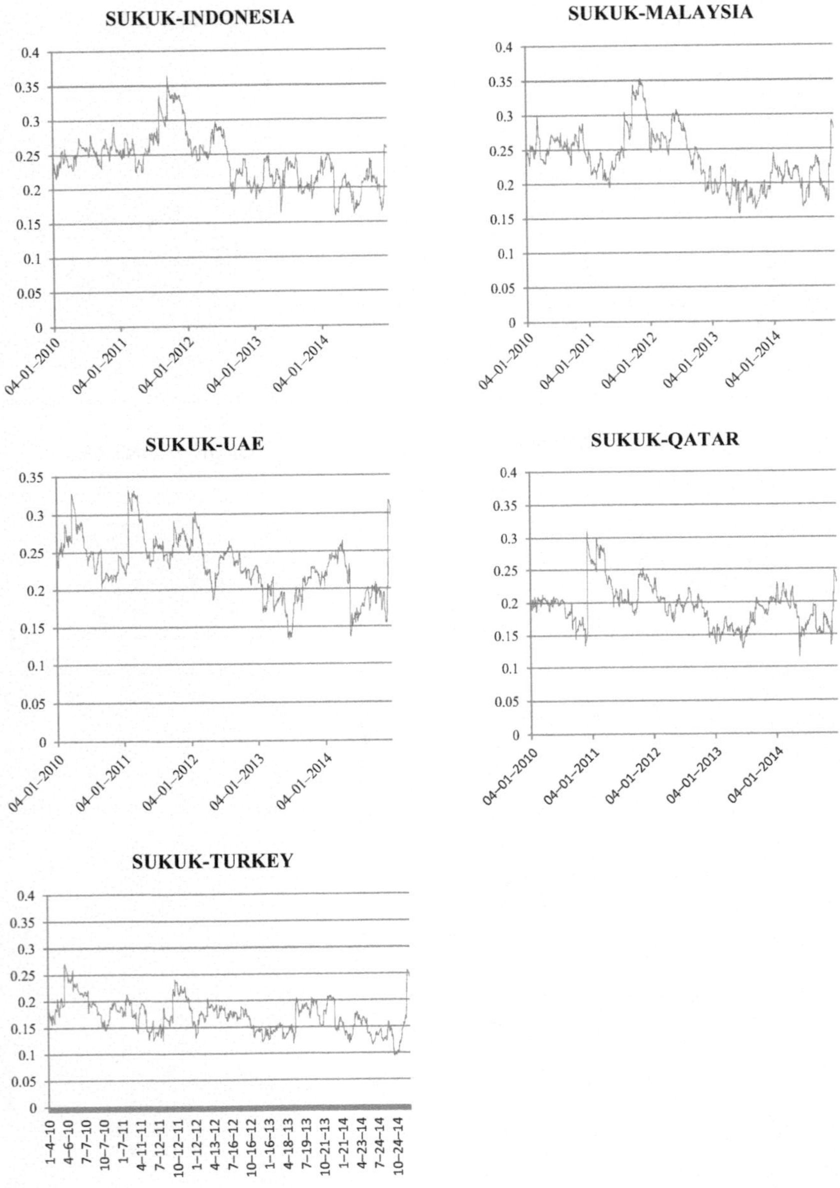

Fig. 3.4 Regional index dynamic correlations (*Source*: Our own elaboration)

quality and *flight-from quality* phenomena, documented by Baur and Lucey (2009) and Connolly et al. (2005) among others, which suggest a negative correlation between bonds and stocks during periods of high stock market volatility.

As shown from the plot (Fig. 3.3), dynamic correlations between Emerging Markets, Frontiers and Asia Pacific stock indexes and the *sukuk* index experienced a different behavior. Indeed, we denote evidence of greater co-movements between these assets in the first three years. Our results are consistent with Kelly et al. (1998), who revealed greater degrees of co-movement between stocks and bonds in emerging markets than in mature markets. According to the authors the reason is related to country risk, which is more relevant in emerging economics and makes domestic bond returns more similar to equities. Focusing on the last two years (2013, 2014), despite the slight increase in volatility linkages, the plot shows a small decrease in dynamic conditional correlations.

Figure 3.4 represents correlations between the *sukuk* index and five stock markets: Turkey, Qatar, UAE, Malaysia, and Indonesia. The correlation between *sukuk*, Turkey, Malaysia, and Indonesia slightly increased after the burst of the European sovereign debt crisis, from a value of 0.25 to 0.35. Moreover, even the volatility linkage has increased in size. At the same time, we do not notice the same upturn in both correlations and volatility linkages with UAE and Qatar stock indexes.

The main explanation for this different behavior is related to the fact that equity indexes from UAE and Qatar were less effected by global factors during the sample period, as suggested from the increased returns experienced in that period.

In 2012 and in the first half of the 2013 emerging stocks faced an exponential increase in returns, just when we can notice a 0.1 decrease in conditional correlations between *sukuk* and all the emerging market indexes. Conditional correlations between *sukuk*, Turkey, UAE, Qatar, and Malaysia stock indexes rose during the market correction experienced after the speculations about the FED tapering.

To sum up, by analyzing the conditional correlations at the regional level, we confirm the same co-movements observed at the global level with emerging markets, frontiers, and the *sukuk* index during the time span.

From the reported discussion, we can draw the following comments. The co-movements between *sukuk* and conventional stocks are different compared with those between conventional bonds and stocks. This behavior is consistent with Islamic bonds structure, based on *profit and loss sharing* and on a real underlying asset. In contrast with previous literature, we would rather therefore consider *sukuk* as an alternative asset class than an asset backed securities. Indeed *Shariah* compliant bonds have unique characteristics as they hybrid financial instruments between conventional bonds and stocks, following both movements. In terms of diversification benefits, we argue that investors could obtain portfolios' benefits including *sukuk* in a well-diversified equity portfolio, given their lower volatility compared to equity. But since volatility linkages between *sukuk* and regional market indexes are stronger during turmoil periods and the co-movements between volatilities and correlations tend to increase risk in the long run, institutional investors have to be careful in dealing with Islamic bonds, and also consider the relatively lower liquidity and higher *bid-ask spreads* of secondary markets in which they are traded.

6 Conclusions

The aim of this paper is to investigate volatility linkages and co-movements between *sukuk* and international conventional stock markets in the aftermath of the global crisis. We also explore, using the DCC GARCH model, the dynamic correlations between a cross-country market capitalization weighted index of *sukuk* listed in developed and developing countries and ten global and emerging market stock indexes during the period 2010–2014.

We extend the literature on *sukuk* and on portfolio benefits obtained by including *Shariah* compliant financial instruments, since this is the first paper investigating the relationship between *sukuk* and conventional stock market indexes. Our main hypothesis, indeed, is that *sukuk* are hybrid bonds, with similar characteristics to both equities and conventional bonds, due to the specific Islamic Finance framework.

Our results suggest that, during the periods of high market volatility, *sukuk* exhibit high correlations with US and EU stock indexes, without experiencing the well-known *flight to quality* phenomenon, that happened with conventional bonds. We also provide evidence that volatility linkages between *sukuk* and regional market indexes are stronger during turmoil periods.

Our findings could be relevant for institutional investors and asset managers that could obtain portfolios' benefits including *sukuk* in a well-diversified equity portfolio, given their lower volatility compared to equity. But since volatility linkages between *sukuk* and regional market indexes are stronger during financial crisis, institutional investors have to be careful in dealing with Islamic bonds. They have also to consider the specific characteristics of the markets in which *sukuk* are traded, especially the lower liquidity and higher *bid-ask spreads*, that could force investors to hold the *Shariah* compliant bonds until maturity. From our analysis it seems that *sukuk* are an alternative asset class that long term investors, such as pension funds, insurance companies, and Sovereign Wealth Funds have to consider to obtain diversification, though adding some risk to overall portfolio.

We have to frame all these remarks within the sample period (2010–2014) considering that the *sukuk* phenomenon hasn't been relevant worldwide before 2010. During this period we have witnessed low inflation, low GDP, interest rates tending to zero in most of the developed countries, and in general low interest rates also in the emerging markets, due to dovish monetary policies and quantitative easing in US and Japan (also in Europe we had some bond buying over the sample period). Correlations of intra and inter- asset classes could be easily affected by this environment and show higher values than in previous periods (for example before the US sub-prime financial crisis). Therefore future research on *sukuk* has to be done, in order to verify if their behavior persists in the long term and in economic cycles not affected by huge crisis.

References

Abdulkader, T., & Nathif, A. (2004). *Islamic bonds: Your guide to structuring, issuing and investing in Sukuk*. Working paper, Economy Institutional Investors.

Achsani, N. M., Effendi, J., & Abidin, Z. (2007). Dynamic interdependence among international Islamic stock market indices: Evidence from 2000–2007. In *Proceeding of the international conference of the Islamic capital markets*. Jakarta, Indonesia: Islamic Research and Training Institute, Islamic Development Bank.

Akhtar, S. M., Jahromi, M., John, K., & Moise, C. E. (2012). *Intensity of volatility linkages in Islamic and conventional markets*. Working paper, AFA 2012 Chicago Meetings Paper.

Aloui, C., Hammoudeh, S., & Hamida, H. B. (2015a). Co-movement between sharia stocks and sukuk in the GCC markets: A time-frequency analysis. *Journal of International Financial Markets, Institutions and Money, 34*, 69–79.

Aloui, C., Hammoudeh, S., & Hamida, H. B. (2015b). Global factors driving structural changes in the co-movement between sharia stocks and sukuk in the Gulf Cooperation Council countries. *North American Journal of Economics and Finance, 31*, 311–329.

Andersson, M., Krylova, E., & Vähämaa, S. (2008). Why does the correlation between stock and bond returns vary over time? *Applied Financial Economics, 18*, 139–151.

Baur, D. G., & Lucey, B. M. (2009). Flights and contagion—An empirical analysis of stock–bond correlations. *Journal of Financial Stability, 5*(4), 339–352.

Bley, J., & Chen, K. H. (2006). Gulf Cooperation Council (GCC) stock markets: The dawn of a new era. *Global Finance Journal, 17*, 75–91.

Bloomberg. (2015). http://www.bloomberg.com/news/articles/2015-03-09/euro-debt-gains-favor-as-telekom-malaysia-sells-islamic-finance

Bollerslev, T. (1986). Generalised autoregressive conditional heteroskedasticity. *Journal of Econometrics, 31*, 307–327.

Bollerslev, T. (1990). Modeling the coherence in short-run nominal exchange rates: A multivariate generalized ARCH model. *The Review of Economics and Statistics, 72*, 498–505.

Bollerslev, T., & Wooldridge, J. (1992). Quasi-maximum likelihood estimation and inference in dynamic models with time-varying covariances. *Econometric Reviews, 11*, 79–143.

Cakir, S., & Raei, F. (2007). *Sukuk vs Eurobonds: Is there a difference in value-at-risk?* Working paper, IMF WP/07/237.

Campbell, J., & Ammer, J. (1993). What moves the stock and bond market? A variance decomposition for long-term asset returns. *Journal of Finance, 48*, 3–37.

Cappiello, L., Engle, R., & Sheppard, K. (2006). Asymmetric dynamics in the correlations of global equity and bond returns. *Journal of Financial Econometrics, 4*(4), 537–572.

Connnoly, R., Stivers, C., & Sun, L. (2005). Stock market uncertainty and the stock–bond return relation. *Journal of Financial and Quantitative Analysis, 40*, 161–194.

Engle, R. (2002). Dynamic conditional correlation: A simple class of multivariate generalized autoregressive conditional heteroskedasticity models. *Journal of Business & Economic Statistics, 20*(3), 339–350.

Engle, R., & Sheppard, K. (2008). *Evaluating the specification of covariance models for large portfolios.* Working paper, New York University.

Fathurahman, H., & Fitriati, R. (2013). Comparative analysis of return on sukuk and conventional bonds. *American Journal of Economics, 3*, 159–163.

GIFR. (2012). *Global Islamic finance report.* http://www.gifr.net/

Glosten, L. R., Jagannathan, R., & Runkle, D. E. (1993). On the relationship between the expected value and the volatility of the nominal excess return on stocks. *Journal of Finance, 48*, 1779–1801.

IFSB. (2009). *Capital adequacy requirements for sukuk securitization and real estate investment.* http://www.ifsb.org/standard/eng_%20IFSB7%20Capital%20Adequacy%20Requirements%20for%20Sukuk,%20Securitasations%20and%20Real%20Estate%20investment%20(Jan2009).pdf

Iqbal, M., & Mirakhor, A. (2007). *An introduction to Islamic finance: Theory and practice.* Chichester: John Wiley & Sons.

Karim, B. A., Kassim, N. A. M., & Arip, M. A. (2010). The subprime crisis and Islamic stock markets integration. *International Journal of Islamic and Middle Eastern Finance and Management, 3*, 363–371.

Keim, D. B., & Stambaugh, R. F. (1986). Predicting returns in the stock and bond markets. *Journal of Financial Economics, 17*, 357–390.

Kelly, J. M., Martins, L. F., & Carlson, J. H. (1998). The relationship between bonds and stocks in emerging countries. *Journal of Portfolio Management, 24*, 110–122.

Kim, H. B., & Kang, S. H. (2012). *Volatility transmission between the sharia stock and sukuk GII markets in Malaysia.* Working paper, SSRN eLibrary.

Kim, S. J., Moshirian, F., & Wu, E. (2006). Evolution of international stock and bond market integration: Influence of the European Monetary Union. *Journal of Banking & Finance, 30*, 1507–1534.

Kwan, S. H. (1996). Firm-specific information and the correlation between individual stocks and bonds. *Journal of Financial Economics, 40*, 63–80.

Li, L. (2004). Macroeconomic factors and the correlation of stock and bond returns. In *Proceeding of the 2004 American Finance Association meeting.*

Majid, M., Yusof, R. M., & Razal, A. N. (2007). Dynamic financial linkages among selected OIC countries. *Journal of Economic Cooperation Among Islamic Countries, 28*, 25–56.

Majid, M., Meera, A. K. M., Omar, M. A., & Aziz, H. A. (2009). Dynamic linkages among ASEAN-5 emerging stock markets. *International Journal of Emerging Markets, 4*, 160–184.

Marashdeh, H. (2005). *Stock market integration in the MENA region: An application of the ARDL bounds testing approach*. Working paper, University of Wollongong.

Markowitz, H. (1952). Portfolio selection. *Journal of Finance, 7*, 77–91.

Markowitz, H. (1959). *Portfolio selection: Efficient diversification of investments* (Cowles foundation monograph). New York: Wiley.

Moody's. (2014). *Sovereign sukuk: Issuance rises as new governments enter Islamic capital markets*. Moody's report.

Mosaid, F., & Boutti, R. (2014). Sukuk and bond performance in Malaysia. *International Journal of Economics and Finance, 6*, 226–234.

MSCI. (2012). *Index calculation methodology for the MSCI equity indices*.

Najeeb, S. F., Bacha, O., & Masih, M. (2014). *Does a held-to-maturity strategy impede effective portfolio diversification for Islamic bond (sukuk) portfolios? A multi-scale continuous wavelet correlation analysis*. Working paper, MPRA, 56956.

Nelson, D. B. (1991). Conditional heteroskedasticity in asset returns: A new approach. *Econometrica, 59*, 347–370.

Rahman, A. A., & Sidek, N. Z. M. (2011). Spillover effect of us Subprime crisis on ASEAN-5 stock markets. In *Business and social science research conference*. Dubai: World Business Institute Australia.

Rusgianto, S., & Ahmad, N. (2013). Volatility behavior of sukuk market: An empirical analysis of the Dow Jones Citigroup sukuk index. *Middle-East Journal of Scientific Research, 13*, 93–97.

Saiti, B. (2013). Estimation of dynamic conditional correlations of Shariah-compliant stock indices through the application of multivariate GARCH approach. *Australian Journal of Basic and Applied Sciences, 7*, 259–267.

Shiller, R., & Beltratti, A. (1992). Stock prices and bond yields. *Journal of Monetary Economics, 30*, 25–46.

Tariq, A., Dar, A., & Dar, H. (2007). Risks of Sukuk structures: Implications for resource mobilization. *Thunderbird International Business Review, 49*, 203–223.

Vishwanath, S. R., & Sabahuddin, A. (2009). An overview of Islamic Sukuk bonds. *Journal of Structured Finance, 14*, 58–67.

Yang, J., Zhou, Y., & Wang, Z. (2009). The stock–bond correlation and macroeconomic conditions: One and a half centuries of evidence. *Journal of Banking & Finance, 33*, 670–680.

Zin, M. Z. M., Sakat, A. A., Ahmad, N. A., Roslan, M., Nor, M., Bhari, A., et al. (2011). The effectiveness of Sukuk in Islamic finance market. *Australian Journal of Basic and Applied Sciences, 5*, 472–478.

4

Bank-Specific, Macroeconomic or Structural Variables: Which Explains Bank Enterprise Lending? The Evidence from Transition Countries

Ewa Miklaszewska and Krzysztof Kil

1 Introduction

The key responsibility of the banking sector is to provide credit services to consumers, corporations, and small firms. While households use debt primarily to finance consumer spending and mortgages, for firms an external source of finance is essential to their investments, particularly within the European financial model, and in the long run is of fundamental importance for GDP growth. Lending to corporations may be less attractive to banks because the risk is higher and the return often lower than in the case of consumer loans, but from the point of view of the whole economy, it is clearly important to provide both types of loan. The aim of this paper is to analyze the factors influencing lending to businesses in the countries of Central and Eastern Europe (CEE). It analyzes

E. Miklaszewska (✉) • K. Kil
Cracow University of Economics, Cracow, Poland
e-mail: uumiklas@cyf-kr.edu.pl

S. Carbó Valverde et al. (eds.), *Bank Funding, Financial Instruments and Decision-Making in the Banking Industry*, Palgrave Macmillan Studies in Banking and Financial Institutions,
DOI 10.1007/978-3-319-30701-5_4

both macroeconomic characteristics and bank-specific variables relevant to loan dynamics and structure. It also proposes a new methodology of analyzing the impact of bank performance on lending policies, focusing not only on balance sheet ratios and a stability/risk measure (Z-score index), but also employing a comprehensive performance index: the Multi-Level Performance (MLP) score. Structural variables on the macro level (bank concentration) and on the micro level (share of relationship lending) are also analyzed.

For the empirical analysis, the paper uses an adjusted dataset on 11 CEE countries, based on the Bankscope database, employing panel data models for unconsolidated banking data. The time frame covers both the pre-crisis period (2004–2008) and post-crisis period (2009–2014), in order to determine whether and to what extent macroeconomic policies and environmental factors affect bank lending. As the global financial crisis arrived in most CEE countries with a lag, 2008 is classified as belonging to the first period.

The outline of this paper is as follows. Section 2 provides an overview of the literature on the determinants of enterprise loan granting; Sect. 3 describes trends in enterprise lending in CEE countries; Sect. 4 explains the data and empirical methodology; Sects. 5 and 6 summarize the empirical results, and Sect. 7 concludes the paper.

2 Factors Influencing Bank Enterprise Lending

For long-term economic growth, efficient bank lending policies are essential. Empirical research suggests that the availability of loans has a positive and statistically significant impact on GDP, although it is sometimes difficult to determine cause-and-effect relationships clearly (Capiello et al. 2010). Many reports published in the post-crisis period have indicated that corporate bank lending plays a primary role in generating economic growth (Beck et al. 2008). Thus, the sharp decline in bank loans to non-financial corporations in highly advanced EU countries during the 2007–2009 crisis, plus their failure to reassume dynamic corporate lending in the post-crisis period, both posed serious policy concerns (Fig. 4.1).

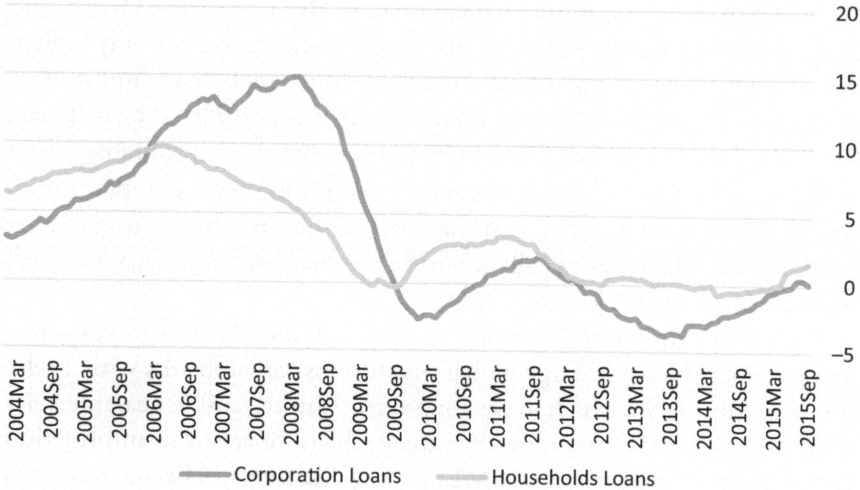

Fig. 4.1 The growth of bank loans to households and to non-financial corporations in the euro area (%)
(*Source:* Own presentation based on: ECB, *Statistical Data Warehouse*, available at: http://sdw.ecb.europa.eu/browse.do?node=bbn143 (accessed 2.11.2015))

Evidence from the global financial crisis of 2008, together with many empirical studies, have clearly indicated that bank lending has a strong effect on growth. Bank balance sheet losses in advanced countries, estimated by the IMF at over US $4 trillion in the period 2009–2010, heralded a strong credit slowdown. Bank credit declined significantly in several regions, including the countries of Central and Eastern Europe, which in the pre-crisis period had experienced a substantial credit boom. Bank credit in OECD countries also slowed down considerably, especially in countries where banks received public support in the form of capital injection (EC 2014).

For countries in the Euro Area, while bank credit is the main source of financing for households (80%), businesses, in contrast, have more diverse sources of funding: 40% is composed of equity instruments, 19% by debt securities and 16% by bank credit (Aisen and Franken 2010; Kok Sørensen et al. 2009). Thus, bank loans are not a primary source of funding, and different types of bank-enterprise relationship have also evolved in Europe, moving away from intense relationship banking towards arms-length contacts, more characteristic of the US system (Rajan and Zingales 2003). For small firms, financial constraints are not only higher, but also act as more of a growth impediment, as small firms find it more difficult to diversify sources of financing. Banks consider the small and medium-sized enterprises (SME) segment as potentially profitable, but it is also burdened with high credit risk. In addition, fierce competition in highly developed countries and macroeconomic instability in emerging economies are factors typically identified as discriminating against small business lending (Beck et al. 2011).

There is an important question of who is more efficient in corporate lending: local banks or large global institutions. Small banks with a relationship approach, which have long-term, direct, and repeatable relationships with SMEs, tend to solve the problem of access to information better, and relationship-based SMEs are also less likely to become subjects of default in times of crisis (Fiordelisi et al. 2013). Research shows that small banks lend more to small and medium-sized enterprises than large banks because of their comparative advantage in processing soft information on SMEs. Large banks have a comparative advantage in lending to large customers. However, transaction-based lending, which relies on hard information and assets, has also been analyzed as a successful alternative lending technique for SMEs (Beck 2013). De Haas et al. (2010) suggest that bank characteristics, such as ownership and size, are important determinants of a bank's customer focus. Large banks, with arms-length lending, enjoy a strong advantage in technology and have a better record of lending in good times. In periods of dynamic growth, global banks can be as effective as local banks in servicing small firms. A SME will choose the more expensive relationship-banking if the services it obtains are valuable. Larger firms will generally seek a mixture of relationship and transaction-based lending in an effort to reduce the cost of borrowing.

3 Enterprise Lending in the CEE Countries

Bank-loans are particularly important in lower-income countries, because they offer inexpensive risk management for standardized risks and can compensate for weaker institutions. When financial markets mature, they are better able to provide tailored, sophisticated products. Thus, as an economy and market infrastructure grow, they support market-based products, and the demand for a broader set of financial tools increases (Gambacorta et al. 2014). For CEE countries, the economic transformation of the 1990s and EU accession in 2004 caused profound economic and social changes, which resulted in the dynamic growth of their banking sectors and capital markets.

Banking markets in the CEE are dominated by foreign-owned, large global banks, which brought in technical and product efficiency and stimulated the rapid development of market procedures and standards in the pre-crisis period. However, foreign-owned banks may also have discriminated against riskier activities, including business-oriented loans, in the post-crisis period. Moreover, large global institutions may not be efficient in processing the soft information required for lending to businesses. While on a global scale, large enterprises are able to finance their growth from non-bank sources, in the less financially sophisticated CEE region, the availability of bank loans, particularly to small firms, is crucial for investments and for generating sustainable economic growth.

In analyzing factors influencing the access and source of corporate credit in CEE countries, it may be observed that internal financing dominates the scene, with relatively low reliance on external sources such as bank loans or direct financing from capital markets. In the pre-crisis period, a relatively low level of bank corporate lending may be explained by the consumer credit boom, which affected the structure of credit portfolios in countries which were experiencing dynamic growth. For most CEE countries this tendency continued into the post-crisis period, (Fig. 4.2), at least until the 2014–2015 recovery, as indicated in Fig. 4.3.

However, many research papers point out that dynamic loan growth significantly affects loan performance, but with a lag. For example, Carbó-Valverde et al. (2011) found a typical lag of two years for the EU banks. Consequently, CEE countries with high growth in corporate loans have also been burdened by high non-performing loan portfolios (e.g. Latvia, Romania, Slovenia or Croatia), as indicated in Fig. 4.4. This causal link poses a strategic risk management and regulatory dilemma for fast-growing economies.

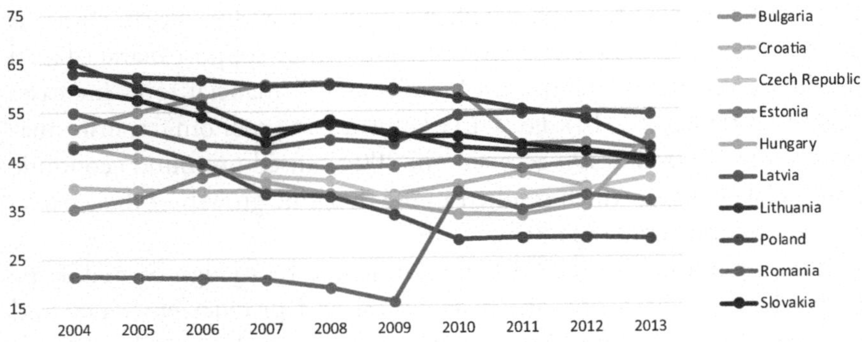

Fig. 4.2 Corporate loans within total loans in CEE countries, 2004–13
(*Source:* Authors' calculations based on Banking Supervisors from Central and Eastern European Countries (BSCEE) reviews (various issues), www.bscee.org

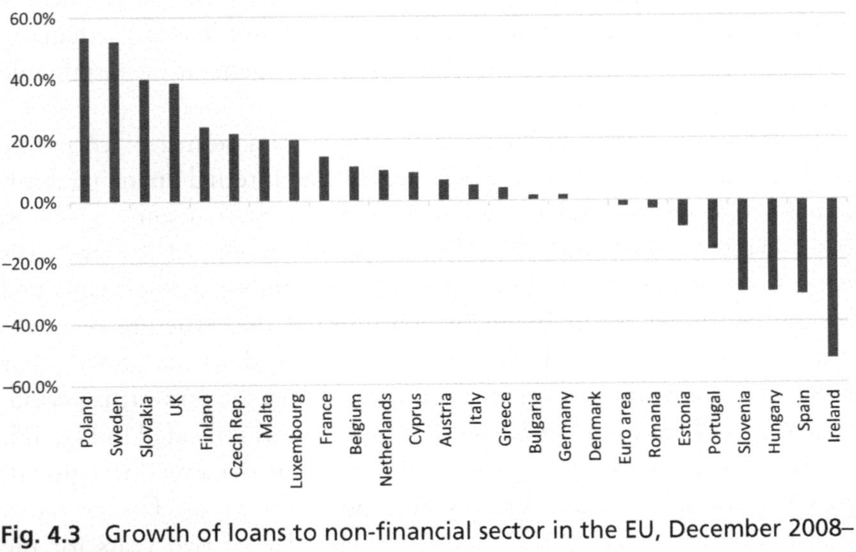

Fig. 4.3 Growth of loans to non-financial sector in the EU, December 2008–March 2015
(*Source:* Own presentation, based on data from NBP (2015))

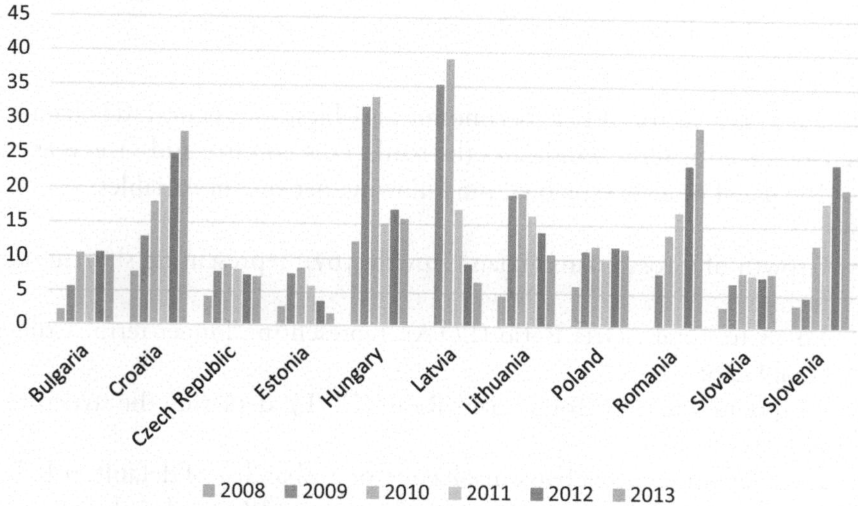

Fig. 4.4 NPL for non-financial corporations in CEE, 2008–2013 (*Source:* Own presentation, based on data from Banking Supervisors from Central and Eastern European Countries (BSCEE) reviews (various issues), www.bscee.org)

4 Empirical Analysis: Assumptions, Variables and Data Selection

The empirical part of the paper focuses on the question of what factors influence the composition of a bank loan portfolio and, in particular, the corporate loan share of this portfolio in CEE countries, based on panel data estimations. Owing to a lack of bank data on SME loans, the models analyzed aggregated data for loans to enterprises, and in order to analyze which factors and to what extent they influence corporate loan accessibility, a number of panel data models were employed, where the dependent variables were, first, overall loan growth and loan to asset ratio, and then corporate loan to total loan ratio. As explanatory variables, two groups of indicators were used: macroeconomic variables and banking sector characteristics, and bank-specific variables. The following model was used in estimations:

$$\text{Dependent variable}_{ijt} = \alpha_0 + \alpha_1 X_{1ijt} + \alpha_2 X_{2ijt} + \varepsilon$$

where X_1 is a vector of macroeconomic variables, X_2—bank-level characteristics, ε error term; i indicates the bank, j the country and t the year.

The panel models explained the following dependent variables:

- Growth of Gross Loans (Loan Growth, yoy): representing short-term factor;
- Loans to Total Assets Ratio (L/TA): representing longer-term, structural factor;
- Corporate Loans to Total Loans Ratio (CL/L): depicting the structure of loan portfolio;
- Z-score: representing bank insolvency, or probability of default, risk. It is defined as the ratio of the return on assets (ROA) plus the capital asset ratio (CAR) for a given year divided by the standard deviation of the return on assets over the period 2004–2014. Low level of Z-score indicates a high default risk.

The analysis was conducted for the period 2004–2014, divided into two sub-periods: the 2004–2008 period of high economic and credit growth, and the period encompassing the consequences of the global crisis and post-crisis recovery of 2009–2014. Bank-level data were extracted from the Bankscope database, with a number of adjustments. Control variables and data sources are summarized in Tables 4.1 and 4.2.

Table 4.1 Dependent variables explained in the panel models

Symbol	Description
Loan growth	Short-term factor: Growth of Gross Loans (yoy)
L/TA	Longer-term structural factor: Loans to Total Assets Ratio
CL/L	Structure of loan portfolio: Corporate Loans to Total Loans Ratio
Z-score	Risk measure: bank insolvency risk (probability of default). The ratio of the return on assets (ROA) plus the capital asset ratio (CAR) for a given year divided by the standard deviation of the return on assets over the period 2004–2014. Low level of Z-score indicate high default risk

Note: Data source: Bankscope

Table 4.2 Control variables used in the models

Symbol	Description	Rationale	Data source
Macroeconomic characteristics			
Δ GDP	Real GDP growth rate	Impact of the business cycle	Eurostat
LT_GBY	Long-term government bond yield (10-year bonds)	Interest rates approximation	Eurostat (for Estonia own estimation)
HICP	Harmonized Index of Consumer Prices	Inflation	Eurostat
HHI	Herfindahl-Hirschman Index for Credit Institutions	Banking market concentration	ECB: Banking Structural Financial Indicators
Coop	Cooperative banks' market share: assets of cooperative banks in total banking assets of a given country	Banking market structural diversification	For 2004–2013 own calculations based on data from: – European Association of Cooperative Banks (EACB); – Banking Supervisors from Central and Eastern European Countries (BSCEE) Reviews – For 2014 approximated
Bank-level characteristics			
ln_TA	Logarithm of Total Assets (in EUR)	Bank size	
L/D	Loans to Deposits ratio	Bank profile	
D/A	Deposits to Assets Ratio	Bank financial strategy and risk	
C/I	Cost to Income Ratio	Cost efficiency	
ROE	Return on Average Equity	Profit efficiency	

(continued)

Table 4.2 (continued)

Symbol	Description	Rationale	Data source
NeII_NoIOI	Net Interest Income/ Total Non-Interest Operating Income	Income diversification	
NPL	Nonperforming loans to total gross loans	Loan portfolio risk	
MLP_Score	Multi-Level Performance Score: basic Calculated as a sum of 5 scores: ROE; C/I; L/A; Z-Score; NPL (in points, methodology explained in the text)	Comprehensive, risk-based bank performance indicator	
MLP (TCR)_Score	Multi-level Performance Score: modified. NPLs replaced by TCR: regulatory risk-based capital ratio	Comprehensive, risk-based bank performance indicator	

Note: Data source: Bankscope

In analyzing factors influencing bank credit policies, the typical control variables used in the post-crisis financial literature are macroeconomic characteristics and bank-level variables, usually narrowly defined. However, the adoption of more comprehensive measures of bank performance and risk might be useful to arrive at a longer-term perspective, as opposed to narrowly defined balance sheet ratios. A frequently used measure included in strategic analysis is the Z-score stability (probability of default) index, well-established in the financial literature, as discussed by Casu et al. (2015). The ratio is defined as return on assets (ROA) plus capital asset ratio (CAR) for a given year, divided by the standard deviation of the return on assets over a given period, or using the rolling windows technique. A high level Z-score indicates low default risk. The value of the index crucially depends on the variability of returns and bank capitalization levels, advantageous to well capitalized traditional banks with stable strategies (and profit-base).

Table 4.3 presents the value of the Z-score index for CEE countries in the analyzed period, where standard deviation was calculated over the 2004–2014 period. For the whole group, 2010 and 2011 are the years of lowest index value, as the crisis arrived in CEE with a lag, although a current value around 16 still indicated the considerable riskiness of CEE banks (as opposed to 20 in 2004). For the whole 2004–2014 period, the lowest value of the index was recorded for Slovenia, where large state-ownership in banking did not enhance bank stability, followed by Hungary. The highest stability recorded was for Croatia, but mostly in the pre-crisis period, Estonia, the Czech Republic, Slovakia, and Poland.

In the financial literature, other stability measures, such as the S-Score (or Bankometer), have recently been proposed. This index is based on Altman's methodology and is defined by the following formula:

$$S = 1.5 * CA + 1.2 * EA + 3.5 * CAR + 0.6 * NPL + 0.3 * CI + 04 * LA$$

where 'S' stands for solvency, CAR stands for capital adequacy ratio, CA stands for capital assets ratio, EA stands for equity to assets, NPL stands for non-performing loans to loans and CI stands for cost to income ratio and LA stands for loans to assets ratio.

The S-score categorizes banks as solvent and insolvent on the basis of IMF recommendations (Evans et al. 2000). The model is focused on capital adequacy, asset quality and profitability (earnings). Every indicator in the formula has a different weighting, depending on their estimated importance and impact on the solvency indicator (Shar 2010). Banks that have an "S" value above 70% are considered solvent, while banks with an "S" value under 50% are considered insolvent and the area between 50 and 70 is defined as a gray area. According to this procedure, a bank that has a capital adequacy ratio between 8% and 40%, capital to assets ratio above 4%, equity to assets ratio greater than 2%, non-performing loans ratio below 15% and loans to assets ratio below 40%, may be categorized as solvent. However, the S-index is heavily based on bank capitalization as its main stability indicator and does not have a simple interpretation, such as in the case of the Z-score.

Table 4.3 Average Z-score level in the CEE region

Country	2004	2005	2006	2007	2008	2009	2010	2011	2012	2013	2014	2004–2014
CZ	19.84	17.21	18.70	19.66	21.24	19.47	19.40	18.25	18.98	17.65	18.90	19.05
BG	12.38	10.75	11.33	8.34	12.49	14.25	14.54	13.63	14.37	14.62	16.93	12.89
EE	22.43	23.71	25.11	18.72	21.57	23.77	20.36	18.31	22.23	23.02	20.33	21.87
HR	34.93	32.50	31.65	30.12	27.88	27.35	16.47	14.97	15.37	14.62	16.16	23.06
HU	10.49	12.33	11.34	9.36	10.14	9.95	10.02	9.76	10.93	10.15	10.18	10.38
LT	13.17	13.52	12.45	17.51	18.14	13.65	7.10	10.08	10.87	10.63	9.46	11.96
LV	25.44	19.44	18.41	13.44	13.56	14.17	8.19	7.54	9.37	10.24	8.44	12.89
PL	24.91	21.54	17.87	16.51	14.55	15.37	16.83	17.30	21.62	20.70	21.91	18.66
RO	13.33	13.14	8.45	9.57	9.77	9.97	14.12	14.03	12.99	11.46	13.46	11.68
SI	9.14	9.50	9.88	9.65	12.76	15.36	5.69	6.56	6.66	4.66	7.46	9.06
SK	19.52	19.91	21.84	17.46	15.84	16.42	27.32	26.71	29.32	27.79	28.48	22.61
CEE group	19.95	18.11	16.85	15.57	16.02	16.33	14.87	14.66	16.02	15.19	15.85	16.22

Source: Own calculations, based on Bankscope, total number of 2756 observations

In the analytical section, the paper employs a new, risk-adjusted, comprehensive performance indicator, called the Multi-Level Performance Score (MLP). It is composed of a sum of scores allocated to five areas vital to bank long-term stability and performance: three efficiency indicators: ROE, C/I and loan accessibility (L/A); and two stability indicators: Z-score and NPL. It is defined by the following formula:

$$\text{MPL} - \text{Score} = \text{ROE} + \text{L}/\text{A}(\text{Loans to Assets}) + \text{C}/\text{I}(\text{Cost to Income}) \\ + \text{Z} - \text{Score} + \text{NPL}.$$

Scores for the MLP index in all five areas are allocated as follows:

- Bank results for each indicator are divided into ten deciles for the whole group in a given year;
- The median for the group has a value of 0 (is neutral);
- Each subsequent decile above the median for ROE, L/A and Z-Score has a score ranging from +1 to +5, while each subsequent decile below the median has a score ranging from −1 to −5;
- For C/I and NPL indicators the signs are the opposite: values above the median are negative from −1 to −5, and below the median positive from +1 to +5 for the last decile;
- By using this scoring methodology, the ratio has a simple interpretation, similar to that of the Z-score: the higher the value of the MLP index, the better.

In computing the MPL-Score, there is a significant problem with data on NPLs, since many banks in CEE do not disclose this indicator. As a consequence, a modified version of the score was also tested in the panel models: an MPL (TCR) Score, in which NPLs were replaced by a total capital ratio (TCR). The number of available observations in the latter increasing from 1550 to 1688. However, as the estimations were not significantly different as regards the basic and modified MLP Score, only the basic score was interpreted in most panels. Tables 4.4 and 4.5 provide MPL scores (basic and modified) for the analyzed CEE countries.

Table 4.4 MLP score (basic)

Country	2004	2005	2006	2007	2008	2009	2010	2011	2012	2013	2014	Av./country 2004–2014
CZ	2.57	4.41	4.32	3	1.72	0.04	9.89	7.82	7.43	5.48	8	4.79
BG	4.25	4.5	3.8	−0.45	−1.93	1.07	1.68	0.67	−1.17	0.59	3.31	0.78
EE	−5.5	1.5	−4.5	−3	−1.17	−1.8	2	8.33	4	9	10.88	3.18
HR	−3.33	−4.5	0.2	−1.54	−1.57	−3.39	0.26	−1.71	−3.41	−4.38	−1.67	−2.26
HU	−1.67	−1.75	1.67	1.13	2.24	4.22	−2.18	−5.38	−6.62	−7.92	−14.57	−1.89
LT	5	3	2.5	6.5	7.67	9	−6.63	−0.43	−1.43	−0.14	−2.71	−0.08
LV	n.a.	5	−6	3.33	0.75	1.18	−10.43	−9.14	−5.36	−1.77	−1.8	−4.09
PL	−0.5	2.88	2.19	3.68	5.04	3	4.54	7.73	8.17	7.81	8.45	5
RO	−1	1.29	−0.89	−0.86	0.23	−0.56	−2.33	−3.74	−5.16	−3.95	−4.53	−2.43
SI	−1.67	−2.6	2.5	−1.91	0.08	−0.5	−1.33	−2.83	−3.94	−6.06	−4.07	−2.34
SK	3.75	1	−0.6	1.14	−0.44	0.8	4	4.82	6.08	7.38	6.9	3.72
Average for CEE	0.6	1.48	1.61	1.01	1.1	0.79	0.62	0.74	0.43	0.71	1.44	0.9

Source: Own calculations. Number of observations: 1550

Table 4.5 MLP (TCR) score (modified)

Country	2004	2005	2006	2007	2008	2009	2010	2011	2012	2013	2014	2004–2014
CZ	5.19	5.89	7.72	5.04	2.40	–0.14	8.21	5.67	3.95	3.32	4.75	4.43
BG	3.67	4.33	1.63	0.85	1.45	1.92	1.47	–1.11	–1.45	–0.16	2.82	0.68
EE	–4.60	1.00	0.20	1.33	1.00	–0.67	–0.50	–2.57	–3.56	0.89	3.57	–0.40
HR	–4.56	0.33	1.42	–0.11	0.43	–2.22	–3.55	–1.96	–4.26	–4.33	–2.33	–2.14
HU	1.36	1.93	0.75	1.14	2.15	2.48	2.07	–1.11	–3.24	–5.20	–10.63	–0.16
LT	1.00	8.00	4.50	4.00	5.33	3.80	–4.13	2.86	0.29	–1.14	–2.71	1.10
LV	3.00	2.25	–3.33	–1.67	0.30	0.67	–6.64	–5.27	–3.73	–2.50	–5.31	–2.87
PL	0.57	1.05	3.21	5.29	6.76	4.21	3.73	7.69	5.79	6.04	7.30	4.80
RO	0.29	0.09	0.77	–0.13	1.57	1.07	–2.56	–4.05	–2.56	–1.81	–4.82	–1.32
SI	–3.71	1.22	1.00	0.36	–0.20	0.00	3.93	1.94	0.31	–2.33	–1.43	0.25
SK	1.64	2.09	2.18	6.50	6.38	5.10	3.50	2.70	3.25	5.42	5.78	3.90
Average for CEE	0.66	2.22	2.20	2.30	2.53	1.30	0.88	0.81	–0.20	0.09	0.24	1.13

Source: Own calculations. Number of observations: 1688

Table 4.6 Comparison of the MPL and Z-scores for the aggregated data in 2004–2014 period for CEE countries

Country	MLP basic	MLP modified	Z-score
PL	5.00	4.80	18.66
CZ	4.79	4.43	19.05
SK	3.72	3.90	22.61
EE	3.18	−0.40	21.87
BG	0.78	−0.68	12.89
LT	−0.08	1.10	11.96
HU	−1.89	−0.16	10.38
HR	−2.26	−2.14	23.06
SI	−2.34	0.25	9.06
RO	−2.43	−1.32	11.68
LV	−4.09	−2.87	12.87

Source: Own calculations

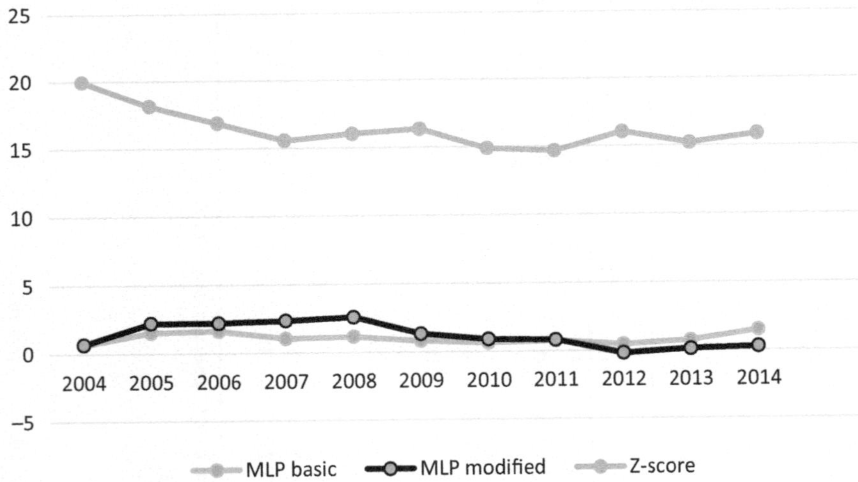

Fig. 4.5 Comparison of aggregate performance scores for CEE countries (*Source:* Own calculations)

An analysis of MLP Scores (Tables 4.4, 4.5 and 4.6 and Fig. 4.5) allows us to make certain interesting observations:

- For MLP both scores, high aggregate values were attained by CEE banks between 2005 and 2008. There was a visible drop in 2009, the lowest value being reached in 2012. 2014, however, witnessed the beginning of a substantial score recovery, indicating the improved performance of CEE banks;

- For individual countries, the highest MPL (basic and modified) scores were attained throughout the whole period by Poland, the Czech Republic, and Slovakia. These countries (except for Poland in 2004 and Slovakia in 2008 on the basic score) have positive index scores every year, above the CEE median, indicating consistently stable results;
- The lowest MLP-Scores values were those of Latvia, followed by Romania, Slovenia, Croatia, and Hungary;
- In the analyzed period, we may observe growing disparities between country scores: for MLP both scores, in 2004 bank scores ranging from -5 to +5, while in 2014 from −14 (Hungary) to +11 (Estonia) for the basic score and from −11 (Hungary) to +7 (Poland) for the modified score;
- For Hungary, there was a dramatic decline in bank performance from 2010 to 2011;
- The biggest difference for MPL basic and modified indices were for Estonia, because of its small NPL indicator;
- There are significant disparities between MLP performance scores and the stability Z-score index, particularly for Croatia, which indicates that a multi-level indicator might be a more useful measure with which to assess longer-term bank potential.

Overall, MLP-Scores proved to be useful integrated performance indicators and were used as control variables in panel models. As the use of both indices produced on average similar results, in most analyses only the basic MLP score was interpreted.

5 Empirical Analysis: Panel Models' Estimations Results

The panel data model was run over the 2004–2014 period and estimated separately for two periods, pre- and post-crisis, in order to capture the impact of the changing macroeconomic conditions.

The global crisis was to a large extent an imported factor for CEE banks, arriving in the region with a time-lag. Hence, the dividing point was placed at 2008–2009, which is also supported by a decline in MLP-Scores for the region from 2009, as presented in Tables 4.4 and 4.5. As a consequence of problems with data accessibility, an unbalanced panel was used in which the number of time-series observations was different across banks. A fixed effects panel data methodology was employed, which holds constant individual differences and stresses the marginal effects of the explanatory variables. The panel model was employed for the 11 Central and East European Countries (CEE), members of the EU, eight which accessed the EU in 2004 (the Czech Republic, Estonia, Hungary, Latvia, Lithuania, Poland, Slovakia and Slovenia), two which accessed in 2007 (Bulgaria and Romania) and Croatia accessed in 2013.

A number of models were run in order to explain three dependent variables:

- Dynamic variable: growth of gross loans (model 1a, 1b), explaining bank reaction to changing conditions,
- Static variable: loans to assets ratio (model 2a, 2b), analyzing which factors influence overall credit policies,
- Corporate loans to total loans ratio (model 3a, 3b), researching factors influencing the availability of business loans.

For each dependent variable, two panel models were run: model (a) with a number of fragmented control variables, and model (b) with a comprehensive MLP score replacing certain balance sheet ratios encompassed in the MLP score. Only for the second dependent variable (L/A) was the MLP score not used, as it encompasses this ratio into its construction. Instead, in order to explain the L/A ratio, two panel models were used: with and without NPL score. Including an NPL score means the number of observation is reduced, since many banks do not disclose this ratio.

In explaining the growth of gross loans in model 1a and 1b (Tables 4.7 and 4.8), many macroeconomic variables, such as dynamic GDP growth, high concentration ration, and growing consumer price index, were significant for the whole period in generating loan growth. Bank-level variables in model 1b, such as size of bank (lnTA) and income diversification (NetII_NoIOI) had a negative influence on the dependent variable, suggesting that large banks with non-diversified incomes might possess lower dynamics of loan growth. Bank individual efficiency ratios were not significant, although the comprehensive

Table 4.7 Panel model 1a: estimations for growth of gross loans

Control variables	2004–2014	2004–2008	2009–2014
Const	312.843***	244.271**	186.020**
	(44.935)	*(96.427)*	*(79.633)*
LT_GBY	−0.404	−1.482	−0.691
	(0.906)	*(5.022)*	*(1.113)*
COOP	4.250	6.862	5.604
	(3.143)	*(6.965)*	*(4.903)*
Δ GDP	0.711**	1.768	−0.574
	(0.332)	*(1.399)*	*(0.454)*
HHI	478.023***	2.365	24.858
	(116.906)	*(341.422)*	*(177.579)*
HICP	1.998***	0.504	0.688
	(0.500)	*(1.839)*	*(0.819)*
ln_TA	−25.343***	−19.177***	−12.018**
	(2.846)	*(5.048)*	*(5.249)*
L/D	0.027**	0.055	0.022
	(0.013)	*(0.038)*	*(0.015)*
D/A	0.151	0.743*	−0.049
	(0.095)	*(0.448)*	*(0.137)*
C/I	−0.014	−0.173	−0.017
	(0.025)	*(0.270)*	*(0.027)*
ROE	0.044	0.427	0.030
	(0.040)	*(0.392)*	*(0.041)*
Z_score	−0.016	−0.038	−0.338
	(0.197)	*(0.731)*	*(0.296)*
NetII_NoIOI	−0.001	−0.007*	−0.001
	(0.001)	*(0.004)*	*(0.001)*
NPL	−0.776***	−0.979	−0.591***
	(0.134)	*(0.650)*	*(0.154)*
R^2	0.438	0.713	0.347
Adjusted R^2	0.305	0.514	0.127
No. of observations	1248	337	906

Note: For all panel models in this section the least squares method with fixed effects was used

***, ** and * correspond to 1%, 5% and 10% significance level

Table 4.8 Panel model 1b: estimations for growth of gross loans, with MLP score

Control variables	2004–2014	2004–2008	2009–2014
Const	266.024***	251.922***	86.212
	(41.901)	*(77.753)*	*(72.892)*
LTGBY	0.176	−1.197	−0.142
	(0.894)	*(4.000)*	*(1.084)*
COOP	2.003	7.896	3.270
	(2.861)	*(6.191)*	*(4.637)*
Δ GDP	0.847***	−0.295	−0.664
	(0.325)	*(1.135)*	*(0.436)*
HHI	253.143***	−339.670	81.029
	(75.620)	*(221.803)*	*(170.686)*
HICP	2.230***	−0.996	0.250
	(0.486)	*(1.505)*	*(0.802)*
ln_TA	−20.312***	−12.702***	−6.583
	(2.713)	*(4.417)*	*(4.926)*
NetII_NoIOI	−0.002***	−0.008**	−0.001
	(0.001)	*(0.003)*	*(0.001)*
MLP_Score	0.791***	0.926*	0.664***
	(0.164)	*(0.479)*	*(0.207)*
R^2	0.385	0.610	0.329
Adjusted R^2	0.245	0.390	0.098
No. of observations	1417	467	945

Note: ***, ** and * correspond to 1%, 5% and 10% significance level

efficiency score, MLP, was significant and had a positive influence on loan growth throughout the whole period and in sub-periods, suggesting that the overall conditions of banking markets are very important for stimulating loan growth.

When analyzing factors influencing the loans to assets ratio (model 2a and 2b), the structural diversification of a banking market, represented by share of cooperative banks and growing interest rates, approximated by LT_GBY, were important (Tables 4.9 and 4.10). In contrast to the previous panel, bank scale had a positive impact on ratio, while GDP growth and market concentration (significant in the pre-crisis period) were negative controls. A large deposit base and high Z-score were important mostly in the pre-crisis period; post-crisis, they had a negative impact on the ratio. ROE also had a negative influence on this ratio. For NPLs, their low level was associated with a higher loan share in the pre-crisis period, and later the converse.

Table 4.9 Panel model 2a: estimations for loans to assets ratio

Control variables	2004–2014	2004–2008	2009–2014
Const	−23.830*	−37.448***	−12.199
	(13.773)	*(12.716)*	*(20.869)*
LT_GBY	0.620*	2.104***	1.332***
	(0.323)	*(0.565)*	*(0.356)*
COOP	4.025***	2.255**	0.419
	(0.953)	*(1.070)*	*(1.559)*
Δ GDP	−0.295**	−0.099	0.165
	(0.116)	*(0.156)*	*(0.143)*
HHI	24.852	−120.148***	-9.420
	(31.118)	*(37.972)*	*(57.976)*
ln_TA	4.874***	5.657***	4.910***
	(0.887)	*(0.728)*	*(1.412)*
L/D	0.013***	0.003	0.011**
	(0.005)	*(0.004)*	*(0.005)*
D/A	0.037	0.141***	-0.011
	(0.029)	*(0.048)*	*(0.037)*
C/I	−0.008	−0.004	−0.003
	(0.008)	*(0.014)*	*(0.008)*
ROE	−0.038***	0.022	−0.405***
	(0.009)	*(0.021)*	*(0.008)*
Z_score	−0.026	0.256***	−0.038
	(0.033)	*(0.071)*	*(0.043)*
R^2	0.622	0.928	0.772
Adjusted R^2	0.560	0.897	0.712
No. of observations	2053	744	1303

Note: ***, ** and * correspond to 1%, 5% and 10% significance level

Looking at the third dependent variable, structure of loan portfolio (CL/TL), model 3a and 3b (Tables 4.11 and 4.12) indicate that GDP and interest rate growth have a positive impact on corporate loan share, similar to that of bank size. Only in the pre-crisis period did low banking concentration and smaller size of banks with a large deposit base positively influence corporate loan share. For the whole period, deposits (D/A) were negatively correlated, while for the Z-score and NPL they were positive. Unlike loan growth, the MLP score has a negative impact on this ratio, highlighting the fact that the good overall condition of banks does not necessarily result in improved accessibility of corporate loans, which may involve a number of inefficiencies for bank profitability (high C/I ratio in pre-crisis period and high NPL ratio in post-crisis period).

Table 4.10 Panel model 2b: estimations for loans to assets ratio, with NPLs

Control variables	2004–2014	2004–2008	2009–2014
Const	−1.016	−9.229	58.281**
	(16.550)	*(19.821)*	*(24.960)*
LT_GBY	1.006***	1.716*	1.449***
	(0.338)	*(0.887)*	*(0.354)*
COOP	1.563	1.938	2.086
	(1.176)	*(1.497)*	*(1.623)*
Δ GDP	−0.203	−0.381	−0.006
	(0.124)	*(0.265)*	*(0.150)*
HHI	−9.735	−193.372**	−96.127
	(44.907)	*(74.720)*	*(58.998)*
ln_TA	4.241***	3.094***	1.513
	(1.030)	*(0.993)*	*(1.643)*
L/D	0.013***	0.013	0.008
	(0.005)	*(0.008)*	*(0.005)*
D/A	−0.063*	0.332***	−0.200***
	(0.036)	*(0.093)*	*(0.045)*
C/I	−0.007	0.079	−0.017**
	(0.008)	*(0.059)*	*(0.008)*
ROE	−0.035***	0.022	−0.029***
	(0.012)	*(0.084)*	*(0.011)*
Z_score	0.058	0.368***	−0.111
	(0.075)	*(0.133)*	*(0.098)*
NPL	0.045	−0.219*	0.104**
	(0.048)	*(0.117)*	*(0.049)*
R^2	0.691	0.911	0.819
Adjusted R^2	0.620	0.850	0.760
No. of observations	1294	352	937

Note: ***, ** and * correspond to 1%, 5% and 10% significance level

The empirical results support theoretical assertions on factors influencing corporate lending, although stressing the importance of some new factors:

- Bank-level variables were largely insignificant and the overall index of bank performance (MPL score) had a negative influence on corporate lending,
- A safe financing base (deposits) was not only unimportant, but actually negative,
- Bank size (lnTA) had a significant impact on the share of corporate loans in the total loan portfolio in the pre-crisis period. However, large banks, which discriminated against corporate loans in the pre-crisis period, reversed this tendency in the post-crisis years.

Table 4.11 Panel model 3a: estimation for corporate loans to total loans ratio

Control variables	2004–2014	2004–2008	2009–2014
Const	−32.477	110.458**	−74.726*
	(26.399)	*(42.943)*	*(38.639)*
LTGBY	1.354***	1.065	0.815
	(0.432)	*(1.136)*	*(0.502)*
COOP	−1.514	2.925	−1.072
	(1.614)	*(1.811)*	*(2.175)*
Δ GDP	0.534***	−0.454	0.213
	(0.163)	*(0.321)*	*(0.220)*
HHI	−34.212	−244.485*	−100.264
	(70.484)	*(130.240)*	*(86.764)*
ln_TA	6.724***	−7.113***	10.833***
	(1.603)	*(2.513)*	*(2.529)*
L/D	0.012*	−0.007	0.020*
	(0.007)	*(0.008)*	*(0.010)*
D/A	−0.227***	0.442***	−0.290***
	(0.054)	*(0.129)*	*(0.068)*
C/I	0.016	0.473***	0.006
	(0.013)	*(0.080)*	*(0.012)*
ROE	−0.011	0.240*	−0.001
	(0.014)	*(0.125)*	*(0.013)*
Z_score	0.326***	0.260	0.072
	(0.093)	*(0.196)*	*(0.129)*
NPL	0.163**	0.144	0.161**
	(0.065)	*(0.158)*	*(0.069)*
R^2	0.787	0.956	0.842
Adjusted R^2	0.721	0.917	0.777
No. of observations	869	199	670

Note: ***, ** and * correspond to 1%, 5% and 10% significance level

6 Banking Market Competitive Characteristics and Enterprise Lending in CEE

In the panel models analyzed in the previous section, the structure of the CEE banking market, represented by a cooperative banking share, was important only as regards the L/A ratio in the pre-crisis period (model 2a). Thus, as a next step, the paper takes a more in-depth look at structural and competitive conditions in CEE banking markets, with the

Table 4.12 Panel model 3b: estimations for CL/TL ratio, with MLP score

Control variables	2004–2014	2004–2008	2009–2014
Const	9.420	100.341***	−63.668
	(24.107)	(31.599)	*(39.327)*
LTGBY	1.287***	2.158*	0.917*
	(0.420)	(1.142)	*(0.503)*
COOP	−0.969	1.555	−1.554
	(1.479)	(1.977)	*(2.199)*
Δ GDP	0.419***	0.036	0.214
	(0.151)	(0.309)	*(0.220)*
HHI	−35.630	−118.187*	−90.967
	(40.751)	(63.395)	*(87.970)*
NetII_NoIOI	0.000	−0.001	0.000
	(0.000)	(0.001)	*(0.000)*
ln_TA	3.349**	−2.467	8.890***
	(1.494)	(2.026)	*(2.619)*
MLP_score	−0.314***	−0.624***	−0.075
	(0.087)	(0.167)	(0.105)
R^2	0.779	0.903	0.844
Adjusted R^2	0.714	0.836	0.780
No. of observations	968	282	686

Note: ***, ** and * correspond to 1%, 5% and 10% significance level

aim of discovering whether market characteristics have influenced corporate loan accessibility. For this further analysis, CEE banking markets were defined as concentrated or diversified, based on two joint criteria:

- Micro-oriented: the share of relationship-lending, defined by access to bank branches;
- Macro-oriented: market concentration level, defined by CR5 ratio.

Relationship-lending is typically defined as a bank repeatedly interacting with clients in order to obtain and exploit proprietary borrower information, and has traditionally been seen as the appropriate tool for banks to reach small and medium-sized enterprises (SMEs). There is a substantial body of research concentrating on the importance of relationship lending for SME loans. Some empirical studies emphasize that small firms in a poor financial state often rely on this relationship while those in a good financial state may choose cheaper transactional banks. There are also indications that firms are more likely to maintain bank relationships in countries with inefficient judicial systems and poor enforcement of creditor rights, but this is also true of countries with strong, but decentralized, banking systems and active public bond markets (Ongena and Smith 2000). Many empirical studies point out that relationship-banking is more stable and anti-cyclical, as relationship-based banks are able to take bigger risks risk during downturns, and in addition, firms with relationship-lending tend to enjoy improved credit availability (Chiaramonte et al. 2013).

Data on relationship-lending is difficult to obtain, hence the paper uses a classification adopted from *T.* Beck et al., where CEE countries were ranked according to relationship-banking share, defined as the number of branches of relationship-banks in a locality, divided by the total number of bank branches in that locality (2014).

The problem of the impact of market concentration on market competitive conditions is even more complex (Pawłowska 2015). One of the most visible developments in recent years has been a strong consolidation in the banking industry, which raises the question of what extent competition is affected by the expansion of the largest banks, and what the long-term impact is of a relative decline in traditional intermediation in favor of complex, tailor-made banking services (Bikker and Spierdijk 2009). Concentration data are easy to obtain, but the interpretation of their importance to market efficiency and stability is less universally accepted, the more so that both EU-27 and CEE-11 groups are not homogeneous in this respect (Fig. 4.6).

Consequently, the CEE-11 group was divided into two subgroups, based on two joint criteria: market concentration and relationship-banking share, in order to analyze whether these factors influence loan growth and structure and affect both groups in the same way. The allocation of countries to both groups is presented in Table 4.13.

When analyzing performance indicators (MLP scores and Z-score) for both these groups, some observable differences emerge (Fig. 4.7). While countries in the Concentrated Banking Group in the 2004–2009 period had a much higher Z-score, they also had the worst performance scores. However, from 2012 the performance indicators have tended to harmonize for both groups.

The next step was to test the importance of the selected explanatory variables for loan accessibility for both groups, measured by two

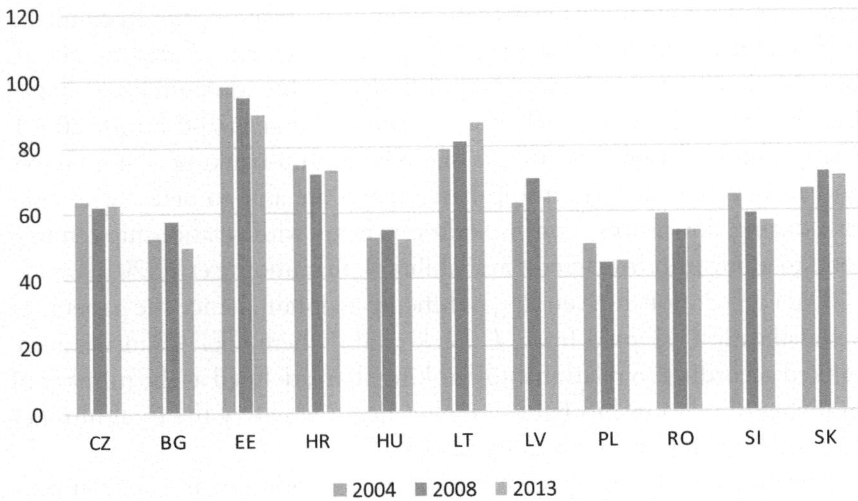

Fig. 4.6 Banking market concentration in CEE-11 countries, CR5 (%) (*Source:* Own presentation, based on ECB: Banking Structural Financial Indicators)

Table 4.13 CEE-11 subgroups: countries with concentrated and diversified banking markets

Country/criteria	(A) Share of relationship banks (Beck score, scale 0–1)[a]	(B) CR-5 ratio
Group 1: Diversified Banking (DBG). Criteria: A>50% and B<60%.		
Czech Republic	0.90	62.2[b]
Bulgaria	0.77	57.8
Slovenia	0.64	59.4
Hungary	0.58	54.8
Poland	0.59	44.0
Romania	0.55	53.2
Group 2: Concentrated Banking (CBG): other countries		
Croatia	0.71	73.4
Lithuania	0.59	80.8
Estonia	0.53	94.1
Latvia	0.45	69.8
Slovak Republic	0.31	71.8

Source: Own presentation, based on (A): Beck et al. (2014), and (B): ECB: Banking Structural Financial Indicators, both for 2008/09

Note: [a]Share of relationship banks is the number of branches of relationship banks in a locality divided by the total number of bank branches in that locality

[b]For the Czech Republic, in the 2nd criterion 62% was accepted, as the 1st indicator was very high

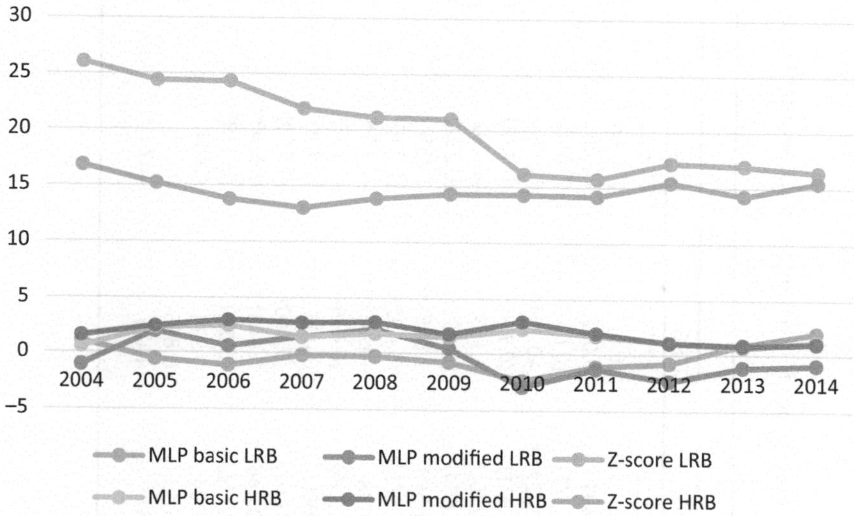

Fig. 4.7 Bank performance of centralized and decentralized banking markets in CEE: the MLP and the Z Scores, 2004–2014
(*Source:* Own calculation based on Bankscope)

dependent variables: loan growth and loan structure (CL/TL), using the panel model with MLP Score, with an additional dependent variable: the stability indicator: Z-score index (Table 4.14).

An analysis of the results of estimations for model 4 shows that the diversified group has been more strongly affected by macroeconomic conditions (particularly GDP growth) in regard to loan growth and structure. For both groups, corporate loan share was influenced by interest rates and price indices. As regards diversified banking group, bank size (log. of assets) was negative for loan growth, but positive in relation to structure (corporate loan share), while the performance index (MLP) showed just the opposite trend: positive for growth and negative for loan structure. The stability index Z-score was positively influenced by structural diversity (cooperative bank share) in DBG. For both groups, the performance index (MLP) had a positive influence on the index, while the growing size of banks had a negative influence on bank stability.

In summary, many factors in both groups affect corporate lending in a similar way. The diversified group was more dependent on business cycle

Table 4.14 Panel model 4: market conditions and loan accessibility in CEE: estimations for concentrated (CBG) and diversified (DBG) group

	Growth of loans		CL/TL		Z-score	
Control variables	DBG	CBG	DBG	CBG	DBG	CBG
Const	360.450***	29.240	1.868	−23.581	27.134***	55.003***
	(45.738)	*(85.578)*	*(23.839)*	*(48.180)*	*(6.675)*	*(16.422)*
Δ GDP	1.544***	0.297	0.374*	0.391	0.012	−0.089
	(0.435)	*(0.490)*	*(0.196)*	*(0.275)*	*(0.067)*	*(0.096)*
HICP	1.486**	3.233***	−0.310	1.142***	−0.191*	0.098
	(0.714)	*(0.665)*	*(0.329)*	*(0.371)*	*(0.110)*	*(0.128)*
LT_GBY	1.485	−0.925	1.569**	1.270 *	0.153	−0.232
	(1.510)	*(1.183)*	*(0.752)*	*(0.654)*	*(0.231)*	*(0.232)*
COOP	3.985	−11.482	−0.985	−1.504	1.096**	1.255
	(3.231)	*(8.711)*	*(1.581)*	*(5.570)*	*(0.493)*	*(1.740)*
ln_TA	−25.642***	−1.209	3.608**	5.138	−1.089**	−2.555**
	(3.022)	*(6.001)*	*(1.499)*	*(3.356)*	*(0.436)*	*(1.153)*
NetII_NoIOI	−0.002**	−0.002	0.000	0.000	0.000	0.000
	(0.001)	*(0.002)*	*(0.000)*	*(0.001)*	*(0.000)*	*(0.000)*
MLP score	0.922***	−0.017	−0.314***	−0.346**	0.149***	0.374***
	(0.197)	*(0.296)*	*(0.097)*	*(0.176)*	*(0.030)*	*(0.058)*
R^2	0.387	0.404	0.827	0.704	0.914	0.884
Adjusted R^2	0.249	0.254	0.773	0.619	0.895	0.855
No. of observation	983	434	637	331	1025	447

Note: ***, ** and * correspond to 1%, 5% and 10% significance level

(GDP growth), which may be advantageous in booming years. Structure of loan portfolio (CL/TL) increased with growing bank size, which may be more favorable for concentrated markets (CBG). However, the stability index Z-score indicated clearly that the growing size of banks had a negative influence on risk, while a positive performance does just the opposite. So the overall conclusions are similar to the previous section that an increase in corporate loans entails substantial risk, and concentrated markets with a dominance of large banks tend to have a bigger CL/TL share. However, their overall performance does suffer and long term riskiness, as measured by the Z-score, increases, while the performance index (MPL) decreases. Diversified banking markets are more influenced by the business cycle and macroeconomic conditions, which positively affect loan growth, but not necessarily corporate loan share.

7 Conclusions

From the empirical analysis presented in the paper it is evident that different factors influence loan growth and longer term credit structure. For loan growth, strong macroeconomic indicators, such as GDP growth, and positive overall bank performance, as indicated by MLP Score, are crucial. In analyzing the factors influencing bank credit structure, in particular corporate loan share, the trends are more complex. A higher L/A ratio brings about an increase in bank size and risk (low deposit to assets ratio and low Z-score, low ROE and high NPLs). The structural diversification of the banking market (share of cooperative banks) and growing interest rates were also of importance in relation to corporate loans.

Looking at the structure of loan portfolio (CL/TL), GDP growth, interest rate growth, increasing bank size, and stability (high Z-score), each had a positive impact on corporate loan share, while bank own deposit base did not. The MLP score had a negative impact on this ratio, indicating that overall good bank performance does not necessarily influence corporate loan accessibility, which may involve a number of inefficiencies as regards bank profitability (such as high C/I ratio in pre-crisis and high NPL ratio in post-crisis period). The models also indicate that the factors influencing corporate loan portfolio changed in the pre- and post-crisis periods, reflecting the evolving environment and changing structure of CEE banking markets.

The link between bank size and risk-taking has been investigated in the literature, e.g. Bhagat et al. (2015) found that size is positively correlated with the risk-taking measures (Z-score), particularly in the pre-crisis (2002–2006) and the crisis (2007–2009) period. A decomposition of the Z-score revealed that financial firms engage in excessive risk-taking mainly through increased leverage (Bhagat et al. 2015). Other research has also indicated that banks with high rates of loan growth were more risky (Mercieca et al. 2007). A study by Köhler (2012) established that banks were more stable if they increased their non-interest income share through a better diversification of income sources, and suggested that supervisors should monitor loan growth carefully on an individual level, since high rates of loan growth are associated with high bank risk-taking. The empirical research presented in this paper supports the above observations.

To summarize, panel data analysis makes it possible to formulate the following policy conclusion: that in order to influence the structure of the loan portfolio and to stimulate corporate loans, an efficient and high-performing banking market, as epitomized by a high MLP Score, is not sufficient. Of greater importance are the favorable macroeconomic environment, increasing scale and the universal profile of banks (low D/A ratio), the last two carrying considerable risk. Hence, there seem to be some inefficiencies in providing corporate loans by traditional, low risk banks, which should be dealt with outside the banking markets.

References

Aisen, A., & Franken, M. (2010). *Bank credit during the 2008 financial crisis: A cross-country comparison* (IMF working paper no. 10/47). Washington, DC: IMF.

Beck, T. (2013). Bank financing for SMEs—lessons from the literature. *National Institute Economic Review Report, 225*, 23–38.

Beck, T., Büyükkarabacak, B., Rioja, F., & Valev, N. (2008). *Who gets the credit? And does it matter? Household vs. firm lending across countries.* The World Bank working paper no. 4661. Washington, DC: The World Bank.

Beck, T., Demirgüç-Kunt, A., Soledad, M., & Peria, M. (2011). Bank financing for SMEs: Evidence across countries and bank ownership types. *Journal of Financial Services Research, 39*, 35–54.

Beck, T., Degryse, H., De Haas, R., & Van Horen, N. (2014). *When arm's length is too far: Relationship banking over the business cycle* (EBRD working paper no. 169). London: EBRD.

Bhagat, S., Bolton, B., & Lu, J. (2015). Size, leverage, and risk-taking of financial institutions. *Journal of Banking & Finance, 59*, 520–537.

Bikker, J. A., & Spierdijk, L. (2009). *Measuring and explaining competition in the financial sector.* Discussion paper series no. 09–01, Koopmans Research Institute, Utrecht University. www.koopmansinstitute.uu.nl

Cappiello, L., Kadareja, A., Kok Sørensen, C., & Protopapa, M. (2010). *Do bank loans and credit standards have an effect on output? A panel approach for the euro area.* ECB working paper no. 1150. Frankfurt am Main: European Central Bank.

Carbó-Valverde, S., Marqués-Ibáñez, D., & Rodríguez Fernández, F. (2011). *Securitization, bank lending and credit quality.* ECB working paper no. 1329. Frankfurt am Main: European Central Bank.

Casu, B., Girardone, C., & Molyneux, P. (2015). *Introduction to banking.* Harlow: Pearson.

Chiaramonte, L., Poli, F., & Oriani, M. (2013). On the relationship between bank business models and financial stability. Evidence from the financial crisis in OECD countries. In J. Falzon (Ed.), *Bank stability, sovereign debt and derivatives.* Basingstoke: Palgrave MacMillan.

De Haas, R., Ferreira, D., & Taci, A. (2010). What determines the composition of banks' loan portfolios? Evidence from transition countries. *Journal of Banking & Finance, 34*, 388.

EC. (2014). *Economic review of the financial regulation agenda.* European Commission Staff Working Document, Brussels, p. 54 and 205.

Evans, O., Leone, A. M., Gill, M., & Hilbers, P. (2000). *Macroprudential indicators of financial system soundness.* IMF staff paper. Washington, DC: IMF.

Fiordelisi, F., Monferrà, S., & Sampagnaro, G. (2013). *Relationship lending and credit quality.* http://ssrn.com/abstract=2210356

Gambacorta, L., Yang, J., & Tsatsaronis, K. (2014). Financial structure and growth. *BIS Quarterly Review*, 21–35.

Köhler, M. (2012). *Which banks are more risky? The impact of loan growth and business model on bank risk-taking.* Deutsche Bundesbank discussion paper no. 33. Deutsche Bundesbank: Frankfurt am Main.

Kok Sørensen, C., Marqués Ibáñez, D., & Ross, C. (2009, January). *Modelling loans to non-financial corporations in the euro area* (ECB working paper series no. 989). Rome: Banca d'Italia.

Mercieca, S., Schaeck, K., & Wolfe, S. (2007). Small European banks: Benefits from diversification? *Journal of Banking & Finance, 31*, 1975–1988.

NBP. (2015). *Financial stability report.* www.nbp.pl/systemfinansowy/rsf072015.pdf

Ongena, S., & Smith, D. C. (2000). What determines the number of bank relationships? Cross country evidence. *Journal of Financial Intermediation, 9*, 25–56.

Pawłowska, M. (2015). *Changes in the size and structure of the European Union banking sector: The role of competition between banks.* NBP working paper no. 205. Warszawa: National Bank of Poland.

Rajan, R., & Zingales, L. (2003). *Banks and markets: The changing character of European finance.* NBER working paper no. 9595. Cambridge, MA: National Bureau of Economic Research.

Shar, A. H. (2010). Performance evaluation of banking sector in Pakistan: An application of bankometer. *International Journal of Business and Management, 5*(9), 81.

5

The Reputable Underwriting Matching in Corporate Bond Issuances: Evidence for Non-financial Bonds

Santiago Carbó-Valverde, Pedro J. Cuadros-Solas, and Francisco Rodríguez-Fernández

1 Introduction

Capital markets are an important source of funding for non-financial corporations. Firms raise funds on these markets to finance their economic activity. The issuance process requires prior knowledge of previous strategic decisions regarding the characteristics of the issuance. The correct definition of these features is crucial because the final terms and conditions obtained in the markets depend on them. Furthermore, the placement process is strategically important because it is the method by which the demand of potential investors is analysed. In this sense, firms

S. Carbó-Valverde
Bangor University, Bangor, UK

P.J. Cuadros-Solas (✉) • F. Rodríguez-Fernández
Universidad de Granada, Granada, Spain
e-mail: pjcuadros@ugr.es

S. Carbó Valverde et al. (eds.), *Bank Funding, Financial Instruments and Decision-Making in the Banking Industry*, Palgrave Macmillan Studies in Banking and Financial Institutions,
DOI 10.1007/978-3-319-30701-5_5

seeking funding through capital markets must reflect on which financial intermediary will be in charge of undertaking the task of distributing the bonds among investors in the primary market. As asymmetric information problems between insiders and outsiders are present in capital markets, the relevance of the placement process is strengthened. All the research, information production, marketing, and market stabilization activities performed by banks appointed as underwriters are conducted with the aim of mitigating these asymmetries.

Many studies have suggested that the reputation of commercial and investment banks is linked to the reputation of its underwriting function. Reputation appears to be decisive in capital markets in order to reduce information asymmetries, because it is reputation that is able to certify that the underwriter valuation of the issue is consistent with inside information (Beatty and Ritter 1986; Booth and Smith 1986; Carter and Manaster 1990; Chemmanur and Fulghieri 1994). They perform this certifying function because highly reputable underwriters are interested in preserving their reputation. Chemmanur and Fulghieri (1994) designed a theoretical model in which underwriters' survival and future incomes are defined by the success of its past issues; poor later performances negatively affect their reputation. A number of studies have agreed on reputation being a determinant factor for the matching of firms and underwriters. In a specific paper on this field, Fernando et al. (2005) argue in favor of a positive assortative selection, in which high quality issuers are matched with reputable underwriters. It also sheds light on the part reputation plays in switching decisions.

Furthermore, the impact of the 2008 financial crisis in the investment banking industry has served to evaluate the role of underwriters. Recent studies have argued that those firms whose equity was placed by underwriters with financial troubles suffered large losses in their stock value (Fernando et al. 2012; Kovner 2012).

Despite the fact that the volume annually issued in the corporate bond markets is larger than in the stock markets, most of the empirical evidence has been obtained for IPOs and SEOs deals. This research aims to provide insight into the role of underwriter reputation in debt markets by analyzing the characteristics of corporate bonds in relation to underwriter reputation. Whether or not reputation plays a significant role in debt markets, those deals underwritten by reputable underwriters must differ from those issued by less reputable underwriters. We present an overview of the corporate bonds markets in Europe during 2007–2013 that argues in favor of the existence of differences in bond main terms by underwriters' reputation. More reputable underwriters placed bonds with larger proceeds. The tenth largest reputable underwriters by market share in the period 2007–2013 placed deals that were 3.31 times larger in size than those underwritten by the lowest reputable banks. Furthermore, the length of the bonds placed by the European market leaders in the underwriting industry was different from the maturity of the bonds underwritten by others with lower market-share. We find that the average maturity of the bonds placed during our sample period by the top ten underwriters was 6.45 times larger (7.82 years vs. 1.21 years) than by those deals underwritten by the lowest underwriters in the league tables.

In order to empirically confirm our suspicions, we use a database of 1,196 non-financial corporate bonds issued in 18 European countries from 2007 to 2013. This database offers detailed information on a deal-level, allowing us to explore econometrically the role of reputation in debt markets. Being consistent with the empirical literature we use market share as proxy of underwriter reputation. We find that bonds placed by reputable underwriters are significantly different from those placed by the less reputable. Univariate statistics show that there are differences in European corporate bonds based on underwriter reputation. More reputable underwriters appear to place bonds with larger proceeds and longer maturity. Using a model that relates underwriter reputation with bonds' characteristics, we study the matching between reputable underwriters and firms after controlling variation for industries and time. Our results suggest that European corporate bonds are statistically different in their main terms (bond size, maturity, callability, and collateralization) by underwriter reputation. Firms and underwriters are not randomly matched in debt markets, there is a self-selection mechanism. Firms placing bonds with large proceeds bonds, with longer maturities, collateralized bonds, and those including a call option are more likely to place these bonds with reputable underwriters.

The remainder of the paper is organized as follows. Section 2 discusses the role of reputation in capital markets and reviews the relevant literature. Section 3 describes the placement process of bonds in the primary markets and provides insight into the current situation of these markets in Europe. Data selection and sample specification as well as the empirical specification are presented in Sect. 4. In the latter section, the results of the main empirical analyses are also reported. Section 5 discusses the findings and concludes the paper.

2 Literature Review

A number of studies have aimed to explain the role of underwriters on capital markets. The finance literature agrees on the existence of information asymmetries problems in capital markets in which issuers and investors face these information problems in capital and debt raising issues. In this sense, the intermediary function performed by these banks helping to reduce the asymmetries between insiders and outsiders helps to explain the role of underwriters (Booth and Smith 1986). Their activity serves to improve the efficiency in the capital markets (Benveniste and Spindt 1989). Furthermore, their role is strengthened because underwriters perform a monitoring function in these markets (Easterbrook 1984; Hansen and Torregrosa 1992).

A large body of the finance literature has linked the functions performed by financial intermediaries in capital markets to its reputation. An underwriter is not merely a distributor as their acquired reputation provides credibility to all their performed functions. The so-called "certification hypothesis" argues that underwriters certify the value of an issuance due to their reputation. Reputation is what guarantees that their valuation of the issue is consistent with inside information (Beatty and Ritter 1986; Booth and Smith 1986; Carter and Manaster 1990; Chemmanur and Fulghieri 1994). Furthermore, opportunistic behaviors by underwriters using their private information for their own benefit are discouraged in the presence of reputation. In this sense, more reputable underwriters are less likely to be involved in dubious practices. Therefore, more reputable underwriters are able to more efficiently reduce the information asymmetries because they are concerned with maintaining their reputation. Underwriters do not merely distribute securities among investors, they perform marketing, certification, and screening functions (Dong et al. 2011).

A large strand of literature has studied how the joint production of underwriting and lending activities affects the certification role of underwriters. The de-regulation of restrictions on commercial bank underwriting activity in the U.S. due to the Gramm-Leach-Bliley Act and the entry of commercial banks into typically investment banking activities in Europe enable the joint production of these services. On the one hand, this joint production might generate a conflict of interest for the underwriter bank. This hypothesis suggests that the presence of lending relationships between the issuer and the underwriter could negatively affect the certification role of the underwriter, as the underwriter is tempted to overprice the deal in order to make it easier for the issuer to repay the loans granted. On the other hand, this joint production could reinforce the certification role of the underwriter as lending relationships enable the bank to make use of its private information to more accurately price the deal. There is no consensus in the literature, some papers have found evidence in favor of the conflict of interest while others have stressed that the certification role is reinforced when credit relationships exist (Drucker and Puri 2005; Gande et al. 1999; Narayanan et al. 2004; Roten and Mullineaux 2002; Schenone 2004; Sufi 2004). In this sense, the reputation of the underwriter could play in favor of the certification role, making reputable underwriters refrain from being involved in opportunistic behaviors. Additionally, lending relationships are also likely to affect the matching between issuers and underwriter. Issuers are more likely to match with a lender bank (Bharath et al. 2007; Drucker and Puri 2005; Ljungqvist et al. 2006).

Apart from previous and current lending relationships, underwriters' reputation also explains the matching that occurs between issuers and underwriters. Regarding reputation, in a specific study on this topic Fernando et al. (2005) argue in favor of a positive assortative selection, in which high quality issuers are matched with reputable underwriters. In fact, the extant studies that have examined the underpricing phenomenon have acknowledged this fact considering underwriter's reputation as endogenous of the matching. Additionally, the role of reputation in the matching is confirmed through switching models which explain why firms are motivated to change underwriters over time. Firms change underwriters in subsequent offerings because they are searching for more reputable underwriters (Krigman et al. 2001; McKenzie and Takaoka 2013).

3 Background: Capital Markets and the Underwriting Industry

The financial innovation that occurred before the financial crisis led to the creation and distribution of new financial products and services. This phenomenon has caused changes in the investment banking industry as it is specialized in trading securities. In this sense, the method used to place debt and equity issues in the primary markets has changed, moving from the "bought deal" to "at the best efforts". From the mid-2000s onwards, but especially after the turmoil, the "bought deal" is not as widely used as it was in the past for the European corporate bonds placements. In this method the bank is committed to buy the bond to later resell. By doing so, the underwriting banks assumed all the risks relating to the placement. Nowadays, in the "at the best efforts" technique the underwriter does not assume all the risks because its commitment only encompasses making an effort to place the issuance.

Issuers, banks and investors are engaged in the underwriting process. The mandate agreement in which the issuer appoints a bank as underwriter determines the offering starting point. Despite the process commonly involving the participation of several banks, with different roles, it is just the lead bank or a group of them responsible for managing the issue, that act as sole or joint-underwriter. Other banks can be designated managers and co-managers assuming basically, selling functions. In the investment banking industry the terms "underwriter", "lead underwriter" and "bookrunner" are used interchangeably. All these terms are used to designate the bank in charge of taking control and responsibility of the placement in contrast to the secondary roles of other banks. Additionally, in syndicated placed offerings the issuer can appoint one of the underwriters as "global coordinator". The greater responsibility held by the underwriter is rewarded by receiving the bulk of the fees. Despite the prevalent role of underwriters, recent studies have also emphasized the importance of adding co-managers for the success of the offering.

The issue placement is a lengthy and complex process that involves the participation of several agents. Besides the lead underwriter other agents perform activities all along the process: auditors, calculation agents, trustees, lawyers, financial advisors, paying agents, and rating agencies. Regarding the timing of the issue, the whole process, depicted in Fig. 5.1 from the mandate agreement to the settlement date, lasts 7 weeks although it might vary from deal to deal depending on several circumstances. Shortly after discussing the main terms of the offering with the issuer, the underwriter assumes all its tasks. First, a research phase is conducted in order to price the bond by analyzing the market behaviour. Frequently underwriters use prior issuances of comparable firms as a reference to help them price the current issuance. Then, a marketing activity named roadshow follows in order to present the deal to potential investors and ultimately to catch their business. These activities lead to the announcement of the issue closely followed by the opening of the books. For approximately 2 weeks, the underwriter collects all the orders received from the interested investors. After allocating investors' orders the final terms are agreed and afterwards the bond is priced. Finally, the underwriter is involved in the market stabilization of the issue until the settlement date.

The volume of the underwriting activity depends on the relevance of the capital markets. Regarding equity markets, there is evidence of recovery in 2013 and 2014 after the issuance size decreased from 2009. In 2014, according to Dealogic, the international equity issuance (IPOs and SEOs) surpassed the 1,000 billion dollars which had not happened since 2010. Debt markets have remained stable around the 10,000 billions

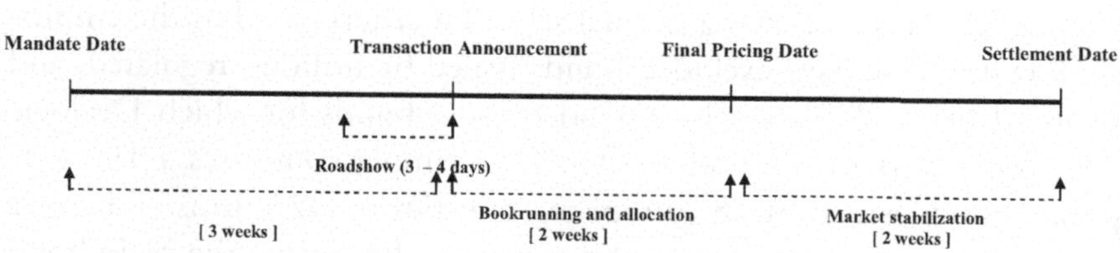

Fig. 5.1 Issuing timeline process

annual issuance since 2009, after the low volumes of 2007–2008. However, the most recent trends show that debt capitals are increasing their importance in Europe. In the Euro-zone, the bond market experienced a 6.21% increase from 2011. Furthermore, the remarkable increase in the volume issued in corporate bonds by non- financial firms might lead to a disintermediation process in which firms fund their activity through capital markets. The economic figures reveal that despite equity markets being very important as indicators of the economic pulse; debt markets are larger in size.

Finally, it is worthwhile noting that underwriting is a particularly profitable activity for investment and commercial banks as incomes from fees are significant. However, from the industry perspective some recent changes have occurred. Traditionally, it was an industry characterized by high levels of concentration in which the "bulge bracket banks" dominated the placements holding large market shares. However, the latest evolution in U.S. and Europe reveals that the market shares of these heavyweight players have decreased while mid-tier banks are gaining ground. The entry of commercial banks into the underwriting activity and the existence of less exclusive relationships in the investment banking industry are the main reasons for the reduction in the concentration.

4 Empirical Evidence

4.1 Database

In order to empirically address the research question, we have used a bond-level dataset of corporate bonds issued in Europe over the period 2007–2013. Data on corporate bonds was collected from Dealogic Debt Capital Markets. Following normal selection criteria used in the empirical literature, we have excluded bonds issued by utilities, regulated, and financial firms. We have also excluded those bonds for which Dealogic does not report to the underwriter. Our sample comprises 1,196 corporate bonds issued in 18 European countries by 323 firms. Table 5.1 offers some summary statistics of our sample. Regarding the main bond

Table 5.1 Descriptive statistics by year

	2007	2008	2009	2010	2011	2012	2013	2007–2013
Mean								
Proceeds ($ million)	885.89	809.33	1120.55	722.5	777.12	744.31	698.25	813.66
Maturity (years)	9.49	6.12	6.14	6.97	6.44	6.76	6.78	6.81
Offer price	99.62	99.61	99.67	99.9	99.87	99.81	100.07	99.83
Yield	5.05	5.54	5.87	5.21	4.83	3.91	3.96	4.75
Coupon	4.88	5.43	5.83	5.16	4.79	3.89	3.97	4.71
Callable	0.12	0.07	0.16	0.24	0.26	0.22	0.37	0.23
Collateral	0.03	0	0	0.01	0.01	0.04	0.06	0.03
High yield	0.05	0	0.11	0.24	0.17	0.18	0.28	0.17
Nº tranches	1.27	1.2	1.21	1.28	1.38	1.3	1.25	1.27
Syndicate UW	2.59	2.47	3.33	3.48	3.64	3.52	3.87	3.41
Bonds	91	103	195	164	138	267	238	1196
Firms	50	47	107	114	90	146	154	323
Countries	10	11	15	15	13	17	15	18
Underwriters	31	30	39	46	46	58	71	97

Source: Dealogic. Own elaboration

characteristics, an average sample bond has a size of $813.656 millions, an average maturity of 6.81 years and a coupon of 4.71 points.

Although measuring reputation in capital markets has been previously discussed in the empirical literature, there has been no unique measure. The use of tombstones announcements to infer the reputation of the underwriter thanks to the position of the bank name is not possible for European corporate bonds. Although these announcements were quite popular in the U.S. there were not so in Europe. Being consistent with the boundaries of placing a bond with a reputable underwriter, it can be assumed that reputation attracts more underwriting contracts. Following this argument, the empirical literature has considered that highly reputable underwriters would be the ones with greater market shares, showing that market share is an accurate proxy for underwriter reputation. Based on the market share, two main measures can be built: a cardinal and an ordinal. In this sense, when market share is used as a continuous variable a cardinal measure is built, while if underwriters are classified in clusters according to their market share an ordinal measure is used. We show in Table 5.2 an overview of the largest underwriters for non-financial deals in Europe during our sample period (2007–2013). This table ranks underwriters by market shares computed on a proceeds base. If a bond is

Table 5.2 Underwriter league table by market share in fixed-corporate bonds (2007–2013)

Position	Underwriter	# deals	# sole UW	# syndicated UW	Proceeds ($ million)	Market share
1	Deutsche Bank	437	24	413	92021	9.4
2	RBS	482	41	441	75227.77	8.06
3	BNP Paribas	397	7	390	68644.64	7.03
4	HSBC	367	7	360	63388.36	6.99
5	Barclays	330	9	321	58469.86	6.32
6	JPMorgan	307	15	292	57576.21	6.2
7	Citi	279	12	267	55551.09	6.04
8	SG Corp. and IB	281	6	275	52056.48	5.28
9	Goldman Sachs	166	9	157	32472.84	3.73
10	Bank of America Merrill Lynch	255	21	234	38811.31	3.59

Source: Dealogic. Own elaboration

syndicate-placed by joint- underwriters, all proceeds are shared among all the underwriters. Although league tables are annually reported, the same group of banks hold the top positions despite some positional changes. This fact provides insight into the structure of the underwriting industry, where reputation is a valuable asset for banks built along time. The three largest underwriters—all of them are European banks- hold around the 25% of the market share. Additionally, this league table shows that half of the total proceeds raised in Europe during our sample period were placed by just seven underwriters. Overall, this table shows the well-known high concentration in the underwriting industry.

4.2 Methodology

In this section, we attempt to answer the question of whether corporate bonds differ by underwriter reputation when considering the main bond terms. By doing so, we are able to explore the differences among bonds according to which underwriters placed the deal. In this sense, we have considered two of the bond-defining terms: size and maturity. Investment bankers agree that these terms are the ones mainly discussed during the mandate agreement meeting between the issuer and the potential underwriter.

Prior empirical literature has found evidence supporting the view that more reputable underwriters have strong relationships with investors (Benveniste et al. 2003; Chen and Wilhelmjr 2008; Ljungqvist and Wilhelm 2002). The more extensive underwriter's network of investors held by more reputable underwriters is likely to explain these facts. Furthermore, Morrison et al. (2014) show that since the 2000s there is a stronger correlation between underwriting market share and banks' connections. Therefore, as large-proceeds-bonds entail a higher complexity for their successful placement due to the large investors demand required to complete the offering, it is highly likely that we see firms appointing reputable underwriters if they are raising a large amount of money. Consequently, if bonds differ by underwriter reputation these differences will be observed in bond size.

In order to gain insight about how bond size differs by underwriter reputation we have computed the average bond size for all the underwriters in our sample. In Fig. 5.2 we have plotted the underwriter market share on their average bond size. As the decrease in market share is marginal as we descend the league tables, being lower than one percent, we have just plotted the top 15 underwriters. Figure 5.2 shows evidence consistent with more reputable underwriters placing large- proceeds- bonds. These results are confirmed after clustering underwriters in groups according to their market share. Figure 5.3 plots the average market share of the clusters on their average bond size. The average proceeds of the bonds placed by the tenth largest underwriters by market share is 1.05 times larger than for the bonds placed by the next ten underwriters (11th–20th) in league tables. Comparing the top ten underwriters with the ones with

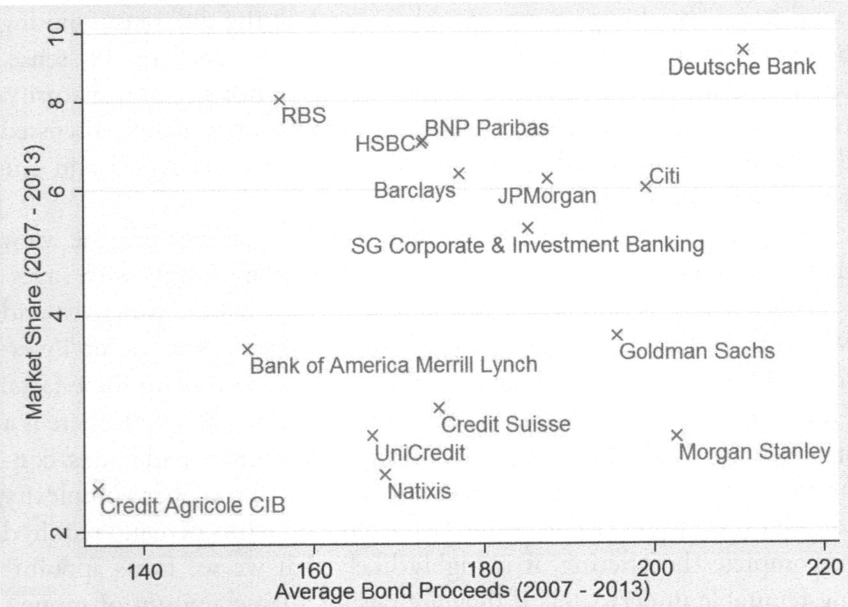

Source: Dealogic. Own elaboration

Fig. 5.2 Average bond proceeds ($ million) by underwriters market share for the top 15 largest underwriters by market share during 2007–2013 (*Source:* Dealogic. Own elaboration)

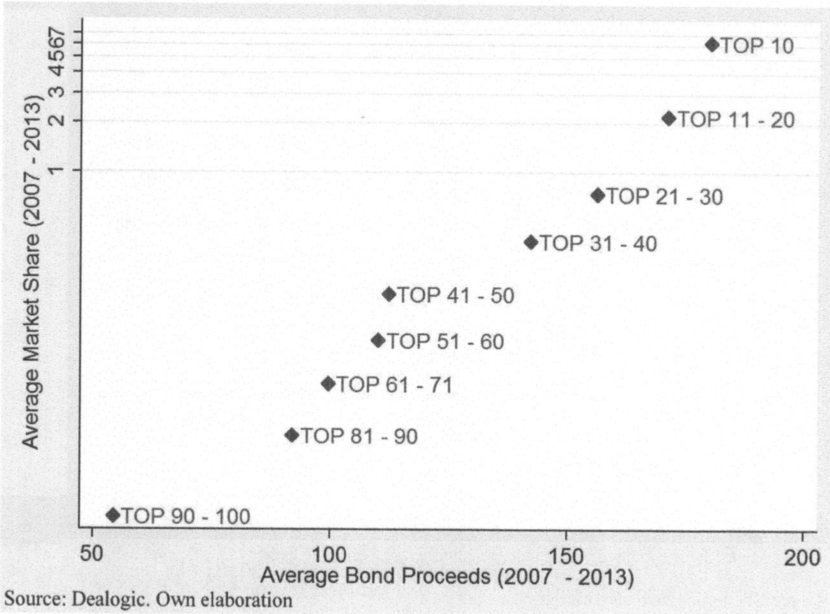

Fig. 5.3 Average bond proceeds ($ million) by cluster of underwriters by market share during 2007–2013
(*Source*: Dealogic. Own elaboration)

the lowest market share reveals that the ratio of the average bond size increases up to 3.16 points in favor of the largest underwriters.

Bond maturity as well as bond size is a defining bond feature due to the relationship between maturity and risk. Issuer default risk increases with debt maturity. In addition, long term bonds entail higher interest risk for investors, because as most of them are fixed rated bonds if market interest rates rise after the issuance, investors will be stuck with a bond which is paying less than other newer bonds. Thus, it is reasonable to assume that bonds with longer maturities require higher intricacy for their placement. Figure 5.4, plots the underwriter market share on average bond maturity for the 15 largest underwriters, showing that underwriters with the largest market share underwrite long-terms bonds. This graph confirms that maturity differs by underwriter reputation. Highly reputable underwriters place longer maturity bonds, as could be expected according to the higher difficulties in terms of placement that they imply.

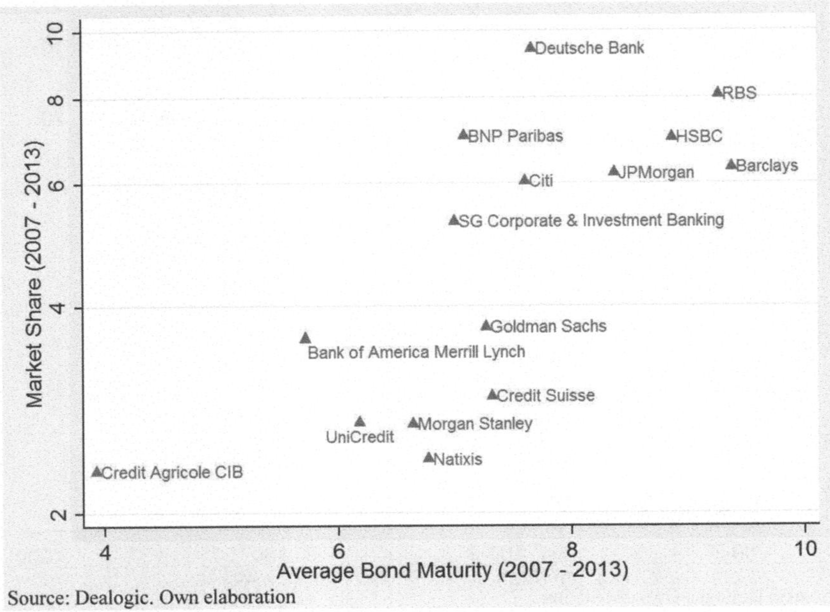

Fig. 5.4 Average bond maturity (years) by underwriters market share for the top 15 largest underwriters by market share during 2007–2013 (*Source:* Dealogic. Own elaboration)

The average market share by underwriters' clusters on average bond size is also depicted in Fig. 5.5, being our results confirmed. While the tenth largest underwriters by market share placed bonds with an average maturity of 7.82 years, the next ten underwriters (11th–20th) in the league rankings placed bonds with an average maturity of 5.97 years. This difference increases as we descend in the ranking positions, the average maturity of the bonds placed by the top ten underwriters is 6.45 (7.82 years vs. 1.21 years) larger than for underwriters with the lowest market shares. In conclusion, an overview of the corporate bonds markets in Europe during 2007–2013 argues in favor of the existence of differences in the bond main terms by underwriters' reputation.

We then computed t-statistics in order to test the difference in means and the Wilcoxon rank sum statistics to test the difference in medians. Prior literature considers a deal to be reputably placed if one of the largest underwriters by market share is appointed as underwriter. We have considered reputable those bonds placed by one of the largest

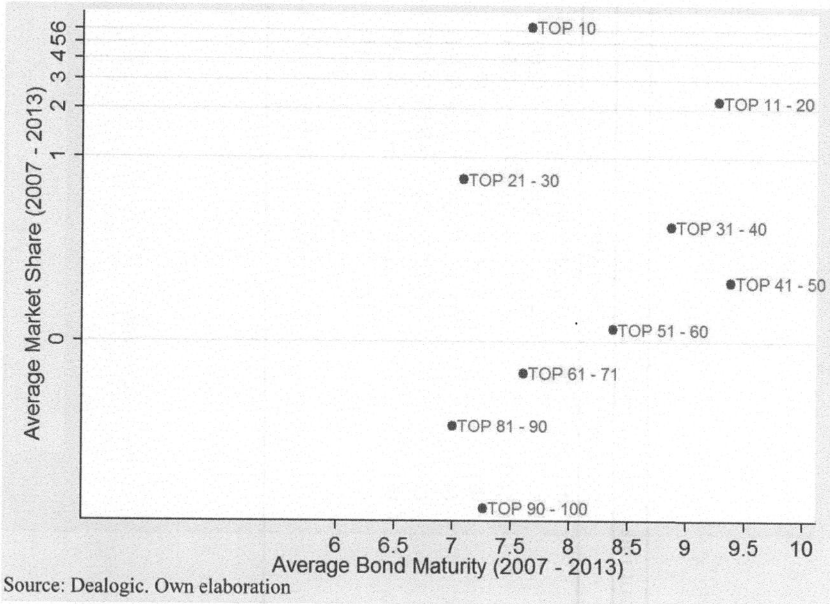

Fig. 5.5 Average bond maturity (years) by cluster of underwriters by market share during 2007–2013
(*Source*: Dealogic. Own elaboration)

underwriters in Table 5.2. These results showed in Table 5.3 suggest that more reputable underwriters place longer-proceeds-bonds with longer maturities and including a call option. Moreover, the tests suggest that more reputable underwriters are less likely to place high-yield bonds. Summing up, the statistical significance of the t-tests and z-tests for the differences in means and median confirms that bonds placed by more reputable underwriters are significantly different from those placed by the less reputable in several bond features.

Then, we run multivariate regressions to confirm the previous univariate findings. Equation 5.1 depicts our model, which explains the issuer—underwriting matching on bond characteristics. Our dependent variable "underwriter reputation" is measured using the underwriter market share. When several banks are appointed as joint-underwriters we use the average market share of the syndicate members. Finally, we control for time by including year dummies and in order to account for issuers' activity, we include industries dummies with SIC codes. In order to obtain robust

Table 5.3 Univariate statistics by underwriter reputation

	More reputable	Less reputable	More reputable	Less reputable		
	Mean	Mean	Median	Median	T-statistics	Z-tests
Proceeds ($ million)	939.32	243.52	669.82	157.84	−20.24 (0.00)	−16.84 (0.00)
Maturity (years)	7.15	5.25	6.5	5	−7.94 (0.00)	−9.26 (0.00)
Offer price	99.8	99.39	99.73	100	1.57 (0.12)	6.13 (0.00)
Yield	4.73	4.86	4.42	4.5	0.83 (0.41)	0.83 (0.41)
Coupon	4.67	4.88	4.38	0	1.31 (0.19)	1.18 (0.24)
Callable	0.26	0.1	0	0	−6.43 (0.00)	−5.01 (0.00)
Collateral	0.03	0.01	0	0	−1.63 (0.11)	−1.29 (0.20)
High yield	0.16	0.22	0	0	−2.12 (0.03)	−2.31 (0.02)
N° tranches	1.3	1.12	1	1	−5.79 (0.00)	−3.69 (0.00)
Syndicate UW	3.78	1.69	4	2	−27.54 (0.00)	−17.49 (0.00)
Total (*n*)	1196					

Source: Dealogic. Own elaboration

errors accounting for the possibility of dependence on bonds issued by the same firm we have clustered errors on a firm-level. We use the OLS (Ordinary Least Square) econometric technique to obtain the estimations.

$$\text{Underwriter Reputation} = \beta_0 + \beta_1 Z_{(\text{bond features})} + \sum_{(h=1)}^{h} \text{Year}_h + \sum_{k=1}^{k} \text{SIC Industries} + e_{(i)} \tag{5.1}$$

Table 5.4 reports the regression results. Large-proceeds-bonds are more likely to be placed by more reputable underwriters. These findings confirm our expectations, as bond size increases so does the placement complexity, thus the higher distribution capabilities of reputable underwriters is likely to explain the results. Additionally, as Fig. 5.3 reveals the possibility of a quadratic relationship between bond size and reputation, we have included bond size^2. As the coefficient on bond size is positive and on bond size^2 is negative we can conclude that there is a concave relationship between size and underwriter reputation. We also find that maturity is statistically significant; so long term bonds are more likely to be placed by reputable underwriters. This result could be explained due to the above-mentioned relationship between maturity and risk, longer maturities bonds are riskier for investors and therefore require the higher capabilities provided by prestigious underwriters. We have also included *maturity*^{2} allowing for the possibility of a non-linear relationship between underwriter reputation and maturity. The positive and statistically significant coefficient of maturity and the negative and statistically significant suggest a concave curvilinear relationship. In addition the multivariate regressions also show that collateralized bonds with a call option are placed by reputable underwriters. Overall, univariate findings are confirmed. After taking account of industries and time variation, we conclude that European corporate bonds are statistically different in their main terms (bond size, maturity, callability, and collateralization) depending on underwriter reputation. These results suggest the existence of a matching mechanism between issuers and underwriters driven by reputation. Firms and underwriters are not randomly matched in debt

Table 5.4 OLS regressions on underwriter reputation

	(I)	(II)
Variables	Model I	Model II
Bond size	0.000522***	0.00127***
	(0.000113)	(0.000228)
Bond size^2		−1.84e-07***
		(4.78e-08)
Maturity	0.0938***	0.174***
	(0.0215)	(0.0429)
Maturity^2		−0.00251***
		(0.000921)
Offer Price	0.0225	0.0345
	(0.0680)	(0.0643)
Yield	0.260	0.253
	(0.305)	(0.303)
Coupon	−0.376	−0.363
	(0.320)	(0.318)
Callability	0.558***	0.496***
	(0.164)	(0.164)
Collateralized	0.837*	0.847*
	(0.442)	(0.444)
Investment Grade	−0.00934	−0.101
	(0.286)	(0.284)
N° Tranches	−0.241*	−0.245*
	(0.145)	(0.139)
Syndicate UW	0.0927**	0.0321
	(0.0381)	(0.0367)
Constant	1.643	−0.0848
	(6.749)	(6.385)
Year dummies	Yes	Yes
Industries dummies	Yes	Yes
Observations	1,126	1,126
R-squared	0.326	0.345

Robust errors clustered by issuer in parentheses
***$p<0.01$, **$p<0.05$, *$p<0.1$

markets, there is a self-selection mechanism. Firms placing bonds with large proceeds, long maturities, collateralized, and including a call option are more likely to place these bonds with reputable underwriters. The issuer-reputable matching predicted by earlier writing depends on bond characteristics. These results also suggest that reputation is likely to play a role in the bond design.

5 Conclusions

Capital markets, composed of equity and debt issues, are a very important funding source as they channel the wealth of savers to those who can put it to long-term productive use. The economic relevance for firms' requirement of sources of funding justifies the studying of how to access to them through a commercial or investment bank acting as underwriter of the issue. Prior literature has studied the role of reputation in capital markets arguing that underwriter reputation is able to solve the asymmetric information problems in capital markets.

This paper investigates the issuer-reputable underwriter matching process studying how European corporate bonds differ by underwriter reputation. We offer an overview of the corporate bonds markets in Europe during 2007–2013 highlighting the differences in bond size and maturity by underwriters' reputation. More prestigious underwriters placed bonds with larger proceeds and longer maturities. We confirm these preliminary results using as laboratory a database that comprises 1,196 non-financial corporate bonds issued from 2007 to 2013 in 18 European countries. We find that bonds placed by reputable underwriters are significantly different from those placed by less reputable. Then, in multivariate regressions that have control over industries and time changes we regress underwriter reputations on a vector of bond features. Our results suggest that European corporate bonds are statistically different in their main terms (bond size, maturity, callability, and collateralization) by underwriter reputation. These findings confirm prior expectations about the existence of a non-random matching in the capital markets between issuers and non- financial companies. Therefore, reputation is likely to play a role in the bond design.

References

Beatty, P., & Ritter, J. R. (1986). Investment and the initial public offerings. *Journal of Financial Economics, 15*(June 1984), 213–232.

Benveniste, L. M., & Spindt, P. A. (1989). How investment bankers determine the offer price and allocation of new issues. *Journal of Financial Economics, 24*, 343–361.

Benveniste, L. M., Ljungqvist, A., Wilhelm, W. J., & Yu, X. (2003). Evidence of information spillovers in the production of investment banking services. *The Journal of Finance, 58*(2), 577–608.

Bharath, S., Dahiya, S., Saunders, A., & Srinivasan, A. (2007). So what do I get? The bank's view of lending relationships. *Journal of Financial Economics, 85*(2), 368–419. doi:10.1016/j.jfineco.2005.08.003.

Booth, J. R., & Smith, R. L. (1986). Capital raising, underwriting and the certification hypothesis. *Journal of Financial Economics, 15*, 261–281.

Carter, R., & Manaster, S. (1990). Initial public offerings and underwriter reputation. *The Journal of Finance, 45*(4), 1045–1067.

Chemmanur, T. J., & Fulghieri, P. (1994). Investment bank reputation, information production, and financial intermediation. *The Journal of Finance, 49*(1), 57–79.

Chen, Z., & Wilhelmjr, W. (2008). A theory of the transition to secondary market trading of IPOs. *Journal of Financial Economics, 90*(3), 219–236. doi:10.1016/j.jfineco.2007.08.006.

Dong, M., Michel, J.-S., & Pandes, J. A. (2011). Underwriter quality and long-run. *Financial Management, 40*, 219–251.

Drucker, S., & Puri, M. (2005). On the benefits of concurrent lending. *The Journal of Finance, 60*(6), 2763–2799.

Easterbrook, F. H. (1984). Two agency-cost explanations of dividends. *American Economic Review, 74*(4), 650. doi:10.2307/1805130.

Fernando, C. S., Gatchev, V. A., & Spindt, P. A. (2005). Wanna dance? How firms and underwriters choose each other. *The Journal of Finance, 60*(5), 2437–2469.

Fernando, C. S., May, A. D., & Megginson, W. L. (2012). The value of investment banking relationships: Evidence from the collapse of Lehman brothers. *The Journal of Finance, 67*(1), 235–270.

Gande, A., Puri, M., & Saunders, A. (1999). Bank entry, competition, and the market for corporate securities underwriting. *Journal of Financial Economics, 54*, 165–195.

Hansen, R. S., & Torregrosa, P. (1992). Underwriter compensation and corporate monitoring. *Journal of Finance, 47*(4), 1537–1555. doi:10.1111/j.1540-6261.1992.tb04669.x.

Kovner, A. (2012). Do underwriters matter? The impact of the near failure of an equity underwriter. *Journal of Financial Intermediation, 21*(3), 507–529. doi:10.1016/j.jfi.2012.01.001.

Krigman, L., Shaw, W. H., & Womack, K. L. (2001). Why do firms switch underwriters? *Journal of Financial Economics, 60*, 245–284.

Ljungqvist, A. P., & Wilhelm, W. J. (2002). IPO allocations: Discriminatory or discretionary? *Journal of Financial Economics, 65*, 167. doi:10.1016/S0304-405X(02)00138-1.

Ljungqvist, A., Marston, F., & Wilhelm, W. J. (2006). Competing for securities underwriting mandates: Banking relationships and analyst recommendations. *The Journal of Finance, 61*(1), 301–340.

McKenzie, C. R., & Takaoka, S. (2013). The matching of lead underwriters and issuing firms in the Japanese corporate bond market. *Mathematics and Computers in Simulation, 93*, 86–97. doi:10.1016/j.matcom.2013.04.009.

Morrison, A. D., Schenone, C., Thegeya, A., & Wilhelm, W. J. (2014). *Investment-banking relationships: Investment-banking relationships: 1933–2007*. (January 8, 2014). Saïd Business School WP 2014-1. Available at SSRN:http://ssrn.com/abstract=2376481

Narayanan, R. P., Rangan, K. P., & Rangan, N. K. (2004). The role of syndicate structure in bank underwriting. *Journal of Financial Economics, 72*(3), 555–580. doi:10.1016/S0304-405X(03)00187-9.

Roten, I. C., & Mullineaux, D. J. (2002). Debt underwriting by commercial bank-affiliated firms and investment banks: More evidence. *Journal of Banking & Finance, 26*(4), 689–718. doi:10.1016/S0378-4266(01)00163-7.

Schenone, C. (2004). The effect of banking relationships on the firm's IPO underpricing. *The Journal of Finance, 59*(6), 2903–2957.

Sufi, A. (2004). *Does joint production of lending and underwriting help or hurt firms? A fixed effects approach*. Unpublished Manuscript.

6

New Financing Instruments to Bridge the Funding Gap: The Lesson from Italy

Elisa Giaretta and Giusy Chesini

1 Introduction

The sovereign debt crisis has worsened funding conditions for banks in distressed countries. This resulted in a reduction of bank loans to companies which created a funding gap—a situation in which deserving companies do not receive the volume of loans that they would get in an efficient market, making obstacles to the birth and growth of companies and overall adverse effects for their economic development.

In addition to the crisis, there are also structural factors in Italy that effect the current funding difficulties. It has become necessary to reduce the use of traditional bank debt and increase the use of market funding instruments.

E. Giaretta (✉) • G. Chesini
University of Verona, Verona, Italy
e-mail: elisa.giaretta@univr.it

S. Carbó Valverde et al. (eds.), *Bank Funding, Financial Instruments and Decision-Making in the Banking Industry*, Palgrave Macmillan Studies in Banking and Financial Institutions,
DOI 10.1007/978-3-319-30701-5_6

From the analyses of the Italian situation, two alternatives to traditional bank debt have been identified to meet the demand for the financing of companies and bridge the funding gap: mini-bonds and companies' networks. These funding tools have been selected as they present the following characteristics: (i) they are innovative, as they have been recently introduced into the Italian legislation; (ii) they have been created for unlisted companies so they are suitable for small and medium-sized enterprises (SMEs); (iii) although they are new instruments, the number of companies that have used these instruments in the last two years is sufficient for statistical analyses.[1]

Mini-bonds are a tool for self-financing for unlisted companies that raise funds from professional investors in exchange of debt securities. This form of financing allows companies to diversify their sources of funding and to reduce their dependence on the banking system. The Italian market for mini-bonds is the largest in Europe, with 95 securities traded on ExtraMot Pro (Borsa Italiana 2015).

Companies' networks consist of a form of hybrid aggregation that allows participants to maintain their independence and individual identity, and helps companies to grow and to reach the appropriate size to compete on global markets. In Italy, from the regulation of network contracts in 2009 to September 2015, 2,348 companies' networks have been established that include 11,879 networked companies (Italian Chamber of Commerce 2015).

Studying a new database of 216 companies in 2013–14, this research analyzes the ability of these funding instruments to improve the financial condition of financed companies through a Student's *T* test and an Ordinary Least Squares (OLS) regression model.

The results of the analyses provide evidence that mini-bonds issuers present a better financial structure when compared to networked companies; however this improvement in the financial structure is achieved despite an increase in the cost of financing, which is not supported by a similar increase in the companies' revenues.

[1] The first parameter let us exclude other form of financing alternative to traditional bank debt, such as private equity, venture capital, leasing, that have not been recently introduced in the legislation. Because of the second parameter we did not consider forms of funding typical of listed companies, such as convertible bonds. Finally, the last parameter let us exclude other (more) innovative funding instruments such as crowdfunding and peer-to-peer lending.

This work contributes to the existing literature in several ways. First, there are few works conducting rigorous empirical research that measures the effects of different sources of funding on companies' financing. Second, the literature on mini-bonds and companies' networks is underdeveloped. Finally, this investigation is aimed specifically at the Italian market.

The remainder of the paper is organized as follows: Sect. 2 studies the literature on funding gaps and describes the funding instruments; Sect. 3 provides data description and research methodology; empirical results are presented and interpreted in Sect. 4; Sect. 5 draws the main conclusions.

2 Literature Review

The financing gap or funding gap is defined as the situation in which deserving companies, because of market imperfections, do not get the amount of loans that theywould get in an efficient market (Gualandri and Schwizer 2008). This situation arises from inadequacies on both the demand and supply of capital channels. The presence of a funding gap translates into obstacles to the birth and growth of companies, with negative consequences for economic development as a whole. The access to funding is important for companies both in the form of overdraft for financing the working capital and in term loans for fixed investments (Cressy 2012).

Small, young companies and new technology-based companies are likely to be most affected by such gaps due to the fact that they are often run by optimistic and inadequately skilled or trained entrepreneur-owner-managers. They may have products based on untested or novel technologies, and are more likely to fail than their larger counterparts (Cressy 2012).

The concept of the funding gap and the interpretation of this measure is not straightforward. The funding gap in the positive or '*P*' definition is an equilibrium, in which the volume of lending is below that which would emerge in a competitive capital market with costless and complete contracting, no private information, and rational expectations: By the normative or '*N*' definition the funding gap is a market failure, the appropriate policy response to which is an increase in the volume of lending (Cressy 2002).

The financing gap is generally defined as the difference between the "capital formation" and the "savings" of the corporate sector over a given period and measures the need for external funds: For a given level of capital formation, whatever funds the corporate sector cannot generate from internal sources (retained earnings or cash flow), it has to raise from other sectors. These funds come typically in the form of loans from the banking sector, trade credit from the rest of the world, issues of shares and corporate bonds placed with households, the financial sector, and the rest of the world (Galizia 2003).

A funding gap occurs when the deficit is a persistent rather than a temporary phenomenon. In fact a temporary gap would be associated, for example, with disequilibrium under competitive conditions as markets adjust to some unpredictable shock to the system. This would not be a market imperfection and be no cause for intervention.

It is important to be aware that the exclusion of borrowers at the lower end of the wealth spectrum is not a situation affecting the funding gap: They are signaling their low quality (De Meza 2002).

Another similar case is the "discouraged borrower effect": a situation in which a borrower wrongly believes that the search for financing would not yield funds, or would yield them only at unacceptable costs. As a result the company does not get funds, although there is no funding gap (Cressy 2012).

Moreover, a funding gap is not credit-rationing, that is defined as a situation in which, as a result of a financial market imperfection, the supply of finance is persistently less than the demand. In this instance the level of the economy is lower than it should be as some profitable projects are not being financed (Cressy 2012). During downturns, banks prefer quality in their borrowers and so create a so called "flight to quality" mechanism that favors larger companies whose greater diversification and fixed assets allow them to borrow more at more favorable terms than their younger, smaller, faster moving counterparts (Fraser 2009).

As a result, the funding gap is an extreme case of financial market failure where demand for finance is greater than supply and prices and other parameters do not adjust to eliminate the difference. Currently, in Italy the specific factors arising from the sovereign debt crisis have led to a funding gap, with difficulties for Italian companies, in particular for SMEs. The continued weakness of the economy is the main risk factor for companies. The reduction of traditional bank lending is still ongoing and a gradual rebalancing of the financial structure of companies is required: it has become necessary to reduce the use of traditional bank debt and to increase the use of different funding instruments through other funding channels. Among the larger and more foreign market-oriented companies there were signs of improvement in economic conditions, SMEs—that are on average less capitalized—are more exposed to the risks arising from the economic situation and the current difficulties of access to credit. Moreover, besides the sovereign debt crisis, the Italian financial system is experiencing some structural problems. It has evolved as a bank-based system with a banking system subject to regionalization rather than globalization, which relies to a limited extent on market-based banking, compared with the more advanced financial system in the EU[2] (Pagoulatos and Quaglia 2010).

The importance of both debt and equity funding being allocated efficiently among companies has been widely stated in the academic and practitioner literatures. However, there a small number of works conducting rigorous empirical research to identify and measure their effects. To the best of our knowledge, the current academic literature aims to describe the funding instruments instead of measuring their impact on companies' financial conditions. The aim of this paper is to bridge this gap, evaluating the effects of funding instruments.

The innovative funding instruments which are alternatives to traditional bank debt, that can play an important role in bridging the funding gap and reactivating the circuit of financing for companies, studied in the present work, are mini-bonds and companies' networks.

---

[2] With market-based banking, Authors consider the extent to which the banks' ability to supply credit to the economy is driven by market pressures on both the asset and liability sides of their balance sheets. As for liabilities they look at the funding base of banks, in particular their reliance on retail deposits or on wholesale markets for funding including inter-bank borrowing from abroad, which increased the banks' dependence on international funding, as for assets, they look at the trading of securities, the presence of toxic assets and the use of structured investment vehicles. As part of the banks' business model they also examine the expansion of their activities abroad in particular the banks' expansion into retail banking in other countries, or into international investment banking, including the investment in securities, many of which subsequently proved toxic.

2.1 Mini-Bonds

The mini-bonds are instruments of self-financing for companies that raises funds from professional investors in exchange for debt securities. This form of funding allows companies, especially SMEs, to diversify their sources of funding and to reduce their dependence on the banking system (Forestieri 2014).

The issuance of mini-bonds is defined in the Italian Legislative decree no. 83/2012, converted into the Italian Law no. 134/2012, aimed at encouraging the development of the funding of the debt market in the medium and long term for SMEs.

The issuers of mini-bonds should be unlisted companies different from banks and micro companies. Consequently, SMEs, as defined by the EU recommendation no. 2003/361/CE of the European Commission of the 6th May 2003,[3] might issue mini-bonds.

Companies may issue mini-bonds for the purpose of collecting savings—the acquisition of funds with reimbursement obligation, raising funds obtained through legal transactions which give the investor the right to the repayment of the amounts delivered—from investors.

As mini-bonds can be issued with a deadline in the medium to long term, they allow a diversification of the nature of the debt which results in an extension of the average maturity of sources of funding. In turn this results in greater consistency between the average maturity of the assets and the average duration of the liabilities, with a general improvement of financial ratios. On a practical level this allows the company to avoid the process of revaluation of loans that banks regularly carry out, and plan more sustainable financial commitments related to debt repayment. In addition, the issue of mini-bonds may allow companies to introduce a potential improvement in the rating ascribed to them and to a consequent increase in the potential for access to bank channels.

There are tax incentives that support the market for mini-bonds, both for investors and for the issuers. In the first case, it provides for the

[3] The category of micro, small and medium-sized enterprises is made up of enterprises which employ fewer than 250 persons and which have an annual turnover not exceeding EUR 50 million, and/or an annual balance sheet total not exceeding EUR 43 million. Within the SME category, a small enterprise is defined as an enterprise which employs fewer than 50 persons and whose annual turnover and/or annual balance sheet total does not exceed EUR 10 million. Within the SME category, a microenterprise is defined as an enterprise which employs fewer than 10 persons and whose annual turnover and/or annual balance sheet total does not exceed EUR 2 million.

application of the system already in force for listed companies and banks; in the second, it provides a broader deductibility of interest and an immediate deductibility of issuance costs.

The requirements for mini-bonds issuers are (i) to be assisted by a financial sponsor; the financial sponsor assists the issuer company in the process of issuance and placement of mini-bonds, assuming commitments to ensure the liquidity of the securities, maintaining a minimum amount of the securities in its portfolio, and also the requirement to make a report every six months, which includes the value of securities and classifies the issuer on the basis of a rating system; (ii) the last balance sheet should be audited by a professional auditor or an auditing firm; and (iii) mini-bonds should be placed exclusively with qualified investors that are not, directly or indirectly, members of the issuer company and are intended only for circulation among these investors.

Companies that want to issue mini-bonds are also required to prepare a business plan that includes the terms of repayment of the mini-bonds.

Normally, the amount of issued bonds should not exceed twice the amount of the equity capital and the legal reserves from the last approved financial statements; however, this limit is not applied to mini-bonds as it may be exceeded whether bonds are to be subscribed for only by professional investors.

Mini-bonds can be issued with a fixed or floating rate and the method of amortization can be bullet or amortizing. Mini-bonds may present a buyback option and they can also be callable bonds.

The first subscription of mini-bonds may be made either by private placement or through public offering.

To access the secondary market it is necessary for the security to be encoded. The assignment of the International Securities Identification Number (ISIN) code from the Bank of Italy meets the need to uniquely identify the issued security, both on domestic and on international markets. This code consists of 12 alphanumeric characters. After the request for the ISIN code, and before the official entrance of the securities in the secondary market, the mini-bond should be centralized at "Monte Titoli": The obligations are to be filed with a single entity in order to allow the transfer-entry form to eliminate the risks and costs associated with the material circulation of securities.

The Italian market segment for the sale of mini-bonds is ExtraMot Pro, part of ExtraMot, and it is reserved to professional investors. It was created in February 2013 by the Italian Stock Exchange as a multilateral trading facility (MTF). ExtraMot Pro is an order-driven market.

The regulatory infrastructure of the market segment offers companies easy and economical access to the capital market. The unique requirements for companies are the publishing of the financial statements of the last two years and an information document containing some essential information. Since the mini-bonds are listed, issuers are required to publish other documents such as: audited financial statements annually; disclosures relating to any change in the rights of the holders of the instruments; and any technical information relating to the characteristics of the instruments. Currently, the Italian mini-bonds market is the largest in Europe, with 95 securities traded on ExtraMot Pro (Borsa Italiana 2015).

From the analyses of mini-bonds issued in 2013–14, it emerges that they present an average outstanding balance of 41 million euros; this ranges between 10,000 euros and 411 million euros. The minimum trading size per mini-bond varies from 1 thousand euros to 4 million euros and on average amounts 148 thousand euros.

The average expiration time of mini-bonds issued in 2013–14 is 2020; however there are mini-bonds that have already expired in 2014 and also mini-bonds that will last a further 20 years.

There is a lot of variety also for the coupon rate applied to mini-bonds issued in 2013–14, that ranges from less than 3% to 12%; on average it is around 6.45% on year base. However, around 89% of mini-bonds issued present a fixed rate, while 11% of the total applied a floating rate.

Mini-bonds that pay the coupon every six months are 70% of total; 17% of mini-bonds pays the coupon annually while only 13% pays it quarterly.

The Bank of Italy (2014) identified requirements for the issue of mini-bonds for Italian companies. These companies should be joint-stock companies with a turnover of at least 10 million Euros, a positive EBITDA in the last 3 years, leverage equal to 3 or less and a ratio of net debt and EBITDA equal to 4 or less. From our calculations, we identified 20,283 companies with the above mentioned requirements in 2013, of which 14,633 (equal to 72% of total) are SMEs (Table 6.1).

Table 6.1 Number of companies that meet the requirement to issue mini-bonds in Italy (Total, SMEs, % SMEs) in 2013

	Companies
SMEs	14,633
Total	20,283
% SMEs on total	72%

2.2 Companies' Networks

Companies' networks consist of an hybrid form of aggregation, which allows participants to maintain their independence and the identity of individual companies and helps them to grow and reach the appropriate size to compete on global markets.

The Italian regulation of companies' networks is included in four Legislative decrees converted into Italian Laws from 2009 to 2012, more particularly the Italian Legislative decree no. 5/2009 converted into the Italian Law no. 33/2009 and modified by the Italian Law no. 99/2009, the Italian Legislative decree no. 78/2010 converted into the Italian Law no. 122/2010, the Italian Legislative decree no. 83/2012 converted into the Italian Law no. 134/2012 and the Italian Legislative decree no. 179/2012 converted into the Italian Law no. 221/2012.

According to the definition contained in the Italian legislation, with the network contract "*more entrepreneurs pursuing the aim of enhancing, individually and collectively, their capacity for innovation and their competitiveness in the market, to that end on the basis of a joint program collaborate in forms and in predetermined areas relevant to the exercise of their own companies or exchange industrial, commercial, technical or technological information or even engage in common one or more activities*".

The purpose of the network contract is to improve individually and/or collectively the participants' ability to innovate and the competitiveness of companies, through vertical integration, horizontal cooperation, or through the conduction of joint activities.

By organizing a companies' network, SMEs get the benefits of large size, without having to carry out M&A. In addition, the formation of companies' networks also helps the process of merging companies, creating the basis for more stable future partnerships (RetImpresa 2013).

Networked companies can benefit from several advantages, including economies of scale. The fixed costs are divided among the networks' participants so companies' structures become more flexible, with positive effects on operational risk and the value of the networked companies (Porter 1998). The companies' networks allow coordinated forms of labor division that in turn permits greater flexibility: networked companies become more able to adapt to technological changes and other external shocks than larger competitors (Marshall 1920). It is important to note that the coordinated sharing of expertise and specialization of labor results in an increase in efficiency and a benefit for the economy as a whole since they eliminate the excess capacity of the system. In the same way, companies' networks avoid costs duplications and overcome the minimum thresholds for R&D investment (D'Aspremont and Jacquemin 1988).

By joining companies' networks, companies can increase their market power and thus their bargaining power; the increased bargaining power in turn leads to an increase in the ability to assert their preferences with counterparts (Becattini 1987).

Also, the establishment of a lasting relationship with the other members of the network reduces both the cost of the search for new partners and the expenses related to the achievement of an agreement (Marshall 1920).

To finance the companies' networks in Italy, the European Investment Bank (EIB) has introduced a tool called "Italian Growth Reti d'impresa", which provides loans to help them finance small and medium-sized companies' investment by SMEs belonging to companies' networks. These are loans in the medium-long term using intermediaries selected by the EIB. Its purpose is to facilitate access to credit for networked companies who want to improve their competitiveness through product innovation and entry into new markets. In practice, this tool provides a reduction in the interest rate for the participants (EIB 2012).

Networked companies are generally able to attract capital on more favorable terms, both in terms of cost and quantity. The growth of total loans should be based on the examination of the network program, and favorable conditions of access to credit-related EIB funding above.

Networked companies should also benefit from a reduction of operational risk which leads to a change in the risk assessment by banks.

Moreover, cost sharing allows you to share the losses, thereby increasing the chances of success (Boari 2007).

Network design is the crucial factor in the success of the network, where the total network transcends the sum of its parts. This leads to the possibility of a rating system that evaluates the network as a whole, and accordingly a rating of the network is not the sum of individual evaluations, but is related to network design. In this regard, the specialized lending introduced with Basel II (2006), gives the banks the possibility of establishing a rating of the network, which considers the system of relationships between companies. The banking system gives a better rating for networked companies that have good innovative joint projects. The networks facilitate access to credit and, therefore allow companies to obtain significant discounts in terms of spread. This view completely changes the approach of the banks in the analysis of company: in addition to the data normally analyzed (for example turnover, leverage, profit, and so on). Banks consider the data from the system of relations in which companies operate. It stresses that it is too expensive for a bank to assess the rating of the network "bottom" or by data such as sales, margins, and other individual data, in order to assess the creditworthiness and then make a further assessment. A reversal of perspective is therefore necessary, starting from the project and from the network program, the preparation of a company plan and a network of "readable relationships" by banks. To implement this process of reversal in the assessment, credit institutions should also use the assessment criteria typical of venture capitalists and private equity funds.

In view of the application of Basel II, the Italian Law no. 266/2005 of 23 December 2005 stressed the importance of companies' networks by facilitating the creation of appropriate external agencies to assess the creditworthiness of the specific companies' networks.

Under the new action areas at which companies are looking, networks catalyze the attention of many companies. In fact, the competitive advantages of a company integrate with and complement those of other undertakings: Come to life projects "meta-company" in which the knowledge and skills of individual companies are at the service of a wider entrepreneurial formula: Finally, it is possible to pool the know-how of all participants, creating complex products integrating different technologies, creating a commercial network common, sharing the costs of R&D, and reaching dimensions more consistent with current markets. Ultimately, the companies' networks create a strategy with which companies can better grasp the enormous opportunities present in global markets.

In Italy, from the introduction of the regulation of the network contract in 2009, there are 2,348 network contracts signed, involving 11,879 companies (Italian Chamber of Commerce 2015). There are 145 contracts signed for financial purposes.

3 Data and Methodology

3.1 Sample Description

The sample includes unlisted companies that have issued mini-bonds in the ExtraMot Pro market segment of Borsa Italiana during the years 2013–14 and companies that have signed a network contract for financial purposes during the years 2013–14.[4] Data for mini-bonds issuers are taken from the website of the Italian Stock Exchange Borsa Italiana, while data for networked companies are taken from the Italian Chamber of Commerce. We merge data with financial information from AIDA Bureau Van Dijk database, which contains balance sheets for Italian companies.

The final sample includes 216 companies that have used one alternative instrument during the period 2013–14 as follows:

- 43 companies that have issued mini-bonds; and
- 218 companies that have signed a network contract for financial purposes.

The distribution of companies in the years is reported in Table 6.2 As we can see from Table 6.2, mini-bond's issuers count for 20% of the total sample. In 2013, mini-bonds issuers where less than 8% of the total sample; however the number of mini-bonds issuers increase from 2013

[4] We select companies that includes the Italian words that start with "finanz" in the purpose of the network contract (e.g finanziamento, finanziamenti, finanziare, finanziario, finanziari, finanziarie, finanza) which states for the English words "finance" and "financing". We find 85 network contracts with the above mentioned characteristics.

Table 6.2 Distribution of companies in 2013 and 2014

	2013	2014	Total
Networked companies	163	55	218
Mini-bonds issuers	14	29	43
Total	177	84	216

Source: Our elaboration on data from Borsa Italiana and the Italian Chamber of Commerce

to 2014, reaching the 34% of the total in 2014. Contrarily, the number of companies that joined a compenies' network included in the sample decrease from 2013 to 2014.

The descriptive statistics for companies analyzed are respectively in Table 6.3 for mini-bonds issuers and Table 6.4 for networked companies. From Tables 6.3 and 6.4 it emerges that in general, mini-bonds issuers present higher average values and greater maximum values for the natural logarithm of Net financial position, the natural logarithm of Operating cash flow, Long term debt index, and Financial costs on sales ratio. The distribution of companies in the geographical area and in the industrial sectors is nearly the same for companies funded by the two different funding methods. Also the ages of the companies in the two samples are similar, despite the networked company that has a maximum value for age which is older than the oldest mini-bonds issuer.

The descriptive statistics for both mini-bonds issuers and networked companies are reported in Table 6.5 for companies funded in 2013 and Table 6.6 for companies that have made financing in 2014. From the analyses of the two tables it emerges that companies funded in 2014 seems to be healthier than companies funded in 2013: the mean values for Net financial position (calculated in natural logarithm), Operating cash flow (natural logarithm), and Long term debt index are highest for companies funded in 2014. Anyway, companies funded in 2014 presents higher mean values and greater standard deviation also, for Financial costs on sales ratio. As regards companies distribution, there is a greater presence of companies from Central Italy and in the service industry for 2014. Moreover, companies funded in 2014 are five years older on average than their counterparts in 2013. It follows that these new types of funding have been firstly adopted by new companies and later they have been extended to other companies.

Table 6.3 Descriptive statistics for mini-bonds issuers in 2013–14

	Obs	Mean	Std. Dev.	Min	Max
Log Net financial position	35	16.44	1.47	13.26	19.09
Log Operating cash flow	34	15.20	1.20	12.76	18.50
Long term debt index	43	0.51	0.24	0.03	0.99
Financial costs on sales ratio	36	10.13	17.89	1.12	90.44
North	43	0.79	0.41	0	1
Centre	43	0.16	0.37	0	1
Age	43	17.90	14.83	0	74
Construction	43	0.09	0.29	0	1
Commerce	43	0.06	0.25	0	1
Services	43	0.41	0.49	0	1

Source: Our elaboration on AIDA Bureau Van Dijk database

Table 6.4 Descriptive statistics for networked companies in 2013–14

	Obs	Mean	Std. Dev.	Min	Max
Log Net financial position	135	12.78	2.06	2,56	19.74
Log Operating cash flow	187	11.44	1.85	5,15	17.10
Long term debt index	218	0.16	0.20	0	0.96
Financial costs on sales ratio	217	2.43	8.65	0	83.68
North	218	0.70	0.45	0	1
Centre	218	0.19	0.39	0	1
Age	218	17.11	14.22	0	92
Construction	218	0.12	0.33	0	1
Commerce	218	0.10	0.30	0	1
Services	218	0.35	0.48	0	1

Source: Our elaboration on AIDA Bureau Van Dijk database

Table 6.5 Descriptive statistics for variable analyzed in 2013

Variable	Obs.	Mean	Std. Dev.	Min	Max
Funding	177	0.08	0.27	0	1
Log Net financial position	117	12.87	2.25	2.56	19.10
Log Operating cash flow	146	11.41	1.83	5.15	16.66
Long term debt index	177	0.19	0.23	0	0.99
Financial costs on sales ratio	172	3.04	9.96	0	83.68
North	177	0.73	0.44	0	1
Centre	177	0.15	0.35	0	1
Age	177	15.88	13.06	0	85
Construction	177	0.10	0.29	0	1
Commerce	177	0.10	0.30	0	1
Services	177	0.41	0.49	0	1

Source: Our elaboration on AIDA Bureau Van Dijk database

Table 6.6 Descriptive statistics for variable analyzed in 2014

Variable	Obs.	Mean	Std. Dev.	Min	Max
Funding	84	0.34	0.4783	0	1
Log Net financial position	53	14.99	2.24	9.92	19.74
Log Operating cash flow	75	13.21	2.45	7.72	18.51
Long term debt index	84	0.28	0.26	0	0.96
Financial costs on sales ratio	81	4.58	12.29	0	90.44
North	84	0.70	0.45	0	1
Centre	84	0.27	0.44	0	1
Age	84	20.12	16.32	0	92
Construction	84	0.17	0.37	0	1
Commerce	84	0.09	0.29	0	1
Services	84	0.28	0.45	0	1

Source: Our elaboration on AIDA Bureau Van Dijk database

3.2 Methodology

As one of the pending issues in research on the funding gap is the analysis of the economic impact of the companies that receive funds as part of their financing, this paper aims to measure the effect of investment in terms of financial conditions. The precise hypothesis to test is whether or not these funding instruments enhance the financial conditions of companies.

To test the hypothesis, the analyses are conducted performing a Student's *T* test for equality and majority of means for the Net financial position, Long term debt index, and financial costs on sales ratio, between companies financed with the two types of funding tools during the funding year. Significant differences of the means of the samples are expected.

Moreover, the study is carried out through an empirical model to find a significant relation between the type of funding and the improvements of the financial conditions over the funding year. The analysis is conducted via the following Ordinary Least Squares (OLS) regression:

$$Y_{i,n} = \beta_0 + \beta_1 \text{Funding} + \beta_2 \text{Control} + u \tag{6.1}$$

where $Y_{i,n}$ is the index that measure the funding conditions for company i in period n; *Funding* is a dummy variable that takes the value 1 when the company has joined a companies' network and 0 when the company has issued mini-bonds; and *Control* indicates the control variables that are the geographical area (North Italy, Central Italy and South Italy), the age of the company during the funding year and the industry (high-level aggregation of ISIC/NACE categories).

The variables used to measure the funding conditions are Net financial position, Long term debt index, and Financial costs on sales ratio.

In the Appendix are variable sources and definitions (Table 6.9) and the correlation matrix for regressors (Tables 6.10, 6.11 and 6.12).

All the analyses are conducted through the use of the Stata 11 software package.

4 Results

The results of the Student's *T* tests for equality and majority of means by the two type of funding analyzed are reported in Table 6.7 We ran the test separately for companies funded in 2013, for companies funded in 2014, and for both companies funded in 2013 and 2014.

The analyses of the Log Net financial position reveal that the samples of mini-bonds issuers and networked companies are different when considering 2013, 2014 and the years 2013 and 2014 together (significant at 0.0000***). In all cases the samples of mini-bonds issuers present higher average values than networked companies (0.0000***).

The same results emerge for Log Operating cash flow and Long term debt index, as the two samples are different considering 2013, 2014 and 2013–14 together (0.0000***) and in all the analyses the samples of mini-bonds issuers present higher average values than networked companies (0.0000***).

As regards the Financial costs on sales ratio, the analysis fails to find differences between mini-bonds issuers and networked companies in 2013 (p-value 0.1159, not statistically significant). However, by considering 2014 and 2013–14 together, the samples present differences in mean (significant at 0.0002*** for 2014 and 0.0000*** for 2013–14). Moreover, the sample of mini-bonds issuers presents higher average values than networked companies (significant at 0.0004*** for 2014 and 0.0000*** for 2013–14).

Table 6.7 Student's *T* test for equality in mean

	2013	2014	2013–14
Log Net financial position	t=−5.7742	t=−6.0190	t=−9.8816
	Degrees of freedom = 115	Ddegrees of freedom = 51	Degrees of freedom = 168
	Pr(MB ≠ NC) = 0.0000***	Pr(MB ≠ NC) = 0.0000***	Pr(MB ≠ NC) = 0.0000***
	Pr(MB > NC) = 0.0000***	Pr(MB > NC) = 0.0000***	Pr(MB > NC) = 0.0000***
	Pr(MB < NC) = 1.0000	Pr(MB < NC) = 1.0000	Pr(MB < NC) = 1.0000
Log Operating cash flow	t=−5.0453	t=−7.3755	t=−11.3555
	Degrees of freedom = 144	Degrees of freedom = 73	Degrees of freedom = 219
	Pr(MB ≠ NC) = 0.0000***	Pr(MB ≠ NC) = 0.0000***	Pr(MB ≠ NC) = 0.0000***
	Pr(MB > NC) = 0.0000***	Pr(MB > NC) = 0.0000***	Pr(MB > NC) = 0.0000***
	Pr(MB < NC) = 1.0000	Pr(MB < NC) = 1.0000	Pr(MB < NC) = 1.0000
Long term debt index	t=−6.2827	t=−7.0687	t=−9.917
	Degrees of freedom = 175	Degrees of freedom = 82	Degrees of freedom = 259
	Pr(MB ≠ NC) = 0.0000***	Pr(MB ≠ NC) = 0.0000***	Pr(MB ≠ NC) = 0.0000***
	Pr(MB > NC) = 0.0000***	Pr(MB > NC) = 0.0000***	Pr(MB > NC) = 0.0000***
	Pr(MB < NC) = 1.0000	Pr(MB < NC) = 1.0000	Pr(MB < NC) = 1.0000
Financial costs on sales ratio	t=−1.2002	t=−3.7241	t=−4.0934
	Degrees of freedom = 170	Degrees of freedom = 79	Degrees of freedom = 251
	Pr(MB ≠ NC) = 0.1159	Pr(MB ≠ NC) = 0.0002***	Pr(MB ≠ NC) = 0.0000***
	Pr(MB > NC) = 0.2317	Pr(MB > NC) = 0.0004***	Pr(MB > NC) = 0.0000***
	Pr(MB < NC) = 0.8841	Pr(MB < NC) = 0.9998	Pr(MB < NC) = 1.0000

Test for majority of the mean of one sample. The samples includes networked companies and mini-bonds issuers

Source: Our elaborations on AIDA Bureau Van Dijk

*p-value<10% **p-value<5% *** p-value<1%

The results of the regressions are summarized in Table 6.8. As we can see from the table, the explanatory variable is always statistically significant.

The relationship between the type of funding and the Net financial position (in natural logarithm) is always positive. The same results emerge when considering the natural logarithm of the Operating cash flow. Moreover, the coefficient of the funding is positive and statistically significant also for the Long term debt index, for the model in 2013, 2014 and 2013–14. It follows that the funding with mini-bonds improves the financial structure of companies in the funding year, in comparison to the financing shown by joining a companies' network.

In the case of Financial costs on sales ratio, however, there is always a positive and statistically significant relationship, meaning that the above-mentioned better financial structure for mini-bonds issuers is achieved by increasing financial costs, not covered by a rise in companies revenues, compared to networked companies.

With regard to the control variables, in the case of the variable North, the coefficient is positive for Long term debt index in 2014 and negative for Financial costs on sales ratio in 2013–14.

The coefficient for Centre is significant and positive for Log Operating cash flow in 2013, Long term debt index in 2014, and Log Net financial position in 2013–14. Only the relationship with Financial costs on sales ratio in 2013–14 is negative and significant, as for the variable North.

The relationship between the age of the company and the Log Net financial position is positive and significant for 2013 and for 2013–14, as for the relationship between Age and Log Operating cash flow. Besides, the age of the company has a negative significant impact on the Long term debt index in 2014.

The value of the Constructions' coefficients is positive and statistically significant in two cases, for the Financial costs on sales ratio in 2013 and in 2013–14.

Both for the coefficient of Commerce and Services, there are on average negative and statistically significant values. Considering 2013 and 2014 together, for Log Operating cash flow and Long term debt index, as for Log Net financial position in 2013, there are values which are negative and significant. Services have a negative impact also for Log Operating cash flow in 2013, Log Operating cash flow, and Long term debt index in 2014 and Log Net financial position in 2013–14.

Table 6.8 OLS regression model

	Log Net financial position (2013)	Log Operating cash flow (2013)	Long term debt index (2013)	Financial costs on sales ratio (2013)	Log Net financial position (2014)	Log Operating cash flow (2014)	Long term debt index (2014)	Financial costs on sales ratio (2014)	Log Net financial position (2013–14)	Log Operating cash flow (2013–14)	Long term debt index (2013–14)	Financial costs on sales ratio (2013–14)
Funding	4.05	3.64	0.35	1.67	3.23	3.13	0.37	1.98	3.40	3.59	0.38	1.96
	(0.000)***	(0.000)***	(0.000)***	(0.000)***	(0.000)***	(0.000)***	(0.000)***	(0.000)****	(0.000)***	(0.000)***	(0.000)***	(0.000)***
North	−0.16	0.65	−0.02	−0.40	1.31	0.30	0.33	−0.93	0.64	−0.08	0.00	−0.53
	(0.749)	(0.114)	(0.623)	(0.200)	(0.493)	(0.817)	(0.017)**	(0.323)	(0.104)	(0.864)	(0.951)	(0.068)*
Centre	0.14	1.44	−0.03	−0.38	1.50	−0.31	0.29	−1.43	0.93	0.39	−0.01	−0.75
	(0.835)	(0.008)***	(0.627)	(0.364)	(0.433)	(0.820)	(0.041)**	(0.149)	(0.046)**	(0.479)	(0.796)	(0.031)**
Age	0.03	0.03	0.00	−0.01	0.02	0.02	−0.00	−0.01	0.03	0.02	−0.00	−0.01
	(0.026)**	(0.014)**	(0.292)	(0.304)	(0.236)	(0.226)	(0.001)***	(0.347)	(0.001)***	(0.028)**	(0.804)	(0.323)
Constructions	−0.29	−0.35	0.04	0.94	0.38	−0.62	−0.06	0.43	−0.54	0.02	0.02	0.71
	(0.581)	(0.435)	(0.494)	(0.008)***	(0.569)	(0.291)	(0.296)	(0.301)	(0.120)	(0.961)	(0.694)	(0.006)***
Commerce	−1.37	−0.58	−0.08	−0.10	0.08	−0.91	−0.10	0.07	−0.61	−0.96	−0.10	−0.05
	(0.009)***	(0.192)	(0.112)	(0.773)	(0.950)	(0.264)	(0.204)	(0.899)	(0.119)	(0.026)**	(0.025)**	(0.865)
Services	−1.63	−1.25	−0.03	−0.12	−0.82	−1.27	−0.15	−0.24	−1.31	−1.43	−0.06	−0.18
	(0.000)***	(0.000)***	(0.330)	(0.568)	(0.231)	(0.032)**	(0.016)**	(0.586)	(0.000)***	(0.000)***	(0.058)*	(0.339)
Year									−0.26	−0.28	0.00	0.17
									(0.305)	(0.359)	(0.897)	(0.355)
Constant	12.93	10.76	0.13	1.61	11.83	11.95	−0.03	2.16	11.12	13.18	0.15	1.58
	(0.000)***	(0.000)***	(0.006)***	(0.000)***	(0.000)***	(0.000)***	(0.820	(0.035)**	(0.000)***	(0.000)***	(0.005)***	(0.000)***
Number of obs.	117	146	177	172	53	75	84	81	221	170	261	253
F	F(7, 109)= 12.09	F(7, 138)= 11.07	F(7, 169)= 5.94	F(7, 164)= 4.10	F(7, 45)= 7.32	F(7, 67)= 12.67	F(7, 76)= 15.14	F(7, 73)= 8.22	F(8, 212)= 28.02	F(8, 161)= 23.42	F(8, 252)= 17.60	F(8, 244)= 11.46
Prob>F	0.0000	0.0000	0.0000	0.0004	0.0000	0.0000	0.0000	0.0000	0.0000	0.0000	0.0000	0.0000

Coefficients and *p*-values (*p*-values in brackets). The sample consists in 216 companies that issued mini-bonds or joined a companies' network in the period 2013–14. The dependent variables are respectively Log Net financial position, Log Operating cash flow, Long term debt index and Financial Costs on sales ratio. The independent variables are *Funding* and control variables related to the funding year, the geographical area, the age of the company and the industry

Source: Our elaborations on AIDA Bureau Van Dijk database

*p-value <10% **p-value <5% *** p-value<1%

Finally, the variable year is not statistically significant, meaning that the results are not different from 2013 and 2014.

We point out that the intercepts present statistically significant values.

5 Conclusions

The funding gap is the situation in which deserving companies do not get the volume of loans that they would get in an efficient market, with related obstacles to the birth and growth of companies. In Italy, following the sovereign debt crisis, the funding conditions for companies have greatly worsened. To meet the demand for the financing of companies and bridge the funding gap, the main funding instruments that are an alternative to bank debt are mini-bonds and companies' networks. A sample of 216 companies that have used one instrument during the period 2013–14 was analysed to test if these funding instruments could enhance the funding conditions of financed companies. By the analyses of the Student *T* test for equality and majority of means by the two types of funding, it emerged that mini-bonds issuers present higher average values than networked companies for Net financial position (in natural logarithm), Operating cash flow (in natural logarithm), Long term debt index, and Financial costs on sales ratio. That means that issuing mini-bonds creates an improvement in the financial structure of companies in the funding year, in comparison to the financing by joining a companies' network. However, the cost of debt for mini-bonds issuers is not covered by the companies' sales, while joining a companies' network creates a better financial costs on sales ratio.

The OLS regression models confirm the previous results as the analyses demonstrate that issuing mini-bonds are synonymous with positive effects on Net financial position (in natural logarithm), Operating cash flow (in natural logarithm), Long term debt index, and Financial costs on sales ratio.

Further, we can assert that there is a trade-off between funding by the issuing of mini-bonds or joining a companies' networks: while the first one is conducive to a better financial structure, this improvement is achieved by increasing financial costs, not covered by a rise in companies revenues, when compared to networked companies.

5.1 Limitations and Further Research

We conclude our work with limitations and suggestions for the direction of future research. The first limitation of this work is the statistical significance of the constant in the regression model. This means that there are important factors that are not included in the models. Moreover, we can further investigate the phenomena within the use of other methodologies and investigate some performance variables. It can also be useful to analyze this issue in other European countries. Furthermore, it could be interesting to analyze the situation of the companies before and after the funding year.

Acknowledgements Authors gratefully acknowledge financial support from "Polo Scientifico Didattico di Studi sull'Impresa" in Vicenza (Italy).

Appendix

Table 6.9 Variable sources and definitions

Variable	Definition	Source
Log Net financial position	Natural logarithm of net financial position defined as Bank debt + Bank long term debt + Other debt + Other long term debt – Cash	AIDA Bureau Van Dijk
Log Operating cash flow	Natural logarithm of operating cash flow defined as Profit or Losses for period + depreciations and amortizations	AIDA Bureau Van Dijk
Long term debt index	Long term debt / (Short term debt + Long term debt)	AIDA Bureau Van Dijk
Financial costs on sales ratio	(Financial costs / (Sales + Other revenues)) * 100	AIDA Bureau Van Dijk
Funding	Dummy variable. It takes the value 0 when the company has signed a network contract and 1 when it has issued mini-bonds	Borsa Italiana and Italian Chamber of Commerce
North	Dummy variable. It takes the value 1 when the company is located in North Italy and 0 when the company is located in Central Italy or South Italy and Italian islands	AIDA Bureau Van Dijk

(*continued*)

Table 6.9 (continued)

Variable	Definition	Source
Centre	Dummy variable. It takes the value 1 when the company is located in Central Italy and 0 when the company is located in North Italy or South Italy and Italian islands	AIDA Bureau Van Dijk
South	Dummy variable. It takes the value 1 when the company is located in South Italy and Italian islands and 0 when the company is located in Central Italy or North Italy. Variable dropped for perfect correlation with North and Centre and taken as benchmark	AIDA Bureau Van Dijk
Age	Age of the company in the funding year	AIDA Bureau Van Dijk
Year	Dummy variable. It takes the value 1 when the company has been funded in 2013 and 0 when the company has been funded in 2014	Borsa Italiana and Italian Chamber of Commerce
Manufacturing	Dummy variable. It takes the value 1 when the company operates in the manufacturing sector (NACE codes 05–39) and 0 otherwise. Variable dropped for perfect correlation with Construction, Commerce and Services and taken as benchmark	AIDA Bureau Van Dijk
Constructions	Dummy variable. It takes the value 1 when the company operates in the constructions sector (NACE codes 41–43) and 0 otherwise	AIDA Bureau Van Dijk
Commerce	Dummy variable. It takes the value 1 when the company operates in the commerce sector (NACE codes 45–56) and 0 otherwise	AIDA Bureau Van Dijk
Services	Dummy variable. It takes the value 1 when the company operates in the service sector (NACE codes 58–99) and 0 otherwise	AIDA Bureau Van Dijk

Table 6.10 Correlation matrix for regressors in 2013

	Log Net financial position	Log Operating cash flow	Long term debt	Financial costs on sales ratio	Funding	North	Centre	Age	Constructions	Commerce	Services
Log Net financial position	1.0000										
Log Operating cash flow	0.7267	1.0000									
Long term debt	0.2538	0.1370	1.0000								
Financial costs on sales ratio	0.2899	0.1273	0.1590	1.0000							
Funding	0.4368	0.4119	0.1210	0.4207	1.0000						
North	−0.0748	−0.0131	−0.2292	0.0086	0.0232	1.0000					
Centre	0.1474	0.1971	0.2574	−0.0637	0.0523	−0.6728	1.0000				
Age	0.2454	0.3178	0.1128	−0.0981	0.0461	−0.1226	0.3330	1.0000			
Constructions	0.0366	−0.0900	0.0008	0.0126	−0.0853	−0.1795	−0.1376	−0.0392	1.0000		
Commerce	−0.1164	0.0148	−0.2088	−0.0598	0.0620	0.1277	−0.0386	−0.0727	−0.1310	1.0000	
Services	−0.2457	−0.3053	0.0869	0.1575	0.1441	−0.0390	0.1507	−0.1880	−0.2458	−0.2458	1.0000

Source: Our elaboration on AIDA Bureau Van Dijk database

Table 6.11 Correlation matrix for regressors in 2014

	Log Net financial position	Log Operating cash flow	Long term debt	Financial costs on sales ratio	Funding	North	Centre	Age	Constructions	Commerce	Services
Log Net financial position	1.0000										
Log Operating cash flow	0.8393	1.0000									
Long term debt	0.4944	0.6535	1.0000								
Financial costs on sales ratio	0.3234	0.2846	0.4604	1.0000							
Funding	0.6577	0.7277	0.6560	0.3374	1.0000						
North	0.2824	0.3343	0.2287	−0.2696	0.2069	1.0000					
Centre	−0.2197	−0.2722	−0.1651	0.2958	−0.1656	−0.9401	1.0000				
Age	0.1875	0.1963	−0.0924	−0.1561	0.0987	0.2146	−0.1817	1.0000			
Constructions	0.0307	−0.1167	−0.0342	0.2001	−0.0751	−0.0117	0.0363	−0.0420	1.0000		
Commerce	−0.0795	−0.1636	−0.2114	−0.1028	−0.1280	−0.3696	0.2114	−0.0471	−0.1416	1.0000	
Services	−0.2528	−0.2141	−0.0998	0.1798	0.0981	−0.2374	0.2715	−0.3002	−0.2263	−0.1522	1.0000

Source: Our elaboration on AIDA Bureau Van Dijk database

Table 6.12 Correlation matrix for regressors in 2013–14

	Log Net financial position	Log Operating cash flow	Long term debt	Financial costs on sales ratio	Funding	North	Centre	Age	Constructions	Commerce	Services	Funding
Log Net financial position	1.0000											
Log Operating cash flow	0.8145	1.0000										
Long term debt	0.4186	0.4176	1.0000									
Financial costs on sales ratio	0.3288	0.2768	0.3568	1.0000								
Funding	0.6340	0.6548	0.4659	0.3992	1.0000							
North	0.0458	0.1069	−0.0592	−0.1393	0.0970	1.0000						
Centre	0.0550	0.0464	0.1086	0.1897	−0.0029	−0.7628	1.0000					
Age	0.2759	0.3121	0.0729	−0.0746	0.1485	0.0025	0.1339	1.0000				
Constructions	0.0675	0.0581	0.0079	0.1384	−0.0270	−0.1174	−0.0552	−0.0255	1.0000			
Commerce	−0.1122	−0.0603	−0.2116	−0.0750	−0.0454	−0.0206	0.0418	−0.0699	−0.1362	1.0000		
Services	−0.2747	−0.2962	−0.0088	0.0969	0.0331	−0.0962	0.1710	−0.2394	−0.2440	−0.2133	1.0000	
Year	−0.4676	−0.4184	−0.2606	−0.2246	−0.4883	−0.0033	−0.1177	−0.1763	−0.0798	0.0438	0.1259	1.0000

Source: Our elaboration on AIDA Bureau Van Dijk database

References

Bank of Italy. (2014). *Centrale dei rischi*. Retrieved from https://www.bancaditalia.it/statistiche/raccolta-dati/centrale-rischi/index.html. Accessed 13 Oct 2015.

Basel II. (2006). *International convergence of capital measurement and capital standards*. Revised International Capital Framework.

Becattini, G. (1987). *Mercato e forze locali: il distretto industriale*. il Mulino: Bologna.

Boari, C. (2007). Reti e relazioni tra imprese, in Economia e gestione delle imprese, il Mulino (pp. 465–498).

Borsa Italiana. (2015). *ExtraMot Pro*. Retrieved from http://www.borsaitaliana.it/obbligazioni/segmento-professionale/extramot-pro/extramot-pro.htm. Accessed 13 Oct 2015.

Cressy, R. (2002). Introduction: Funding gaps: A symposium. *Economic Journal, 112*, F1–F16.D.L. 179 of 18.10.2012, converted in L. 221 del 17.12.2012, art. 30.

Cressy, R. (2012). *Funding gaps* (The Oxford handbook of entrepreneurial finance, pp. 255–304). Oxford: Oxford University Press.

D'Aspremont, C., & Jacquemin, A. (1988). Cooperative and noncooperative R and D in duopoly with spillovers. *The American Economic Review, 78*, 1133–1137.

De Meza, D. (2002). Overlending? *The Economic Journal, 112*(477), F17–F31.

European Investment Bank. (2012). *Italia growth reti d'impresa*. Retrieved from http://www.eib.org/projects/pipeline/2013/20130286.htm. Accessed 15 June 2015.

Forestieri, G. (2014). *I nuovi canali di finanziamento delle imprese*. Mini-bonds, cartolarizzazioni, capitale di rischio.

Fraser, S. (2009). *Small firms in the credit crisis: Evidence from the UK survey of SME finances*. Coventry: Warwick Business School (ESRC grant no. RES-177-25-0007).

Galizia, F. (2003). *Measuring the 'financing gap' of European corporations*. An update. No. 2003/02. Economic and financial reports/European Investment Bank.

Gualandri, E., & Schwizer, P. (2008). Bridging the equity gap: il caso delle PMI innovative. *Studi e note di economia, 13*(1-2008), 101–138.

Italian Chamber of Commerce. (2015). *Contratti di Rete, Registro delle imprese.* Retrieved from http://contrattidirete.registroimprese.it/reti/#. Accessed 13 Oct 2015.

Italian Law no. 266/2005 of 23 December 2005 ('Legge Finanziaria 2006').

Italian Legislative decree no. 5/2009 converted into the Italian Law no. 33/2009 and modified by the Italian Law no. 99/2009.

Italian Legislative decree no. 78/2010 converted into the Italian Law no. 122/2010.

Italian Legislative decree no. 83/2012 converted into the Italian Law no. 134/2012.

Italian Legislative decree no. 179/2012 converted into the Italian Law no. 221/2012.

Marshall, A. (1920). *Principles of economics: An introductory volume.* London: Macmillan.

Pagoulatos, G., & Quaglia, L. (2010). *Italy and Greece: Financial crisis as sovereign debt crisis.* Conference paper.

Porter, M. E. (1998). Clusters and the new economics of competition. *Boston: Harvard Business Review, 76*(6), 77–90.

RetImpresa. (2013). Il Management delle Reti d'Impresa - Il Management delle Reti d'Impresa dalla costituzione alla gestione operativa.

7

Microfinance Investment Vehicles: How Far Are They from OECD Social Impact Investment Definition?

Mario La Torre and Helen Chiappini

1 Introduction

Social Impact investments (SIIs) are characterized as investments that generate both social value and financial return (Freireich and Fulton 2009). According to the Social Impact Investment Task Force (SIITF 2014) definition, SIIs are investments made into companies and organizations, sometimes through funds, with the intention of generating measurable social and environmental impact, as well as financial return (Global Impact Investing Network or GIIN 2014; Social Impact Investment Task Force or SIITF 2014). In particular, the SIITF (2014) states that impact investments "stay in the middle of an impact continuum" between philanthropic and sustainable investments.

M. La Torre • H. Chiappini (✉)
Sapienza University of Rome, Rome, Italy
e-mail: helen.chiappini@uniroma1.it

S. Carbó Valverde et al. (eds.), *Bank Funding, Financial Instruments and Decision-Making in the Banking Industry*, Palgrave Macmillan Studies in Banking and Financial Institutions,
DOI 10.1007/978-3-319-30701-5_7

Academic research in the field of impact investment is still at an early stage of development (Emerson and Spitzer 2007; Moore et al. 2012; Nicholls 2010; Hochstadter and Scheck 2014).

The lack of clear boundaries between impact investments and other investments (Hochstadter and Scheck 2014; Eurosif 2012) emphasizes the need to create an accurate framework that serves to protect and encourage impact investors (Freireich and Fulton 2009; Drexler and Noble 2013) and the market growth (Saltuk et al. 2014; Eurosif 2014).

Recently the Organisation for Economic Cooperation and Development (OECD 2015) set up a narrow definition of impact investing, fixing features and eligibility conditions to classify an investment as "impact investment". In particular, OECD identifies seven variables—Beneficiary Context, Social Target Area, Characteristics of Goods/Services, Delivery Organization Intent, Measurability of Social Impact, Investor Intent, and Return Expectation—which collectively define a "social impact oriented investment".

Existing data, based on institutional investor surveys, show impact investing as a growing market. The market size amounts to approximately $60 billion worldwide (Saltuk et al. 2015) and €20.2 billion in Europe (Eurosif 2014). One of the major developed sectors is access to financial services and microfinance that account for 27% of the impact investing market (Saltuk et al. 2015). The latest survey—based on more than 300 "impact based" vehicles,[1] and promoted by GIIN (2015)—shows that access to financial services represents the overall "impact theme" for 170 investment vehicles (56% of the total number of vehicles analyzed). In particular, microfinance and microcredit are declared as an "impact theme" by 50 investment vehicles.[2]

Despite the size of the microfinance impact investment market and the relevant role played by microfinance investment vehicles (MIVs), the somewhat unclear boundaries of social impact investments highlight the vulnerability of investors and the need to increase the investor's

[1] Investment vehicles includes both Funds and SICAVs.

[2] Other relevant issues are access to basic services (136 investment vehicles), employment generation (117 investment vehicles), green technology (93 investment vehicles), environmental market and sustainable real assets (88 investment vehicles), sustainable consumer products (63 investment vehicles), followed by other themes (97 investment vehicles).

protection scheme. Social investors could be cheated by the improper use of the label "social impact MIVs". This could be used only with the purpose to promote or to increase the reputation of such investments.

The aim of this study is to examine if MIVs, listed on the market and identified as "impact investments oriented" through the registration in the GIIN or through the publication of an impact report, are compliant with the recent definition of social impact investment suggested by OECD (2015). The methodology applied is content analysis and the ten MIVs have been selected using the Reuters search tool.

The OECD identified a "minimum standard" that should be followed by the market agents in order to define an investment as "social impact investment". The research contributes to the existing literature on social impact investment providing an examination of the level of compliance of listed social oriented MIVs to the features of social impact investments pictured by OECD.

The chapter is organized as follows: the second section proposes a literature review and rationality of the analysis of microfinance impact investments; the third section describes data and methodology used to finalize this research, while the fourth section covers the main findings of content analysis. The fifth section gives a critical discussion of the main evidence. The last section contains the conclusion.

2 Literature on SII and Rationality of the Analysis

Social Impact investments are those which generate both social value and financial return (Freireich and Fulton 2009). According to the SIITF (2014), SIIs are investments made into companies and organizations, sometimes through funds, with the intention of generating a measurable social and environmental impact, alongside a financial return. Thus, social impact should be intentionally pursued and clearly measurable.

Anyway, the overall literature on social impact investments is at an early stage of development (Emerson and Spitzer 2007; Moore et al. 2012; Nicholls 2010; Hochstadter and Sheeck 2014; OECD 2015).

Boundaries among impact investments and other types of investments are not clearly defined (Hochstadter and Scheck 2014; Eurosif 2012): on the one hand, impact investments share the "social impact component" with grants and the "financial return component" both with traditional investments and with socially responsible investments (SRIs). It can be said that impact investments were born to answer the inability of grants to "reach the scale needed to address the world's problems" (O'Donohoe et al. 2010). Under this perspective, SIIs are able to attract for-profit investors—like institutional investors—increasing the amount of social investments and the number of beneficiaries.

SRIs include non-financial criteria inside the investment selection process: "unlike conventional types of investments, SRI apply a set of investment screens to select or exclude assets based on ecological, social, corporate governance or ethical criteria" (Renneboog. et al. 2008). Nevertheless, O'Donohoe et al. (2010) consider SRIs able to minimize the negative social effect of investments, but not able to proactively create a positive impact.

Evidence shows that SRIs and SIIs are differentiated not only on a proactive basis, but also by the dimension and nature of an investment, return expectation and risk-return profile (Hochstadter e Scheck 2014). Socially responsible investors expect a return that is near the market return, while impact investors accept less return (Ashta 2012). For these reasons SRIs can be defined "financial first" investment and SIIs "impact first" (Freireich and Fulton 2009).

Recently, the OECD (2015) has set-up a new framework for SIIs, in which they are described as "a transaction between an investor and investee" (first line of beneficiaries or delivery organization) in a social area. The last beneficiaries should be "at risk populations" and the goods and services provided should have a mixture of public and private characteristics. These transactions involve financial intermediaries. The delivery organization should "at least inscribe a compulsory reporting clause of its social activity in the statutes, as well as provide a formal evaluation of social impact. In parallel, investors should at least have a compulsory reporting clause for social impact investments and have return expectations above or equal to zero, but not above the market rate return" (OECD 2015).

The SIITF (2014) describes impact investments as a new market characterized by "a combination of demand (for capital to finance impact-driven organizations), supply (of impact capital) and intermediaries". Impact driven organizations can typically be financed with different types of capital, which varies mainly according to the level of development of financial markets. The analyses conducted by the National Advisory Boards (NAB) to SIITF have demonstrated that in some more developed markets (i.e. U.K or U.S.A.) there exist more complex financial forms of impact capital, like social impact bonds. Instead in more traditional markets (i.e. Italy and France) forms of capital used in the social impact market are less evolved (France NAB 2014; Italy NAB 2014; U.K. NAB 2014; U.S.A. NAB 2014). The vision of impact investments as a new market contrasts with the view of impact investment as an asset class (O'Donohoe et al. 2010), but also with the general idea of impact investments as an investment strategy (Drexler and Noble 2013; Eurosif 2014).

Microfinance is one of the main "impact themes" (GIIN 2015) and it is defined as a provision of different financial services—e.g. loan, saving, leasing, insurance—to poor people, and the financially excluded (La Torre and Vento 2006).

Microfinance, especially microcredit, has attracted an increasing level of attention according to the Microcredit Summit Campaign (1997) which fixed the goal of escaping from extreme poverty for 100 million of the poorest households, and the declaration of the International Year of Microcredit in 2005.

On the one hand, microfinance is a way to eradicate poverty and to increase financial inclusion; on the other hand, it represents a double bottom line investment opportunity (Jung and Eriksson 2006). Thus, the investment in microfinance pursues both financial and social return. This aspect allows overlapping social impact investments and microfinance investments, at least when the creation of social impact is intentional and measured. The dimensional growth of microfinance institutions (MFIs) and the transformation from Non-Governmental Organizations (NGOs) to more commercial and financial sustainable institutions (La Torre and Vento 2006) have changed both the financing need of MFIs and their financial structures. Thus MFIs financial structure has seen an increasing level of debt and equity financing (Fehr D. and Hishigsuren 2006) that flows into MFIs also through mutual funds and other different typologies of microfinance investment vehicles (MIVs). From the impact investor's prospective, to buy a quote of mutual funds or other MIVs, also represents a way to differentiate the investment in microfinance institutions (Goodman 2006), diversifying the invested portfolio, for example, in terms of geographic area, asset class, and financial risk.

The literature on microfinance vehicles shows both MIVs "financial first" and "impact first oriented". In particular, Goodman (2006) recognized three different categories of microfinance vehicles: commercial microfinance investment vehicles, quasi-commercial investment vehicles, and microfinance development vehicles. The aim of the two first categories is "to provide a financial return to socially responsible and commercial private and institutional investors, while maintaining key social and development objectives". Microfinance development vehicles support the development of MFIs and the financial inclusion without "emphasize financial return" (Goodman 2006).

3 Impact Investing and Microfinance Vehicles

The OECD (2015) has restricted the perimeter in which SIIs can fall, building up a clear framework. In particular, OECD selected seven key variables to label an investment as social impact investment: social target area, beneficiary context, good and service characteristics, delivery organization intent, measurability of social impact, investor intent, and the level of return expectation as follows.

3.1 Social Target Area

OECD shows a list of social target areas addressed by SIIs: ageing, disability, health, children and families, public order and safety, housing, unemployment, education and training. This list can be expanded when transactions are provided in "underserved or developing areas, regions or countries" (OECD 2015). In fact, in these typologies of region, also agriculture, environment and energy, water and sanitation, information and communication technologies, and financial services can be considered as social areas improving the scarce living conditions of the population.

3.2 Beneficiary Context

Beneficiary should be "at risk population". Income level is a necessary but not sufficient condition. Another element is social demographic risk, "that may result in costly social exclusion if not managed or supported properly". At risk population could live indifferently in underserved, developing, or developed areas.

3.3 Good/Service

Good or service should present "some degree of publicness", thus they should provide a social impact and efficiency gains. On the one hand they "address the social needs" on individual or society bases, improving life outcome; on the other hand, they involve reduction of social costs or improvement in effectiveness.

3.4 Delivery Organization Intent

To be considered as social impact investment oriented, delivery organization should evidence the intention of obtaining a social outcome. Thus, incidental outcome of delivery organization are "out" of OECD's (2015) social impact definition. Also, "having the intent stated on the mission is not enough to be considered SII" oriented.

Delivery organization should put in place a "compulsory reporting of social outcomes", including in the organization statute the precise duty of social accountability to shareholders. It also can require, and obtain external certification and/or consider "legally binding constraints" in order to follow the "impact route" and prevent social mission drift.

3.5 Measurability of Social Impact

Measurability of social impact requires a formal impact evaluation process and a monetary or non-monetary evaluation of social impact. To explain formal impact evaluation, OECD (2015) used the framework provided by the Working Group Impact Measurement (WGIM 2014) established under the Social Impact Investment Task Force. OECD explained that this process starts with the definition of impact goals and finishes with the accountability of social impact and the provision of feedback from stakeholders. Other phases concern selection of indicators, collecting, storing and validating data, and verification of quality data.

On the contrary, transactions that do not consider social impact measurement are not in the perimeter of SII. Similarly, transactions that present informal evaluation and lack of measurement are out of the OECD definition.

3.6 Investor Intent

As for delivery organization, investors should demonstrate an intentional intent to obtain a social outcome. Incidental social outcome and social intent expressed in statements are not sufficient to consider an investor as a social impact investor. Only compulsory reporting—that results from the duty of accountability—and legally binding constraints can provide an effective demonstration of the social intent of investors.

3.7 Return Expectation

Social impact investment should be characterized by a return of capital or by a financial return that is above or in line with market rate return. If an investment does not give a return, it falls into the philanthropy perimeter; when the SII investment profit is higher than market rate return, it falls in the area of traditional investments.

According to this definitional framework, it is possible to outline the following functioning scheme of a microfinance impact investment vehicle (Fig. 7.1). Impact MIVs invest in MFIs (delivery organizations) with the intentional aim of reducing financial exclusion and poverty. Thus,

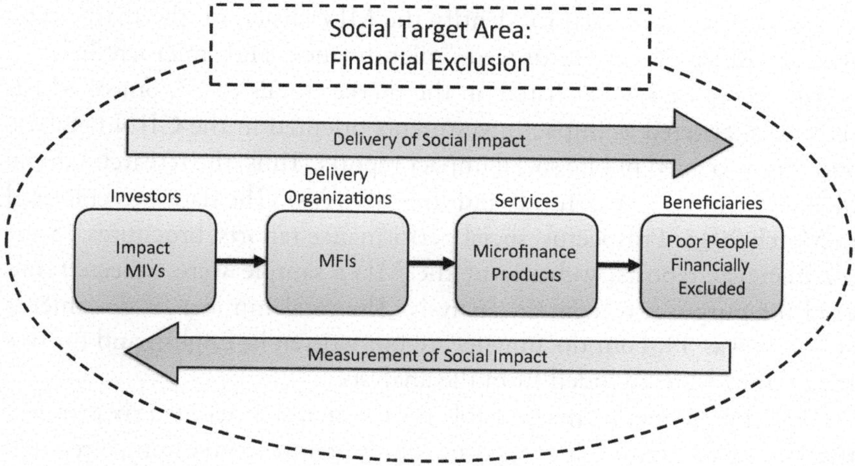

Fig. 7.1 Microfinance impact investment vehicles (*Source*: Author elaboration)

according to the OECD classification, the social area in which they operate is financial exclusion. MFIs provide microfinance products to beneficiaries, which are typically poor and/or financially excluded. Through this process Impact MIVs create a social impact that can be measured with different levels of accuracy and included in a formal or an informal measurement process. Nevertheless, to be defined as impact investment oriented it is necessary that MIVs meet all the conditions identified by OECD.

4 Data and Methodology

In order to test if MIVs are compliant with the recent definition of social impact investment suggested by OECD (2015), data was collected and analyzed as shown in the following sections.

4.1 Data

The research sample includes MIVs listed on the market and identified as "impact investments" oriented through the registration in the GIIN database or through the publication of an impact report.

The research tool used to identify the MIVs listed on the market was Reuters. Research-key words were "microfinance" and "microcredit".

The recognized MIVs listed on the market totals to 17, out of which six were registered as impact investments oriented in the GIIN database and four provided public social impact reports. Thus, the research sample included ten MIVs (six funds and four SICAVs). The data was collected in March 2015. Prospectus, social performance reports, brochures, investor manager reports, websites of the MIVs sample were collected and used for purposes of content analysis. The total number of documents collected was 39. Four documents are not written in English and for this reason they were excluded from the analysis.

Thus the 35 documents available for the analysis included six prospectus, two social performance reports, four brochures, three annual reports, eleven factsheets and monthly/quarterly reports, and nine websites.

4.2 Methodology

The methodology applied was content analysis on prospectus, social performance reports, brochures, investor management reports and websites of the MIVs sample. Content analysis is a research method that allows one to summarize a multitude of texts into a restricted number of categories, following specific rules of coding (Berelson 1952; GAO 1996; Krippendorff 1980; Weber 1990). In this research, content analysis is applied, first of all in deductive way, because the categories are extrapolated from the existing knowledge and the aim of the study is to test a theory (Kyngas and Vanhanen 1999). In fact, this study tested the "compliance" of impact oriented vehicles with the new OECD (2015) impact investing definition, starting with the eligibility conditions, defined by OECD (2015). These conditions refer to different social impact investing characteristics, grouped as follows: beneficiary context, social target area, characteristics of good/service, delivery organization intent, measurability of social impact, investor intent and return expectation.

In order to verify the existence a good degree of compliance with the OECD definition text analysis should recognize that:

(1) The investment is in the social target area identified in the OECD definition (ageing, disability, children and family, criminal and

justice, unemployment, affordable housing, education and training) or in other areas not listed, when the investment is realized in developing countries;

(2) Target beneficiaries who belong to a risk population, may result in low income levels and in social exclusion;

(3) Goods or services provided by impact investment should present "some degree of publicness" which means to improve individual or society life outcome and to obtain saving in social costs and/or improvement in efficacy;

(4) The delivery organization should include in the organizations statute the precise duty of social accountability to shareholders. It can also have an external certification and/or consider "legally binding constraints";

(5) Formal measurement process of social impact is implemented and monetary or non- monetary evaluation is provided. The existence of measurement process is evaluated from the investor prospective. MIV has the role of grouping together social impact information provided by delivery organizations. Furthermore, MIV has the role of implementing a measurement policy that should be followed by any delivery organization included in the MIV portfolio;

(6) The investor should include in the statute the duty of social accountability to shareholders and/or include some legal constraints;

(7) The return expectation should be at least return of capital or above/ in line with the current market rate.

Nevertheless, the existence of various collateral categories emerged conducting the research. These categories were mapped using a content analysis inductive approach.

Thus, this research definitely combines a predominant deductive approach with a residual inductive approach of content analysis.

Table 7.1 provides a full description of categories used in the content analysis. Definitions are included for each category, allowing "stability" and "reproducibility" of the analysis[3] (Stemler 2001).

[3] Stemler (2001) recognized these two variables as dimensions of research 'Reliability'. In particular, stability refers to the possibility for the same researcher to obtain same results 'try after try'; reproducibility means obtain same content analysis results changing researchers.

Table 7.1 OECD (2015) eligibility criteria for social impact investing

Categories	Provisional categories	Definitions	IN or OUT
Social target area	Social areas	Ageing, disability, children and family, criminal and justice, unemployment, affordable housing, education and training	IN
	Others in developing context	Other social areas in developing context	IN
	Others in developed context	Other social areas in developed context	OUT
Beneficiaries	At risk population	Combination of socio-demographic risks (not just income and wealth factors) that may results in costly social exclusion if not managed or supported properly	IN
	Population not at risk	No socio-demographic risks	OUT
Good service	Public	Consumption of a good/service has social impact on the society as a whole and results in systemic efficiency gains	OUT
	Degree of publicness	Consumption of a good/service improves individual or society life outcome and obtains saving in social costs and/or improvement in efficacy	IN
	Private	Consumption of a good/service has a social impact at individual level only and does not result in meaningful systemic efficiency gains	OUT

Categories	Provisional categories	Definitions	IN or OUT
Delivery organization	Incidental outcome	Unexpected or incidental social outcome	OUT
	Social mission intent	Attainment of social goals is expressed in the vision and/or in a set of investment criteria that go beyond financial criteria	OUT
	Sensibility to accountability	Demonstrate the use of measurement tool	OUT
	Compulsory reporting	Some form of reporting to shareholder expressed in the statements or in other documents	IN
	External certification label	External certification of social impact	IN
	Legally binding constraints	Specific legally clause that help to maintain social mission intent	IN
Measurability of social impact	No Measurement	No measurement of social impact applied	OUT
	Informal evaluation, not valued	Used a measurement tool that provides a non-monetary evaluation of social impact	OUT
	Formal evaluation but not valued	Implemented a process of evaluation and used a tool of measurement that provides a non-monetary evaluation of social impact	IN
	Formal evaluation and valued	Implemented a process of evaluation and used a tool of measurement that provides a monetary evaluation of social impact	IN

(*continued*)

Table 7.1 (continued)

Categories	Provisional categories	Definitions	IN or OUT
Investor intent	Incidental social outcomes	Unexpected or incidental social outcome	OUT
	Social intent expressed in statement	Attainment of social goals is expressed in the vision and/or in a set of investment criteria that go beyond financial criteria	OUT
	Compulsory reporting	Some form of reporting to shareholder expressed in the statements or in other documents	IN
	Legally binding constraints	Specific legally clause that help to maintain social mission intent	IN
Return expectation	Grants	Non-repayable investment	OUT
	Return of capital	Stated purpose to obtain the return of capital	IN
	Profit =< market RR	Stated purpose to do not exceeding risk adjusted market rate return	IN
	Profit > market RR	Stated purpose to exceeding risk adjusted market rate return	OUT
	No comparation with market RR	Not provided comparison between expected return and Market RR	OUT
	No information about return expectation	Not provided information about return expectation	OUT

Source: Adapted from OECD (2015)

For each category text code was reported in a final coding table summarized in the Appendix Table 7.3.

5 Main Findings of Content Analysis

This section shows the main findings for each of the seven variables proposed by OECD and for the entirety of MIVs.

5.1 Social Target Area

Social target area as recognized by the analyzed MIVs is the provision of financial services to the financially excluded. The provision of financial services is indirect and it is obtained through financing of MFIs. Six MIVs detail that regions of intervention are developing and/or emerging countries and/or transaction countries but two of them state that the MFIs are "usually domiciled in developing countries" (ResponsAbility Global Microfinance 2015b; ResponsAbility Microfinance Leaders 2015c) and in another section they indicate that they invest in microfinance institutions worldwide.

One MIV does not say anything about the location of financing; stating that it "lend funds to local microfinance institutions that independently manage their own client portfolios" (Finethic Microfinance Fund 2015a). Three MIVs made a list of geographic areas (Africa, Asia, Eastern Europe, and Latin America) without specifying if all were disadvantaged areas.

5.2 Beneficiary

Documents analyzed refer only to delivery organizations: the microfinance institutions. Through these descriptions they marginally identify the final line of beneficiaries: microcredit recipients. Sometimes it is possible to recognize only a general description of beneficiaries: who "supports a wide range of business ideas of microbusiness owners" (IIV MikrofinanzFonds 2015b) and "designated target groups" (ResponsAbility Global Microfinance 2015b). In other cases documents provide a list of beneficiaries: "investing in microfinance institutions providing financial services to low-income people and boosting micro, small and medium enterprises, and producers cooperatives fair trade oriented and/or organic oriented" (Etimos Fund 2015). The miscellaneous terminology used to describe the second line of beneficiaries consists of "low income groups often unserved" (Blue Orchard Microfinance Fund 2015), "economically active poor social classes" (Dual Return 2014b) and "impoverished population groups" (EMF Microfinance Fund AGmvK 2012). The geographical regions are only recognizable looking at the description of domicile of MIFs.

Specific reference to beneficiaries is made only by two MIVs: "the fund aims at delivering a full range of financial services to the underserved in developing countries and countries in transaction" (Triodos Microfinance Fund 2015b) and "the fund facilitates and promotes the generation of income for economically active, but impoverished population groups by facilitating and promoting the important associated access to financial services" (EMF Microfinance Fund AGmvK 2012).

5.3 Good/Service

Goods and services are commonly microfinance products, like microcredit, microleasing, microinsurance, and microsavings. The role of microfinance and the specific characteristics of microfinance products are described by eight MIVs. In particular, all of these MIVs state that microfinance allows people that normally do not have access to the financial sector to gain access to financial services. The other two MIVs in the sample do not describe the goods/services provided through the MIV investment.

Among the MIVs that describe microfinance products, one describes microfinance as "an alternative strategy for fostering economic development" (Finethic Microfinance Fund 2015a); other two MIVs described microfinance as something that allow "a positive self-reinforcing cycle" explaining that through microfinance "micro and small employers are able to work and therefore stabilize their cash flows, create jobs, and increase their standard of living" (Dual Return 2014a). A similar concept is expressed by one MIV that describes microfinance as an "instrument to help them themselves" as well as an instrument for "self-determination" (EMF Microfinance Fund AGmvK 2012).

5.4 Delivery Organization Intent

The delivery organizations intent is analyzable, indirectly, through the MIVs documents. Three MIVs state that MFIs are signatories of SMART Campaign's Client Protection.[4] One of them also pays attention to

[4] 'The Client Protection Principles articulate the standards of care that clients should expect to receive when doing business with a financial service provider'. These principles are: 'Appropriate product design and delivery, prevention of over-indebtedness, transparency, responsible pricing,

transparency and ethics: "we demand greatest transparency throughout the investment cycle, work closely with the MFIs and put value on a healthy structure of credit recipient … only those MFIs that meet the required ethical and social criteria are considered for investment. We thus look for profitable microfinance institutions with a sustainable focus and non-pure profit maximization" (IIV MikrofinanzFonds 2015b).

One MIV outlines that the MFIs in which it invests are "successful, promising and socially responsible MFIs" (EMF Microfinance Fund AGmvK 2012) without describing how to materially recognize these aspects. The environmental protection aspect is mentioned by one MIV: "the fund also invests in greenfield MFIs" (Triodos Microfinance Fund 2014). Among the Smart Campaign signatories, two MIVs recognized: "in terms of social responsibility of MFIs … the fund use Symbiotics social rating of social performance measurement tools consisting of 100 qualitative and quantitative indicators, which are expressed through seven dimensions namely: social governance, labor climate, financial inclusion, client protection, product quality, community engagement, environmental protection and policies" (Dual Return 2014a). "The fund aims to have a high level of social impact and therefore the social performance measurement tool is always taken into account within the investment decision making process" (Dual Return 2014a). In this case the social intent of delivery organizations is only presumable. Another MIV, in the description of its investment process, states that they pay attention to the social performance of the MFIs, thus the delivery organizations have accountability for the social results. One MIV directly describes the delivery organization's sensibility to social impact writing that "various MFIs are developing cost-effective, innovative systems to evaluate their specific impact on their clients' lives" (Triodos Microfinance Fund 2015b).

5.5 Measurability of Social Impact

Social impact represents a key feature of SII. The analysis of the MIVs sample shows that one MIV does not measure social impact substantially. In fact, the MIV provides information about the geographical areas in

fair and respectful treatment of clients, privacy of clients data, mechanism for complaint resolution' (The Smart Campaign 2015).

which it invests. Five MIVs give some social impact information but without describing the social impact measurement process or without recognizing the existence of a formal measurement process. Among these MIVs, two define the section of social impact measurement as "social performance indicators" (Responsibility Global Microfinance 2014; Responsibility Microfinance Leaders 2015b), one as "social performance" (Triodos Microfinance Fund 2015a) and another one as "social indicator" (EMF Microfinance Fund AGmvK 2013). The last MIV of this group provides an "Investment Manager Report", that includes only social information. The Report is divided into two different sections: "social inclusion and outreach (breadth & depth)" and "client & product information" (EMF Microfinance Fund AGmvK 2013).

Three MIVs treat the measurement of social impact as a process, despite linking the measurement to the investment process. One MIV states that "social performance assessment is a fundamental part of the investment process, standing alongside our financial performance assessment to make sound investment decisions to help micro entrepreneurs and SMEs prosper with access to a fair and inclusive financial system" (Blue Orchard Microfinance Fund 2014) and another one writes that "the fund aim to have high level of social impact and therefore the social performance tools are always taken into account while the investment decision making process" (Dual Return 2014a). The last MIV explains that the MIV "use Symbiotics rating tool for measuring and monitoring social impact" (Dual Return 2014a). In these cases the names of the social impact section are: "social performance data for MFIs in managed funds"; "social impact"; "portfolio and social impact" (Dual Return 2014a).

The evaluation of social impact for the MIVs sample includes: in eight cases indicators of the percentage of female/male clients and percentage of loan disbursed in rural/urban areas; in six cases average loan disbursed and in five cases the number of clients of MFIs. Only in three cases do the MIVs provide information about the number of micro entrepreneurs and in two cases information about the number of MFIs and clients activities.

Other indicators, showed only by one MIV are: "number of saving clients reached; total of servers served; total number of MFIs employees; % of MFIs endorsing the Smart Campaign; % of MFIs with an exclusion policy of lending; % of MFIs reporting to the MIX on social inclusion;

% of MFI with social rating; % of MFIs with environmental policy and eco-products; social rating; microloan in USD; number of countries; average GDP per capita; average microfinance gross loan portfolio; loan products and individual or group lending" (Blue Orchard Microfinance Fund).

For one, MIV information about social impact was not available on a standalone basis; in fact information is grouped by the MIVs managed by the Company.

5.6 Investor Intent

The content analysis of the investors' intent shows a clear picture of MIVs goals. Only one MIV in the sample states the intention of generating social value and at the same time refers to the measurement of social impact. In particular, the MIV states: "the overall objective of the fund is to offer investors a financially and socially sound investment in the microfinance sector mainly through investment in MFIs. The fund has the prospect of an attractive financial return combined with the opportunity for the investors to make a pro-active, measurable and sustainable contribution to the development of the microfinance sector into an inclusive financial sector in which the majority of people have access to financial services" (Triodos Microfinance Fund 2014). In the other cases social intent is only stated in documents and websites, without any information about measurability of social impact. One example could be: "the overall objective of the fund is to offer to socially responsible investors financially and socially sound investments to contribute to the sustainable development of emerging market economies by facilitating investments in micro and small enterprises and producers. The fund aims to achieve its objective by investing on a broadly diversified basis in short- to medium-term senior debt instruments" (Etimos Fund 2015) but also the "Fund aims to support microfinance institutions to expand and to extend their outreach to poorer people, improve the quality and appropriateness of financial services, and encourage the development of savings, insurance and payment services" (Blue Orchard Microfinance Fund 2015). Other MIVs state: "the fund aims to generate a sustained, long-term real rise in the value of its assets, while at the same time and to an equal extent striving to contribute towards the creation of prosperity among the underprivileged population groups in developing and emerging countries by indirectly financing entrepreneurial activities in these locations … Pursue a dual investment goal combining to poverty reduction and achieving development policy objectives made possible through microcredits" (EMF Microfinance Fund AGmvK 2012).

In some MIVs the intent is more general: "the administration of the fund focuses on credit transactions with carefully selected microfinance institutions and related micro-sector institutions" (IIV Mikrofinanzfonds 2015c).

Two MIVs seem to be "borderline", in fact reading the prospectus they look like traditional MIVs: "the essential objectives of the funds are to conclude loan transactions" (Dual Return 2014b) and "the essential objectives of the funds are to conclude loan transactions in local currency" (Dual Return 2014b). Nevertheless, the social reports state that the: "fund selects its partner and investment for social and sustainable principles. The fund is dedicated to the concept of responsible investment and is committed to develop and implement environmental, social and governance (ESG) principles in daily fund management contributing to increasing transparency in the microfinance industry" and "the policy of the fund … is to contribute to sustainable growth of microfinance institutions in emerging and frontier markets and to provide investors with competitive financial and social returns derived from a portfolio of investment broadly diversified across many currencies, MFIs and micro-entrepreneurs" (Dual Return 2014a).

5.7 Return Expectation

Return expectation is a central topic for financial investments. In the case of impact investments, a financial return is admitted as long as it is not higher than market rate return. The MIVs analyzed show a wide range of different target returns: "6 month Libor+ 300–400 basis points" (Blue Orchard Microfinance Fund 2015); "Libor +6%' (Dual Return 2015); 'Euribor +2%' (Dual Return 2015)[5]; '3–5% p.a. over a horizon

[5] The return goal of Dual Return Vision Microfinance is 'Euribor+2%'; while the Dual Return Local Currency goal is 'libor+6%'.

of five years" (ResponsAbility Global Microfinance 2015a); "4–7% p.a. over a horizon of five years" (Responsibility Microfinance Leaders 2015a); "average annual return in Euro of 6–9%" (Triodos Microfinance Fund 2015a). One MIV published a generic description of target returns and stated that it "strives for a sustainable, long-term real appreciation of its assets that is higher than the corresponding market level" (EMF Microfinance Fund AGmvK 2015). Another MIV does not give any information about the return expectation but it states in the brochure that "the fund has provided investors with consistent and predictable returns. Broad diversification, the lack of currency risk, and investment limited to granting loans have enabled the fund to attain its long-term goal of a return matching Libor+300 basis points, with no negative returns at all" (Finethic Microfinance Fund 2015a). For another MIV it is impossible to recognize any information in English about the return expectation; only realized performances are described.

6 Discussion of Results

Microfinance impact investment vehicles were analyzed using content analysis methodology that showed a clear picture of MIVs compliance to the OECD definition of impact investment.

6.1 Social Target Area

The social target area of the analyzed MIVs is financial inclusion. OECD admitted this social area only in developing countries and underserved areas. Only six MIVs specifically state that financial services are provided in developing countries and two of them, state that the investments in developing countries are not exclusive. For three other MIVs it is possible to presume that they invest in disadvantaged areas, because they identify only the countries in which they invest (Africa, Asia, Eastern Europe, and Latin America) without describing the level of financial inclusion in that area or the degree of socio-economic development. *To summarize, nine MIVs in the sample could be admitted as "impact investments" using a broad OECD social area definition.*

6.2 Beneficiaries

The description of beneficiaries is often provided through the description of MFIs' clients. There are a lot of different words used to describe beneficiaries: "low income people" (Etimos Fund 2015), "low income groups often unserved" (Blue Orchard Microfinance Fund 2015), "economically active poor social classes" (Triodos Microfinance Fund 2015b), "impoverished population groups" (Dual Return 2014b). Nevertheless, the OCED definition states that social impact investing should be designated for at risk populations and to be considered "at risk" income level is necessary but not a sufficient condition. Another condition should be social demographic characteristics that can lead to social exclusion costs.

Only two MIVs match the OECD criteria and two other MIVs are close to matching the OECD requirements. In fact, they recognized "low income groups often unserved" (Blue Orchard Microfinance Fund 2015) as beneficiaries, "communities or individuals who traditionally have had no access to financial services" (Finethic Microfinance Fund 2015a) or they specifically refer to the improvement of living conditions and indirectly to the social cost reductions. In particular, it is stated: "the fund facilitates and promotes the generation of income for economically active, but impoverished population groups by facilitating and promoting the important associated access to financial services" (EMF Microfinance Fund AGmvK 2012). The MIVs description fails to consider the specific demographic characteristics that lead to social exclusion. They refer only to financial exclusion that could be considered as a dimension of social exclusion.

6.3 Goods and Services

Goods and services, provided through the initial investment in delivery organizations (MFIs) are microfinance products. They show some degree of publicness because they generally allow people—who are financially excluded—to access and use financial services. Nevertheless, the OECD definition specifically recognizes that goods and services provided thanks to social impact investing should have a public utility (addressing social needs) and efficiency gains (allowing reduction of costs for public administrations or efficacy gain).

The research recognizes that beyond the generic definition (provided by eight MIVs) of microfinance products as an instrument that allows access to financial services for people that normally have no access to the financial system, only one MIV specifies the development goals of microfinance as "an alternative strategy for fostering economic development" (Finethic Microfinance Fund 2015a). Nothing was mentioned about the cost reduction theme and efficacy of the products. *Thus, despite generic descriptions of microfinance roles and characteristics, only one MIV appears to be in the perimeter of social impact investing. Nevertheless, the MIVs analyzed are still far from the OECD definition.* The other MIVs are closer to the traditional definition of private goods, than to the definition of "some degree of publicness".

6.4 Delivery Organizations Intent

Social intent of delivery organizations is explored using the MIVs description. On a voluntary or non-voluntary basis only three MIVs recognize that the financed delivery organizations report on or pay attention to social impact. Among them only one MIV directly describes the sensibility of delivery organization to social impact stating that "various MFIs are developing cost-effective, innovative systems to evaluate their specific impact on their client's lives" (Blue Orchard Microfinance Fund 2013). The other two MIVs link the social impact evaluation to the financing process of the MIVs. Thus, indirectly, it is possible to recognize an accountability process on the overall impact theme. For two other MIVs, social intent is generically deducible in the mission of MFIs. The OECD definition requires that delivery organizations include in the statute the duty of compulsory reporting of social intent or include specific clauses in order to prevent social mission drift or obtain an external certification of social impact. *One MIV directly recognized that a number of financed MFIs are developing hard measurement methodologies, however, it is not possible to classify it as "compulsory reporting" following the OECD definition.*

6.5 Impact Measurement

Informal evaluation and non- measurement of social impact outnumber formal evaluation of social impact. In fact, in one case social performance is measured only using the number and typologies of countries in which the MIV invest; in another case the MIV does not provide information about social impact. Only in three cases was social impact measurement described as a process, even though it is part of the investment process. Nevertheless, in these cases, indicators do not allow for a valuation, in a monetary sense, of social impact.

According to the OECD definition, the measurement process should be formal and the indicators should allow the monetary or non-monetary measurability of social impact. *In the research sample only three MIVs are close to being compliant with these requirements.*

6.6 Investor Intent

In the framework of impact MIVs, the investor is the MIV itself. The OECD definition requires impact investor's to provide compulsory reporting or consider some legal constraints in order to prevent mission drifts.

In the research sample, only one MIV is close to being considered an impact investor according to the OECD definition. The MIV states "the overall objective of the fund is to offer investors a financially and socially sound investment in the microfinance sector mainly through investment in MFIs. The fund has the prospect of an attractive financial return combined with the opportunity for the investors to make a pro-active measurable and sustainable contribution to the development of the microfinance sector into an inclusive financial sector in which the majority of people have access to financial services" (Triodos Microfinance Fund 2014). In this case the accountability of social impact is considered a relevant topic by the investor, while in the other nine cases the social intent is expressed in the statement, thus they are not admitted as impact investors according to the OECD definition. Furthermore, among them, two MIVs are "borderline": Reading the prospectus they seem to generate incidental social outcomes, while reading the social reports the social intent is formally described.

6.7 Return Expectation

Considering the return aspect, eight MIVs give information on the return expectation and two MIVs do not provide any information about it. Nevertheless, no MIV compares the return expectation with the market rate return, nor does any of the MIV's state that the return expectation is equal to the return of capital or equal or less than the market rate return. *Thus, no MIV is compliant with the OECD definition of social impact investing return expectations.*

6.8 Synthetic Results

MIVs that fall within the perimeter of "impact investments" as defined by OECD (2015) are relatively few (Table 7.2). No one MIV is completely aligned to the OECD definition of social impact investments. Two MIVs meet three eligibility conditions, and four MIVs are compliant with two eligibility conditions fixed by OECD. The other MIVs are aligned only with one OECD eligibility condition.

The OECD definition of impact investing is in line with the prevalent literature on SII (Freireich and Fulton 2009; GIIN 2015), as well as with the suggestions of the Social Impact Investment Task Force (SIITF 2014), but has also developed a stricter perimeter, defining characteristics of delivery organizations, beneficiaries, and goods/services. Nevertheless, this scheme is not a legal framework and is relatively new, thus a gap between theoretical framework and practical vehicle management was expected.

Results of this research are in line with Hochstadter and Sheck's (2014) investigation of literature review on SII. In particular, the unclear identification of target beneficiaries as well as the unclear characteristics of delivery organizations. Hochstadter and Sheck (2014) wrote "Interestingly, however, a number of texts define impact investing without referring to the recipient of the investment capital or remaining vague with regard to what characterized an impact investee". The clear definition of target beneficiaries is essential in order to guide the realization of a social impact.

Table 7.2 Synthesis of results

MIVs	Social target area	Beneficiary context	Goods/ services	Delivery organization	Measurability	Investor intent	Return	Total
Blue Orchard Microfinance Fund	☺	☺			☺			3
Dual Return Vision Microfinance Fund	☺				☺			2
Dual Return Local Currency	☺				☺			2
EMF Microfinance Fund AGmvK	☺	☺						2
Etimos Fund	☺							1
Finethic Microfinance Fund		☺	☺					2
IIV Mikrofinanzfonds	☺							1
ResponsAbility Global Microfinance Fund	☺							1
ResponsAbility Microfinance Leaders	☺							1
Triodos Microfinance Fund	☺	☺				☺		3
Total	**9**	**4**	**1**	**0**	**3**	**1**	**0**	

Source: Author Elaboration

The investor intent is well expressed in the MIVs mission, in line with the literature (Hochstadter and Sheck 2014), but it does not allow MIVs to fall within the perimeter of the OECD eligibility conditions.

The review of literature on SIIs (Hochstadter and Sheck 2014) is in line with the return expectation condition defined by OECD (2015). Unlike, the practical MIVs analysis shows that no one MIV compare the return expectation with the level of market rate return.

7 Conclusion

The aim of this study was to investigate if MIVs listed on the market are compliant with the definition of social impact investment promoted by OECD (2015).

This research contributes to the literature on impact investing, by providing a clear image of microfinance impact investment vehicles listed on the market and separately describing the level of convergence for the different elements of impact investing: social target area, beneficiary, goods and service, delivery organization intent, measurement of social impact, investor intent, and last but not least return expectation.

There is still much to do in order to "mind the gap" between practical fund management and the OECD definition. The area in which it is possible to recognize major conformity is the social target area (nine out of ten MIVs are compliant with the OECD definition). The analysis of beneficiaries was conducted considering financial exclusion as a dimension of social exclusion and without penalization for the lack of specific demographic conditions. Nevertheless, the results show that less than half of MIVs (four) fall in the perimeter of the OECD definition. Furthermore, despite the innate features of microfinance products, only one out of ten MIVs financing products are near to be considered "impact products" in alignment with OECD.

Formal evaluation of social impact provided by the MIV investment is also rare: only three MIVs consider measurement as a process, although inside the investment process. Furthermore, no MIV monetize the social impact.

The intent of delivery organizations and investors represents a gray area because MIVs do not directly recognize that MFIs reporting on social impact and only one MIV compulsory reports on its intent.

Lastly, the expectation of financial return is the most critical area. No fund compares the expected return with the market rate return and sometimes it is impossible to recognize information at all on the return expectation.

It is possible to conclude that, no one MIV is completely aligned to the OECD definition of social impact investments. Two MIVs meet the requirements of three eligibility conditions, and four MIVs respect two eligibility conditions fixed by OECD. The others MIVs are aligned only with one OECD eligibility condition.

More generally, the analyzed MIVs displayed a consistent lack of information and public documents. In order to bridge the gap, the GIIN should play a relevant role. MIVs aspiring to be listed in the GIIN database should be asked to disclose their approach to the OECD variables. Furthermore, a list of documents and information should be required and published by the GIIN to process the registration as "impact investments".

In the short-medium term the GIIN and other associations should promote a standardized information tool and became guarantors of the impact investing market transparency.

Expanding the analysis to other MIVs inscribed as impact investments in the GIIN database could also bring more significant results to the analysis carried out in this research.

Appendix

Table 7.3 Social target area

Categories	Provisional categories	Codes	Funds
Social target area	Ageing, disability, children and family, criminal and justice, unemployment, affordable housing		
	Others in developing context	'invest … in microfinance institutions located in Africa, Asia, Eastern Europe and Latin America … that offer access to financial services'; 'invest … in microfinance industry … predominantly in Latin America, Central and Eastern Europe, Asia and Africa'; 'invest … in microfinance industry … predominantly in Latin America, Central and Eastern Europe, Asia and Africa'; 'invest money … in successful and promising … MFIs … that … provide specific financial services … in … developing and emerging countries …'; 'developing and transition countries … providing financial services …'; 'small and medium-sized microfinance institutions (MFIs) in various emerging and developing market … in Africa, Asia and Latin America';	BlueOrchard Microfinance Fund; Dual Return Fund-Vision Microfinance; Dual Return Local Currency; EMF Microfinance Fund AGmvK; Etimos Fund; IIVMikrofinanzfonds; Responsibility Global Microfinance Fund; Responsibility Microfinance Leaders; Triodos Microfinance Fund

(continued)

Table 7.3 (continued)

Categories	Provisional categories	Codes	Funds
		'access to financial services … beneficiary institutions (MFIs or SMEs) are usually domiciled in developing and transition countries, primarily in the following region: Latin America, Africa, Central and Eastern Europe, Asia'; 'access to financial services … beneficiary institutions (MFIs or SMEs) are usually domiciled in developing and transition countries, primarily in the following region: Latin America, Africa, Central and Eastern Europe, Asia'; 'investment in the Microfinance sector mainly through investments in MFIs … in developing countries and countries in transition'	
	Others in developed context	'lend funds to local microfinance institutions that independently manage their own client portfolios'	Finethic Microfinance Fund

Table 7.4 Beneficiaries

Categories	Provisional categories	Codes	Funds
Beneficiaries	At risk population (social demographics, location and income)	'invests … In microfinance institutions located in Africa, Asia, Eastern Europe and Latin America … Microfinance institutions offer access to financial services to low-income groups often unserved by mainstream banks'; 'investing its assets in successful, promising and social responsible MFIs and FT trade oriented producers and traders. In this conjunction, the fund facilitates and promotes the generation of income for economically active, but impoverished population groups by facilitating and promoting the important associated access to financial services …'; 'by providing loans to individuals or communities of individuals who traditionally have had no access to financial services'; 'delivering a full range of financial services to the underserved in developing countries and countries in transaction'	BlueOrchard Microfinance Fund; EMF Microfinance fund AGmvK; Finethic Microfinance Fund; Triodos Microfinance Fund

(*continued*)

Table 7.4 (continued)

Categories	Provisional categories	Codes	Funds
	Population not at risk	'refinancing MFIs … Microfinance may be defined as the provision of financial services for economically active poor social classes in developing land and countries in transaction … assets are invested predominantly in Latin America, Central and Eastern Europe, Asia and Africa'; 'refinancing MFIs … Microfinance may be defined as the provision of financial services for economically active poor social classes in developing land and countries in transaction … assets are invested predominantly in Latin America, Central and Eastern Europe, Asia and Africa'; 'investing in microfinance institutions providing financial services to low-income people and boosting micro, small and medium enterprises, and in producers cooperatives fair trade oriented and/or organic oriented'; 'supports a wide range of business ideas of micro business owners in Africa, Asia and Latin America'; 'invest … in … MFIs domiciled in in developing and transition countries, primarily in the following region: Latin America, Africa, Central and Eastern Europe, Asia … that provide specific financial services for the designated target group'; 'invest … in … MFIs … domiciled in in developing and transition countries, primarily in the following region: Latin America, Africa, Central and Eastern Europe, Asia … that provide specific financial services for the designated target group';	Dual Return Fund-Vision Microfinance; Dual Return Local Currency; Etimos Fund Global Microfinance; IIV Mikrofinanzfonds; Responsibility global microfinance fund; Responsibility microfinance leaders

Table 7.5 Good and service

Categories	Provisional categories	Codes	Funds
Good/service	Public		
	Degree of publicness	'Microfinance … has cemented its role as an alternative strategy for fostering economic development. It is predicated on the notion that it is more efficient to finance entrepreneurial initiatives in order to improve the fortunes of people in the most disadvantaged parts of the world in a sustainable way rather than simply doling out aid without seeking to create value. By providing loans to individuals or communities of individuals who traditionally have had no access to financial services, microbanks provide these micro-entrepreneurs with the opportunity to build profitable businesses which, it successful, will ensure financial independence for those individual micro-entrepreneurs in the future'	Finethic Microfinance Fund
	Private	Contributing to developing financial inclusion in emerging economies … microfinance institutions offer access to financial services to low income groups'; 'Microfinance may be defined as the provision of financial services for economically active poor social classes in developing lands and countries in transition. By providing capital for people who are excluded from the official banking sector and economic development, the possibility of a positive self-reinforcing cycle is afforded, i.e. financial security, savings and growth. Micro and small employers are able to work and therefore stabilise their cash flows, create jobs and increase their standard of living'; 'Microfinance may be defined as the provision of financial services for economically active poor social classes in developing lands and countries in transition. By providing capital for people who are excluded from the official banking sector and economic development, the possibility of a positive self-reinforcing cycle is afforded, i.e. financial security, savings and growth. Micro and small employers are able to work and therefore stabilize their cash flows, create jobs and increase their standard of living';	BlueOrchard Microfinance Fund; Dual Return Fund-Vision Microfinance; Dual Return Local Currency; EMF Microfinance Fund AGmvK; Responsibility Global Microfinance Fund; Responsibility Microfinance Leaders; Triodos Microfinance Fund

(continued)

Table 7.5 (continued)

Categories	Provisional categories	Codes	Funds
		'Microfinance comprises various types of financial services for micro-clients in developing countries, emerging and transitional countries. It can be defined as the provision of financial services to economically active poor populations in these countries. These micro-clients normally have no or only limited access to financial services. MF offer them an instrument to help them themselves as well as an instrument for self-determination. The access to financial services is a chance to be entrepreneurial … The fund facilitates and promotes the generation of income for economically active, but impoverished population groups by facilitating and promoting the important associated access to financial services through the investment activities of the fund'; 'Microfinance (MF) comprises a number of types of financial services for small customers in developing and transition countries. These customers normally have no or only limited access to these services'. 'Microfinance (MF) comprises a number of types of financial services for small customers in developing and transition countries. These customers normally have no or only limited access to these services'; 'Microfinance offers poor people access to basic financial services such as loans, savings, money transfer services and micro insurance. People living in poverty, like everyone else, need a diverse range of financial services to run their businesses, build assets, smooth consumption, and manage risks'	

Table 7.6 Delivery organization

Categories	Provisional categories	Codes	Funds
Delivery organization	Incidental outcome		
	Social mission intent	'86% of the portfolio's investee MFIs are signatories of the SMART Campaign's Client Protection Principles'; '86% of the portfolio's investee MFIs are signatories of the SMART Campaign's Client Protection Principles'; 'The Fund pursues its purpose by investing its assets in successful, promising and socially responsible MFI and FT trade oriented producers and traders' … the fund invests primarily in profitable and consequently sustainable institutions'; 'We demand greatest transparency throughout the investment cycle, work closely with the MFIs and put value on a healthy structure of credit recipient … only those MFIs that meet the required ethical and social criteria are considered for investment. We thus look for profitable microfinance institutions with a sustainable focus and non-pure profit maximization. The MFIs guarantee these social standards by signing the client protective principles of the SMART Campaign'; 'MFIs … that are financially sustainable. The fund also invest in greenfield MFIs'	Dual Return Fund-Vision Microfinance; Dual Return Local Currency; EMF Microfinance Fund AGmvK; IIVMikrofinanzfonds; Triodos Microfinance Fund

(*continued*)

Table 7.6 (continued)

Categories	Provisional categories	Codes	Funds
	Sensibility to accountability	'Various MFIs are developing cost-effective, innovative systems to evaluate their specific impact on their clients' lives'. 'In terms of social responsibility of MFIs … the fund use Symbiotics' social rating tool for measuring and monitoring social impact. The tool consisting of 100 qualitative and quantitative indicators which are expressed through seven dimensions namely: social governance, labor climate, financial inclusion, client protection, product quality, community engagement, environmental protection and policies. All MFI's activities in the fund are monitored in all seven dimension and get as well as an overall grade between 1 star and 5 stars. The fund aims to have a high level of social impact and therefore the social performance measurement tools is always taking into account within the investment decision making process'. 'In terms of social responsibility of MFIs … the fund use Symbiotics' social rating tool for measuring and monitoring social impact. The tool consisting of 100 qualitative and quantitative indicators which are expressed through seven dimensions namely: social governance, labor climate, financial inclusion, client protection, product quality, community engagement, environmental protection and policies. All MFI's activities in the fund are monitored in all seven dimension and get as well as an overall grade between 1 star and 5 stars. The fund aim to have a high level of social impact and therefore the social performance measurement tools is always taking into account while the investment decision making process'; 'Social performance of the MFI'	BlueOrchard Microfinance Fund; Dual Return Fund-Vision Microfinance; Dual Return Local Currency; Finethic Microfinance Fund; Responsibility Microfinance Leaders

	Compulsory reporting
	External certification label
	Lagally binding constrints

Table 7.7 Measurability of social impact

Categories	Provisional categories	Codes	Funds
Measurability of social impact	No measurement	'Country Breakdown (loan to MFI), Geographic zone';	Finethic Microfinance Fund
	Informal evaluation, not valued	'Investment manager report. Indicators: Country (number of countries, average GDP per capita); MFI (number of microfinance, Average MFI gross loan portfolio); MSME (Number of clients financed by the fund; average loan size); client gender; client location (rural and urban); client activities (agriculture, production, trade, services, other), loan product (micro-enterprise, SMEs, consumer lending, housing loan, other products); methodology (individual, group)'; 'We look for profitable microfinance institutions with a sustainable focus and not pure profit maximization. Social indicators: target regions, Share women/men; average loan amount; share rural/urban areas'; 'Social performance indicators of the fund: micro entrepreneurs; number of clients of MFI; average loan disbursed in USD; % rural/urban clients; % female'; 'Social performance indicators of the fund: micro entrepreneurs; number of clients of MFI; average loan disbursed in USD; % rural/urban clients; % female'; 'Social performance: number of loan clients reached by the MFIs in the fund's portfolio; percentage female loan clients; percentage rural clients; average loan amount; number of savings clients reached by the MFIs in fund's portfolio'	EMF Microfinance Fund AGmvK; IIVMikrofinanzfonds; Responsibility Global Microfinance Fund; Responsibility Microfinance Leaders; Triodos Microfinance Fund

Formal evaluation but not valued	'Social performance assessment is a fundamental part of the investment process, standing alongside our Financial Performance assessment to make sound investment decisions to help microentrepreneurs and SMEs prosper with access to a fair and inclusive financial system. Social performance data for MFIs in managed funds: total number of borrowers served; total numbers of servers served; total number of MFI employees; % of MFIs borrowers who are female; % of MFIs borrowers who live in rural areas; % of MFIs endorsing the Smart Campaign; % of MFIs with an exclusion policy on lending; % of MFIs reporting to the MIX on social indicators; % of MFIs with a social rating; % of MFIs with environmental policy and or eco products … Activities financed by MFIs and regional portfolio break-down. 'The fund aim to have a high level of social impact and therefore the social performance tools is always taking into account while the investment decision making process. social impact: number of micro-entrepreneurs; including their families, microloans size in USD; number of MFIs, Emerging markets countries, social rating, % clients rural/urban; %woman/Men/legal entities; issued microloan in USD; Client activities; Methodology (individual/small groups)'; 'Use Symbiotics rating tool for measuring and monitoring social impact. Portfolio and social impact: Microfinance portfolio region summary; client gender; client location (rural/urban)'	BlueOrchard Microfinance Fund; Dual Return Fund-Vision Microfinance; Dual Return Local Currency;
Formal evaluation and valued		

Table 7.8 Investor intent

Categories	Provisional categories	Codes	Funds
Investor intent	Incidental social outcomes	'The essential objective of the fund is to conclude loan transactions … showed a sound financial and operational performance and delivered a positive social impact by improving the economic conditions of unbanked people in many developing countries;' 'The essential objective of the fund is to conclude loan transactions in local currency'	Dual Return Fund-Vision Microfinance; Dual Return Local Currency;
	Social intent expressed in statement	'Through its investments, the Fund aims to support microfinance institutions to expand and to extend their outreach to poorer people, improve the quality and appropriateness of financial services, and encourage the development of savings, insurance and payment services'< 'Selects its partner and investment for social and sustainable principles. The fund is dedicated to the concept of responsible investment and is committed to develop and implement environmental, social and governance (ESG) principles in daily fund management contributing to increasing transparency in the microfinance industry'; 'The policy of the fund …, is to contribute to sustainable growth of microfinance institutions in emerging and frontier markets and to provide investors with competitive financial and social returns derived from a portfolio of investment broadly diversified across many currencies, MFIs and micro-entrepreneurs'; 'The fund aim to generate a sustained, long-term real rise in the value of its assets, while at the same time and to an equal extent striving to contribute towards the creation of prosperity among the underprivileged population groups in developing and emerging countries by indirectly financing entrepreneurial activities in these locations … Pursue a dual investment goal combining to poverty reduction and achieving development policy objectives made possible through microcredits'; 'The overall objective of the Fund is to offer to socially responsible investors financially and socially sound investments to contribute to the sustainable development of emerging market economies by facilitating investments in micro and small enterprises and producers. The Sub-Fund aims to achieve its objective by investing on a broadly diversified basis in short- to medium-term senior debt instruments; 'The Fund's objective is to invest its assets in the field of microfinance. More specifically, the purpose of the Fund is to finance unlisted MFIs or assimilated projects aiming at the development of economic activities of micro-entrepreneurs, located around the world, especially in emerging countries, either directly by providing equity and debt financing	BlueOrchard Microfinance Fund; Dual Return Fund-Vision Microfinance; Dual Return Local Currency; EMF Microfinance Fund AGmvK; Etimos Fund Global Microfinance; Finethic Microfinance Fund; IIVMikrofinanzfonds; Responsibility Global Microfinance Fund; Responsibility Microfinance Leaders

Compulsory reporting	or indirectly by investing in investment vehicles active in the field of the microfinance, particularly by subscribing to structured credit products issued by these vehicles such as collateralised debt obligations;' 'The administration of the fund focuses on credit transactions with carefully selected microfinance institutions and related micro-sector institutions'; 'The fund aim at achieving a real increase in value over the long term; at the same time by promoting entrepreneurial activity they seek to contribute to reducing poverty in developing and transition countries. The long-term goal i an increase in the value of the investment as well as socio-economic benefits'; 'The fund aim at achieving a real increase in value over the long term; at the same time, by promoting entrepreneurial activity they seek to contribute to reducing poverty in developing and transition countries. The goal is to achieve financial growth and social added value in the long term''The overall objective of the sub-fund is to offer investors a financially and socially sound investment in the microfinance sector mainly through investment in MFIs. The fund has the prospect of an attractive financial return combined with the opportunity for the investors to make a pro-active, measurable and sustainable contribution to the development of microfinance sector into a inclusive financial sector in which the majority of people have access to financial services'	Triodos Microfinance Fund
Legally binding constraints		

Table 7.9 Return expectation

Categories	Provisional categories	Codes	Funds
Return expectation	Grants		
	Return of capital		
	Profit ≤ market RR		
	Profit > market RR		
	No comparation with market RR	'The fund target return is 6 M LIBOR +300–400 basis points p.a.'; 'The performance goal is set at Euribor + 2%'; 'Performance goal of Libor + 6%'; 'Strives for a sustainable, long-term real appreciation of its assets that is higher than the corresponding money market level'; 'Benchmark LIBOR EUR month'; '3–5% p.a. over a horizon of five years'; '4–7% p.a. over a horizon of five years'; 'average annual return in Euro of 6–9%'	BlueOrchard Microfinance Fund; Dual Return Fund-Vision Microfinance; Dual Return Local Currency; EMF Microfinance Fund AGmvK; Etimos Fund Global Microfinance; Responsibility Global Microfinance Fund; Responsibility Microfinance Leaders; Triodos Microfinance Fund
	No return expectation	'Fund has provided investors with consistent and predictable returns. Broad diversification, the lack of currency risk and investment limited to granting loans have enabled the sub-fund to attain its long-term goal of a return matching LIBOR+300 basis points, with no negative returns at all'	Finethic Microfinance Fund

References

Ashta, A. (2012). Co-creation for impact investment in microfinance. *Strategic Change, 21*(1/2), 71–81.

Berelson, B. (1952). *Content analysis in communication research.* Glencoe: Free Press.

Blue Orchard Microfinance Fund. (2013). Achieving social objective. Available at: http://www.blueorchard.com/wpcontent/uploads/2015/06/BO-SPR-2013-RN.pdf

Blue Orchard Microfinance Fund. (2014). *Rising our spirit. Social performance report 2014.* Available at: http://www.blueorchard.com/social-performance-report-2014/. Accessed 18 Mar 2015.

Blue Orchard Microfinance Fund. (2015). *Web site.* Available at: http://www.blueorchard.com/investment-solutions/investment-fund/. Accessed 18 Mar 2015.

Drexler, M., & Noble, A. (2013). *From the margin to the mainstream. Assessment of the impact investment sector and opportunities to engage mainstream investors.* Cologny: World Economic Forum. Available at: http://www3.weforum.org/docs/WEF_II_FromMarginsMainstream_Report_2013.pdf. Accessed 12 Mar 2015.

Dual Return. (2014a). *Audited annual report.* Available at: http://www.vision-microfinance.com/en/dual-return-fund/vision-microfinance/. Accessed 12 Mar 2015.

Dual Return. (2014b). *Prospectus.* http://www.visionmicrofinance.com/en/dual-return-fund/vision-microfinance/. Accessed 12 Mar 2015.

Dual Return. (2015). *Website.* http://www.visionmicrofinance.com/en/dual-return-fund/vision-microfinance/. Accessed 12 Mar 2015.

Emerson, J., & Spitzer, J. (2007). *From fragmentation to function: Critical concepts and writings on social capital markets' structure, operation and innovation.* Working Paper. Oxford: Skoll Centre for Social Entrepreneurship.

EMF, Microfinance Fund AGmvK. (2012). *Prospectus.* Available at: http://www.enabling.li/wpcontent/uploads/2013/03/EMF_Investment_Report_Nov12_Class_A_T.pdf. Accessed 12 Mar 2015.

EMF, Microfinance Fund AGmvK. (2013). *Investment manager report.* Available at: http://www.enabling.li/wpcontent/uploads/2013/03/EMF_Investment_Report_Feb13_Class_A_T.pdf. Accessed 12 Mar 2015.

EMF, Microfinance Fund AGmvK. (2015). *Brochure.* Available at: http://www.enabling.li/?page_id=391. Accessed 18 Mar 2015.

Etimos Fund. (2015). *Website*. Available at: http//www.etimos.it/eng/. Accessed 18 Mar 2015.

Eurosif. (2012). *European SRI study*. Available at: http://www.eurosif.org/publication/european-sri-study-2012/. Accessed 20 Feb 2015.

Eurosif. (2014). *European SRI study*. Available at: http://www.eurosif.org/wp-content/uploads/2014/09/Eurosif-SRI-Study-20142.pdf. Accessed 20 Feb 2015.

Fehr, D. W., & Hishigsuren, G. (2006). Raising capital for microfinance: Sources of funding and opportunities for equity financing. *Journal of Developmental Entrepreneurship, 11*(2), 133–143.

Finethic Microfinance Fund. (2015a). *Broshure*. Available at: https://www.fundo.ch/en/services/product/cashflow-driven/finethic_microfinance. Accessed 18 Mar 2015.

France National Advisory Board to Social Impact Investment Taskforce. (2014). *The hows and whys of social impact investing*. Available at: http://www.socialimpactinvestment.org/. Accessed 20 Feb 2015.

Freireich, J., & Fulton, K. (2009). *Investing for social and environmental impact*. Cambridge, MA. Available at: http://monitorinstitute.com/downloads/what-we-think/impact-investing/Impact_Investing.pdf. Accessed 12 Jan 2015.

GAO. (1996). *Content analysis a methodology for structuring and analyzing written material. Program evaluation and methodology division*. Washington, DC: United States General Accounting Office.

Global Impact Investment Network. (2014). *About impact investing*. New York. Available at: http://www.thegiin.org/. Accessed 18 Jan 2015.

Global Impact Investment Network. (2015). *Impact base snapshot. An analysis of 300+ impact investing funds*. New York. Available at: http://www.thegiin.org/assets/documents/pub/ImpactBaseSnapshot.pdf. Accessed 3 Mar 2015.

Goodman, P. (2006). Microfinance investment funds: Objectives, players, potential. In I. Matthäus-Maier & J. D. Von Pischke (Eds.), *Microfinance investment funds* (pp. 11–45). New York: Springer.

Hochstadter, A. K., & Scheck, B. (2014). What's in a name: An analysis of impact investing understanding by academics and practitioners. *Journal of Business Ethics, 132*, 449–475.

IIV MikrofinanzFonds. (2015b). *Website*. Available at: http://www.investinvisions.com/invest-in-visions-microfinance-fonds. Accessed 18 Mar 2015.

IIV MikrofinanzFonds. (2015c). *Reuters description*. Available at: http://www.investinvisions.com/invest-in-visions-microfinance-fonds. Accessed 18 Mar 2015.

Italy National Advisory Board to Social Impact Investment Taskforce. (2014). *La finanza che include: gli investimenti ad impatto sociale per una nuova economia*. Available at: http://www.socialimpactinvestment.org/. Accessed at 3 November 2014.

Jung, P., & Eriksson, P. (2006). Microfinane loan obligations. Structured finance for microfinance investment. In V. Robbè & P. Ali (Eds.), *Innovation in securitization yearbook 2006* (pp. 179–188). Alphen aan Den Rijn: Kluwer Law International.

Krippendorff, K. (1980). *Content analysis: An introduction to its methodology*. Newbury Park: Sage.

Kyngas, H., & Vanhanen, L. (1999). Content analysis (Finnish). *Hoitotiede, 11*, 3–12.

La Torre, M., & Vento, G. A. (2006). *Microfinance*. London: Palgrave Macmillan.

Moore, M. L., Westley, F. R., & Nicholls, A. (2012). The social finance and social nexus. *Journal of social Entrepreneruship, 3*(2), 115–132.

Nicholls, A. (2010). The institutionalization of social investment: The interplay of investment logics and investor rationalities. *Journal of Social Entrepreneurship, 1*(1), 70–100.

O'Donohoe, N., Leijonjufvud, C., Saltuk, Y., Bugg-Levine, A., & Brandenburg, M. (2010). *Impact investment*. New York: J.P. Morgan. Available at: http://ventureatlanta.org/wp-content/uploads/2011/11/JP-Morgan-impact_investments_nov2010.pdf. Accessed 14 Jan 2015.

OECD. (2015). *Social impact investment. Building the evidence base*. Paris. Available at: http://www.oecd.org/sti/ind/social-impact-investment.pdf. Accessed 18 Feb 2015

Renneboog, L., Horst, T. J., & Zhang, C. (2008). Socially responsible investments: Institutional aspects, performance and investor. *Journal of banking and finance, 32*, 1723–1742.

ResponsAbility Global Microfinance Fund. (2014). *Monthly report*. Available at: http://www.responsability.com/investing/en/1061/responsAbility-Global-Microfinance-Fund.htm?Product=19665. Accessed 18 Mar 2015.

ResponsAbility Global Microfinance Fund. (2015a). *Fund portrait*. Available at: http://www.responsability.com/investing/en/1061/responsAbility-Global-Microfinance-Fund.htm?Product=19665. Accessed 18 Mar 2015.

ResponsAbility Global Microfinance Fund. (2015b). *Prospectus*. Available at: http://www.responsability.com/investing/en/1061/responsAbility-Global-Microfinance-Fund.htm?Product=19665. Accessed 18 Mar 2015.

ResponsAbility Microfinance Leaders. (2015a). *Fund portrait*. Available at: http://www.responsability.com/investing/en/1061/responsAbility-SICAV-Lux-Microfinance-Leaders.htm?Product=20013. Accessed 18 Mar 2015.

ResponsAbility Microfinance Leaders. (2015b). *Monthly report*. Available at: http://www.responsability.com/investing/en/1061/responsAbility-SICAV-Lux-Microfinance-Leaders.htm?Product=20013. Accessed 18 Mar 2015.

ResponsAbility Microfinance Leaders. (2015c). *Prospectus*. Available at: http://www.responsability.com/investing/en/1061/responsAbility-SICAV-Lux-Microfinance-Leaders.htm?Product=20013. Accessed 18 Mar 2015.

Saltuk, Y., El Idrissi, A., Bouri, A., Mudaliar, A., & Schiff, H. (2014). *Spotting on the market. The impact Investor survey*. New York: J.P. Morgan. Available at. http://www.thegiin.org/assets/documents/pub/2014MarketSpotlight.PDF. Accessed 14 Jan 2015.

Saltuk, Y., El Idrissi, A., Bouri, A., Mudaliar, A., & Schiff, H. (2015). *Eyes on the horizon. The impact investor survey*. New York: J.P. Morgan. Available at: http://www.thegiin.org/assets/documents/pub/2015.04%20Eyes%20on%20the%20Horizon.pdf. Accessed 10 May 2015.

Social Impact Investment Task Force. (2014). *Impact investment: The invisible heart of markets*. London. Available at: http://www.socialimpactinvestment.org/. Accessed 3 Nov 2014.

Stemler, S. (2001). An overview of content analysis. Practical assessment. *Research & Evaluation, 7*(17), 137.

The Smart Campaign. (2015). The client protection principles. Available at: http://www.smartcampaign.org/storage/documents/smart_campaign_cpps.pdf

Triodos Microfinance Fund. (2014). *Audited annual report*. Available at: https://www.triodos.com/downloads/investment-management/funds-for-distribution-partners/microfinance-fund/annual-reports/microfinance-fund-annual-report-2014.pdf. Accessed 18 Mar 2015.

Triodos Microfinance Fund. (2015a). *Factsheet*. Available at: https://www.triodos.com/en/investment-management/our-funds/institutional-investor/microfinance-fund/about-the-fund/. Accessed 18 Mar 2015.

Triodos Microfinance Fund. (2015b). *Prospectus*. https://www.triodos.com/en/investment-management/our-funds/institutional-investor/microfinance-fund/about-the-fund/. Accessed 18 Mar 2015.

UK National Advisory Board to Social Impact Taskforce. (2014). *Building a social impact investment market. The UK experience*. Available at: http://www.socialimpactinvestment.org/. Accessed 15 Dec 2015.

USA National Advisory Board to Social Impact Taskforce. (2014). *Private capital. Public good*. Available at: http://www.socialimpactinvestment.org/. Accessed 14 Dec 2015.

Weber, R. P. (1990). *Basic content analysis* (2nd ed.). Newbury Park: Sage.
Working Group Impact Measurement. (2014). Measuring impact. Subject paper. London. Available at: http://www.socialimpactinvestment.org/. Accessed 14 Dec 2015.

8

Intellectual Capital Disclosure and IPO Results: Is It a Matter of Classification?

Cristiana Cardi, Camilla Mazzoli, and Sabrina Severini

1 Introduction

Although Intellectual Capital (IC) reporting remains largely a voluntary and relatively uncommon practice, its use has increased over the years, since it is thought to improve the evaluation of a company's business activities, as well as its possible future developments. In particular, by reducing the information asymmetry between the firm and its stakeholders, a large IC disclosure is expected to improve the IPO results in terms of the amount of money that the listing firm is able to raise.

To our knowledge, very few studies have attempted to provide empirical evidence of the relationship between the IC disclosure and the IPO results, and the results of the few studies that have been done are

C. Cardi • C. Mazzoli (✉) • S. Severini
Università Politecnica delle Marche, Ancona, Italy
e-mail: c.mazzoli@univpm.it

S. Carbó Valverde et al. (eds.), *Bank Funding, Financial Instruments and Decision-Making in the Banking Industry*, Palgrave Macmillan Studies in Banking and Financial Institutions,
DOI 10.1007/978-3-319-30701-5_8

inconsistent, possibly due to the different IC classifications employed. In particular, Dimovski and Brooks (2006) analyzed a sample of Australian IPOs issued between 1994 and 1999 and found that greater disclosure about intangible assets (represented by goodwill, brand name, trademarks, patents, and capitalized R&D) reduced the uncertainty of the IPO and, in turn, the underpricing. This finding is consistent with the body of literature that commenced with the study by Benveniste and Spindt (1989). They maintained that firms with greater uncertainty surrounding the true value of the shares (firms that disclose less information in the IPO) are more likely to experience revisions in their offer prices and to trade far from their true value on their first day of trading.[1] Similar results were reported by Hanley and Hoberg (2010), who examined a sample of 2112 US IPOs issued between 1996 and 2005; they found that offers issuing more non-financial information in the pre-market period have more accurate and narrower initial filing price ranges and, as a consequence, lower price adjustment and lower underpricing. Opposite results, however, were obtained by Singh and Van der Zahn (2007), who empirically examined a sample of 334 Singapore IPOs launched between 1994 and 2004. Contrary to their expectations, they found that larger IC disclosure (measured using their own classification based on that of Williams 2001; Beaulieu et al. 2002; Bukh et al. 2005) is associated with a larger underpricing. They also provide possible explanations for the positive link they exhibit in terms of litigation risk, marketing-advertising strategy, and extensive bidding up by "unsophisticated" traders. Consistent with these findings, Cardi and Mazzoli (2015) studied the contents of the listing prospectuses for a sample of 74 Italian IPOs issued between 2004 and 2014 and found that the lower the information asymmetry (that is resulting from a large IC disclosure), the larger the price adjustment, especially in relation to information regarding firms' processes and IT. Moreover, they found that the level of disclosure also impacts the secondary market price, giving rise to a larger underpricing, especially when information about research and development is disclosed. More generally, they maintain that a large IC disclosure improves the IPO results, increasing the amount of money raised.

[1] This also happens because underwriters, who are unsure of the price of an issue, are likely to set wider offer ranges to provide greater flexibility in setting the final offer price (Hanley 1993).

In brief, part of the literature maintains that greater IC disclosure is likely to increase the amount of money left on the table by means of a larger underpricing. Other studies support a positive effect of IC disclosure on the IPO results: that is, by disclosing more information, the firm attenuates the information asymmetry towards investors and partly reduces the underpricing by means of a larger price adjustment. These inconsistencies in the literature may be ascribed to the different IC variables being considered (ranging from a complete set of variables to just a few items) and to the different IC classifications employed; indeed, not only is IC disclosure a voluntary practice, but a conventional IC classification format has yet to be established. As a consequence, not only are firms allowed to disclose IC information in different ways, but the apparent results of IC may even appear to vary depending on the classification method used to explore the information.

Here, we analyzed the impact of IC disclosure on IPO results using two different IC classifications: the six-dimension classification suggested by Cordazzo (2007) and the three-dimension classification introduced by Li et al. (2008). This allowed us to assess whether the results changed as a function of the classification system used and therefore whether the inconsistencies revealed between previous studies could be attributed to the manner in which the IC information is categorized.

Our results show that the effects of the IC disclosure on the IPO results are comprehensively stable across different IC classifications. Consistent with Cardi and Mazzoli (2015), primary market investors mainly appreciate “hard (technical) information” that provides solid data about how a firm is structured and how it works, while secondary market investors are more influenced by “soft (communicative) information” that describe the relationships between a firm and its stakeholders as well as their research and development activities. Nevertheless, differences were identified between the two classifications employed in terms of what is considered “hard” or “soft” information, making it impossible to provide firms with operative recommendations about what kinds of IC information they should disclose in their prospectus in order to entice primary and secondary market investors.

The remainder of the paper is organized as follows: in Sect. 2, we provide a review of the literature; in Sect. 3 we describe our data and methodology; a discussion of the key findings is presented in Sect. 4. Section 5 concludes.

2 Previous Literature

Intellectual capital is increasingly recognized as a driver to create and maintain competitive advantage and shareholder value (Tayles et al. 2007; Bontis 2001). In particular, part of the literature on IC stresses the link between the intangible assets of a firm and its structure and performance (CIMA 2001; Marr and Schiuma 2001), reflecting the importance that knowledge assets play in enhancing organizations' competitive advantage. Furthermore, it is recognized that the disclosure of IC variables helps reduce uncertainty about future prospects and facilitates a more precise valuation of the company (Bukh 2003). Previous literature has revealed a growing gap between the market and book values of firms (Holland 2003; Beattie and Thomson 2004; Lev 2001; Gu and Lev 2004). This might suggest that traditional financial reporting models are not able to comprehensively convey the complete information about a wide range of value creating assets (Francis and Schipper 1999; Lev and Zarowin 1999; Barsky et al. 2003), thus stressing the importance of including intangible asset information when evaluating a firm's value.

Despite the large consensus on the importance of IC disclosure, two main drawbacks affect its employment: On the one hand, IC disclosure still constitutes a voluntary practice and no standard framework exists that could be used by firms to disclose such information; on the other hand, different IC variables and IC classifications have been proposed over the years, generating a large heterogeneity depending on the field in which they are applied.

In reference to the first point, standard company balance sheets do not provide for the reporting of most intangible assets (Lev and Zarowin 1999) and traditional financial reports are not suitable for analyzing intellectual capital (Riegler and Hollerschmid 2006). As such, firms disclose non-financial information using their own frameworks, thus generating IC reports that include different items that are then difficult to compare with each other.

Moreover, previous literature has not yet reached a consensus about the classification of the single IC items, thus generating large heterogeneity. Some authors maintain that the concept of IC should be categorized into three major categories: human, structural, and relational capital (Sveiby 1997; Meritum 2002; Lev and Zambon 2003; Boedker et al. 2005). Others, such as Guthrie and Petty (2000), have offered a categorization that considers internal structure, external structure, and human capital; but many other classification schemes have also been proposed over the last 16 years (Stewart 1997; Chiucchi 2004; Previati and Vezzani 2007). As pointed out by Rastogi (2003) and Swart (2006), while a categorization of the intangible assets is useful in many ways, we can only understand the true value of the IC items by considering the dynamic intercorrelations between such elements.

The disclosure of IC information is a key point in IPOs: a large amount of information asymmetry surrounds companies that decide to go public (Guo et al. 2005; Singh and Van der Zahn 2007; See and Rashid 2011) and non-financial information is likely to reduce such information asymmetry towards investors, thus influencing the IPO results. A recent stream of literature has focused on investigating the role of IC disclosure on the IPO results, as measured by the amount of money raised. Dimovski and Brooks (2004, 2006) were the first to investigate the relationship between IC information disclosed in the IPO prospectuses and the IPO success in terms of underpricing. They examined 262 Australian IPOs issued between 1994 and 1999 and found a negative correlation between the underpricing and the information reported about a set of intangible variables (brand name, trademarks, patents, and capitalized R&D). They recognized that providing information about non-financial assets is of great importance in order to reduce the uncertainty surrounding the IPO, thus helping the company to "leave less money on the table". Similar results were reported by Hanley and Hoberg (2010), who examined a sample of 2112 US IPOs issued between 1996 and 2005; they found that offers with larger non-financial information disclosed in the pre-market period have more accurate and a narrower initial filing price range and, as a consequence, a smaller price adjustment and less underpricing. Another study dealing with the link between IC disclosure and underpricing is that by Singh and Van Der Zahn (2007). Although they hypothesized that a negative relationship would exist between IC variables and the level of underpricing, their empirical evidence revealed the opposite: Positive correlation exists between underpricing and the disclosure of IC information. The findings of Cardi and Mazzoli (2015) were also consistent with these results. They examined 74 Italian IPOs and studied the effects of a larger IC disclosure on both the primary and secondary markets by separating the effects produced on the issue price and the market price. They found that a larger IC disclosure impacted the primary market investors in terms of an increase in the price adjustment, especially when it related to "hard (technical) information" regarding a firm's processes or IT. They also demonstrated that IC disclosure can impact the market price, leading to an increase in underpricing, particularly when "soft (communicative) information" is revealed about research and development activities.

The inconsistencies in the results provided by the above-mentioned studies in terms of the effects of the IC disclosure on the amount of money raised could partly be explained by the use of different measures of IPO results (that is price adjustment, underpricing or, at times, both), but also, and perhaps more so, by the different IC items and classifications employed. In particular, Dimovski and Brooks (2004, 2006) made use of two dummy variables without any reference to the IC classifications documented in the literature. Singh and Van Der Zahn (2007) adopted their own single IC disclosure index, based on three existing indices (proposed by: Williams 2001; Beaulieu et al. 2002; Bukh et al. 2005), which comprises six IC categories and 81 items. Hanley and Hoberg (2010) examined the content of the listing prospectuses in terms of the disclosure of risk factors, the use of proceeds, and the management's discussion and analysis, while Cardi and Mazzoli (2015) built an IC disclosure index, according to the method proposed by Cordazzo (2007), based on 87 IC items grouped into six IC dimensions.

Based on the framework proposed by Cardi and Mazzoli (2015), who separated the effects of IC disclosure on the primary and secondary market investors' behavior, here we study the effects of two different IC classifications on the IPO results in terms of both the price adjustment and the underpricing. We expect to see different results emerging according to the classification method employed.

3 Data and Methodology

The aim of this paper was to investigate whether the positive effects of IC disclosure on the IPO results, documented by recent literature, were consistent for different IC classifications. To this end, we carried out an empirical analysis on a sample of 74 firms that went public on the Italian Stock Exchange (Borsa Italiana) for the first time between 2004 and 2014. The effects of IC disclosure on the IPO outcome were analyzed for each firm using two different IC classifications: that proposed by Cordazzo (2007) and that introduced by Li et al. (2008). We focused on Italian firms for the following two reasons: First, the Italian economy is largely built on IC assets and thus represents an interesting market to study in this context[2]; second, linguistic misunderstandings could affect our analysis of the listing prospectuses, thus by examining prospectus contents in Italian only, we can guarantee the highest level of comprehension and thereby eliminate this potential problem. For each of the firms included in the sample, we obtained the IPO prospectus from Borsa Italiana. We then carried out a contents analysis of the prospectuses using two different IC classifications. Additional information about the economic characteristics of the firms included in the sample and details of each IPO were obtained from Thomson DataStream, Borsa Italiana, and a proprietary database from Universoft (Bergamo University)—this latter database has already been employed in previous studies, (see Vismara et al. 2012, for a detailed description of the database) (Table 8.1 provides a description of the variables used).

The first classification we employed was that proposed by Cordazzo (2007), which comprises 87 items grouped into the following six dimensions:

1. Human resources (29 items);
2. Customers (16 items);
3. Information technology (5 items);
4. Processes (8 items);
5. Research and Development (10 items);
6. Strategies (19 items).

[2] Cerisola et al. (2013) show that Italian firms generally exceed other EU countries in terms of reporting data on European intellectual property rights and product innovation. This could be the result of several Italian government initiatives, in place since 1999, which promote Italian organizations to invest in IC; in particular, R&D projects (Bozzolan et al. 2003).

Table 8.1 List of control variables

	Variable	Label	Description	Source	Model
IPO	IPO year	DUMMY_YEAR	Dummy variable (value of 1 for years with a number of IPOs higher than the average number for the whole sample period)	Universoft	UP
	Size of offer	SIZE	Number of shares offered in the IPO divided by the number of shares outstanding	Universoft	PA & UP
	Underwriter's reputation	UW_REP	Number of IPOs leaded by the underwriter divided by total number of IPOs in the whole sample period	Universoft	PA & UP
	Institutional demand	INST_DEM	Percentage of shares asked by institutional investors divided by the total number of shares asked by retail institutional and employee investors	Universoft	PA & UP
	Interval	INT	Number of days from prospectus registration to listing date	Borsa Italiana	PA & UP
	Venture capital backed	VC	Dummy variable (value of 1 if at least one VC is involved in the IPO)	Universoft	PA & UP
	% range	RANGE	Bookbuilding price range divided by the range midpoint	Universoft	PA

(*continued*)

Table 8.1 (continued)

	Variable	Label	Description	Source	Model
FIRM	Return on equity	ROE	Return on equity of the company as an average of the last three years	Thomson Datastream	PA
	Volatility of earnings	CVEARN	Standard deviation of earnings in the three years before the IPO.	Universoft	UP
	Debt ratio	DEBT	Debt ratio of the company as an average of the last three years	Thomson Datastream	PA & UP
	Years of activity	AGE	Number of years the company has been operating in the market	Thomson Datastream	PA & UP
	IC intensive sectors	IC_INT	Dummy to identify IC intensive sectors	Universoft	PA & UP
	Technology based sector	TECH	Dummy variable (value of 1 if the firm belongs to a technology based sector)	Universoft	PA & UP
	Market share	MRKTSHR	Firm's total assets divided by the sum of total assets for firms belonging to the same industrial sector	Universoft	PA & UP

Table 8.1 reports the name, label, description and the source of each control variable used to describe the IPO and the FIRM characteristics. The far right column (Model) indicates the models in which each variable was used: PA is the Price Adjustment model (8.4 and 8.5) and UP is the underpricing model (8.7 and 8.8). The IC intensive sectors comprise the following: banks, financial sector, health care, media, software components, support service, technolo gical equipment, and pharmaceuticals; in accordance with Mangena et al. (2010)

The second classification used was that proposed by Li et al. (2008), which includes 61 items grouped into just three dimensions:

1. Human Capital (22 items);
2. Relational Capital (21 items);
3. Structural Capital (18 items).

The two classifications differ in many ways: the six-dimension methodology by Cordazzo (2007) was devised with the specific aim of investigating IC disclosure in Italian IPO prospectuses. In contrast, Li et al. (2008) developed their classification with the aim of studying the relationship between IC disclosure, information asymmetry, and the cost of capital. In the first case, the items are able to take into account the particularities of the Italian IPO market, because the 87 indicators result from the combination of two frameworks: The content analysis proposed by Bukh et al. (2001) and by AIAF (2002). The second IC classification scheme can be considered as more traditional, and it is more commonly found and generally accepted in the literature.

For both classifications, we carried out a content analysis of the listing prospectuses, whereby a score (ranging from zero to three) was assigned to each of the indicators, reflecting the level of information provided. A score of three was given for items described in great detail, a score of two was assigned when the item was described in detail, a score of one when it was discussed in general terms only, finally a score of zero was assigned when the item was not described at all (Orens et al. 2010). Although this form of evaluation is more subjective than that based on the volume or frequency of reported information, it ensures that irrelevant or redundant generalities are not considered as strategic disclosure (Botosan 1997; Brammer and Pavelin 2006). Moreover, an in-depth analysis of the prospectuses is of great importance since, while some non-financial information has to be included in the listing prospectus by law, it is the firms themselves that decide the breadth and depth of the information they provide. Data collection and the coding process were carried out by the authors. Coding instructions and a standardized coding worksheet were jointly created and agreed on by the authors. Internal consistency estimates show that the variance in the single disclosure indexes is quite systematic (Cronbach's alpha = 0.83).[3]

Once all of the evaluations had been collected, we built different IC disclosure indexes for each dimension that the two classifications consider, as follows:

$$\text{ICDI}\_C_k = \frac{\sum_{i=1}^{n} \text{SC}_i}{n*3} \tag{8.1}$$

$$\text{ICDI}\_L_k = \frac{\sum_{i=1}^{n} \text{SC}_i}{n*3} \tag{8.2}$$

where:

ICDI_C_k is the disclosure index for each of the six dimensions we consider in the classification proposed by Cordazzo (2007) (ICDI_{RD}; ICDI_{IT}; $\text{ICDI}_{\text{PROC}}$; ICDI_{HR}; $\text{ICDI}_{\text{CUSTOM}}$; $\text{ICDI}_{\text{STRAT}}$); ICDI_$L_k$ is for the three dimensions we consider in the classification suggested by Li et al. (2008) (ICDI_{HC}; ICDI_{RC}; ICDI_{SC})[4]; i are the single items belonging to each of the k-IC dimensions (ranging from 1 to a generic n, depending on the k-IC dimensions considered); and SC_i is the score attributed to the specific item (ranging from zero to three).

We then used the 9 IC disclosure indexes as independent variables for two different set of regressions, one of which used the price adjustment (PA) as its dependent variable and the other used the underpricing (UP). The price adjustment measures the percentage difference between the final offer price and the mid-point of the price range, as illustrated in Eq. (8.3).

---

[3] Previous papers have identified 0.7 as an acceptable threshold for the scale reliability coefficient (for example, see Nunnaly 1978), although a value of 0.64 has also been accepted (Botosan 1997).

[4] For the classification based on Cordazzo (2007): ICDI_RD (research and development); ICDI_IT (information technology); ICDI_PROC (processes); ICDI_HR (human resources); ICDI_CUSTOM (customers); and ICDI_STRAT (strategies). For the classification based on Li et al. (2008): ICDI_HC (human capital); ICDI_RC (relational capital); and ICDI_SC (structural capital).

$$PA = (OP - MFP) / MFP \tag{8.3}$$

where: PA is the price adjustment; OP is the final offer price of the IPO; and MFP is the midpoint of the initial filing price range $[(\text{higher price} + \text{lower price})/2]$.

The models describes by Eqs. (8.4) and (8.5) investigate the effect of IC disclosure on the price adjustment when different IC classifications are employed.

$$PA = \alpha + \beta IPO + \gamma FIRM + \chi ICDI\_C_k + \varepsilon \tag{8.4}$$

$$PA = \alpha + \beta IPO + \gamma FIRM + \chi ICDI\_L_k + \varepsilon \tag{8.5}$$

The dependent variable is the price adjustment (PA) and independent variables are divided into three groups. The first and second groups (IPO and FIRM) include a set of the control variables, commonly used in the IPO literature, and they provide information about the characteristics of the IPO and of the listing firm, respectively (as described in Table 8.1). The third group of explanatory variables ($ICDI\_C_k$) describes the degree of IC disclosure in terms of the six dimensions suggested by Cordazzo (2007), as described by Eq. (8.1), and in terms of the three dimensions suggested by Li et al. (2008), as described by Eq. (8.2).

The very same regressions were then re-run using the underpricing (UP) as the dependent variable, measured as the percentage difference between the closing price at the end of the first trading day and the IPO offer price net of the market performance on the same day,[5] as described by Eq. (8.4).

$$UP = (MP - OP) / OP \tag{8.6}$$

where UP is the underpricing that the listing firm generates by selling shares at a discount on the expected market price net of the market

[5] We make use of the FTSE MIB index to calculate the market performance.

performance on the same day; MP is the first day closing market price; and OP is the final offer price.

$$\mathrm{UP} = \alpha + \beta \mathrm{PA} + \gamma \mathrm{IPO} + \delta \mathrm{FIRM} + \chi \mathrm{ICDI\_}C_k + \varepsilon \tag{8.7}$$

$$\mathrm{UP} = \alpha + \beta \mathrm{PA} + \gamma \mathrm{IPO} + \delta \mathrm{FIRM} + \chi \mathrm{ICDI\_}L_k + \varepsilon \tag{8.8}$$

The independent variables are the same as described in Eqs. (8.4) and (8.5). The PA is added to the UP regression in order to take into account the bookbuilding results, as suggested in previous literature (Hanley 1993).

Table 8.1 provides a description of the single control variables included in the IPO and FIRM categories. Of the IPO characteristics included in the analysis, DUMMY_YEAR is a dummy variable that has a value of 1 for years with a number of IPOs higher than the average number for the whole sample period and that signals hot IPO periods, as suggested by Lowry and Murphy (2007). SIZE is calculated as the number of shares offered in the IPO divided by the number of shares outstanding; we expect it to be negatively related to the price adjustment due to the low probability of rationing (Hanley 1993).

The reputation of the underwriter (UW_REP) is expected to influence the way the offer price is set: Underwriters are rewarded a percentage of the total amount of money raised, so the better their reputation, the stronger their market power, that is the power to price IPOs far from their intrinsic value (Chemmanur and Krishnan 2012). An underwriter's reputation has also been found to increase first day returns (Carter et al. 1998; Liu and Ritter 2011). Nevertheless, since national underwriters are excluded from any comprehensive ranking of international underwriters (Boreiko and Lombardo 2011), as a proxy of each underwriter's reputation, we use the number of IPOs managed by each underwriter divided by the total number of IPOs issued over the sample period (2004–2014), as suggested by Signori et al. (2013).

The interest of institutional investors is considered in terms of the demand coming from funds, as a percentage of the total demand coming from retail investors and employees (INST_DEM), and in terms of the time interval (INT) between prospectus registration and the listing date (Wyatt 2014). We expect to observe a positive association between the PA and INST_DEM and a negative association between the PA and INT. Finally, we include some variables that tell us about the uncertainty surrounding an IPO; in particular, the presence of venture capitalists in the listing firm (VC) is likely to produce a positive effect on the price adjustment as investors are more willing to accept higher offer prices if the IPO is associated with less uncertainty (Guo et al. 2005). At the same time, the magnitude of the filing price range (RANGE) is expected to be negatively related to the PA; larger filing ranges are usually associated with greater uncertainty in the IPO results (Hanley 1993). Moving on to the variables related to the firm's characteristics, we control for firms belonging to the IC intensive sectors (IC_INT), according to the classification proposed by Mangena et al. (2010), and we also include the age of the firm (AGE), which has previously been documented to signal the uncertainty of the IPO (Hanley and Hoberg 2008). Here, we expect AGE to be negatively related to the price adjustment, as mature firms that have been operating in the market for many years may be less appealing in terms of future growth and, as a consequence, their offer price is more likely to be kept low in order to induce investors to negotiate.

We also include a series of control variables that tell us about the "quality" of the listing firm in order to avoid any possible self-selection biases; since it is the issuing firm that decides the type and the amount of IC information it discloses, better quality firms may be more likely to disclose more IC information, as suggested by Barton and Waymire (2004). One of the quality variables we include in the analysis is Return On Equity (ROE); ROE is expected to take on a positive sign because managers are more likely to disclose information voluntarily when their firms are performing well (Dye 2001; Miller 2002). Furthermore, the incentive for managers to supply more information increases when the levels of shareholder–debtholder agency conflicts increase. Agency conflicts potentially intensify according to the amount of leverage (DEBT) in the firm's capital structure; we can, therefore, predict that managers of more indebted firms will issue higher quality reports (as in Barton and Waymire 2004).

Moreover, in accordance with Barton and Waymire (2004), we added a tech dummy (TECH) and the market share (MKTSHR). TECH is a dummy variable that takes on a value of one if the firm belongs to a technology based sector, and MRKSHR is the firm's total assets divided by the sum of total assets for firms belonging to the same industrial sector.

The groups of explanatory variables for the underpricing models (8.7 and 8.8) are almost the same as those used for the price adjustment Eqs. (8.4 and 8.5), the first exception is that PA is added in the latter in order to take into account the bookbuilding results (see Hanley 1993). Others slight differences in the variables can be observed owing to the specific dependent variable we are considering. In particular, we added earnings volatility (CVEARN) as a quality variable, as suggested by Barton and Waymire (2004), and we removed ROE (a quality variable very similar to CVEARN and therefore its inclusion would be repetitive) and RANGE (which is already taken into consideration in the PA). CVEARN is calculated as the standard deviation of earnings over the three years prior to the IPO.

As multicollinearity represents a huge problem in multivariate regressions, we systematically computed and checked the VIF coefficients in the regression models, and obtained encouraging results.

Table 8.2 IPOs by year

Listing date	N° of firms
2004	7
2005	12
2006	20
2007	23
2008	5
2009	1
2010	2
2011	1
2012	1
2013	2
2014	0
Total number of IPOs	74
Average number of IPOs	6.7

This table presents descriptive statistics of IPOs issued in Borsa Italiana by year

4 Results

4.1 Descriptive Statistics for IC Disclosure

Below, we report some descriptive statistics for our sample. In particular, Table 8.2 shows the distribution of IPOs over the years examined.

Table 8.2 shows that the period between 2005 and 2007 was a hot IPO period, with a number of IPOs per year that was much higher than the average number for the whole sample period (2004–2014). Tables 8.3 and 8.4 inform about the level of IC disclosure for the firms belonging to our sample, depending on the IC classification that is used (six-dimensions in Table 8.3 and three-dimensions in Table 8.4). In par-

Table 8.3 Descriptive statistics for single IC disclosure indexes in the six-dimensions IC classification

	Mean	Std. dev.	Median	Min	Max	Obs
ICDI_HR	0.313	0.102	0.298	0.172	0.793	74
ICDI_RD	0.316	0.201	0.233	0	0.933	74
ICDI_PROC	0.296	0.178	0.252	0.042	0.75	74
ICDI_IT	0.259	0.257	0.133	0	1	74
ICDI_CUST	0.308	0.192	0.239	0.042	0.75	74
ICDI_STRAT	0.358	0.14	0.359	0.123	0.649	74

Here reported the Mean, Standard Deviation, Median, Minimum and Maximum Values and the number of observations for the six IC dimensions considered into the analysis: *ICDI_RD* research and development, *ICDI_IT* information technology, *ICDI_PROC* processes, *ICDI_HR* human resources, *ICDI_CUST* customers, *ICDI_STRAT* strategies

Table 8.4 Descriptive statistics for single IC disclosure indexes in the three-dimensions IC classification

	Mean	Std. dev.	Median	Min	Max	Obs
ICDI_HC	0.177	0.032	0.167	0.091	0.273	74
ICDI_RC	0.404	0.131	0.4	0.15	0.733	74
ICDI_SC	0.457	0.128	0.451	0.176	0.745	74

Here reported the Mean, Standard Deviation, Median, Minimum and Maximum Values and the number of observations for the three IC dimensions considered into the analysis: *ICDI_HC* Human Capital, *ICDI_RC* Relational Capital, *ICDI_SC* Structural Capital

ticular, it shows that firms tend, on average, to disclose more frequently IC information regarding strategies and research and development in the six-dimensions classification, while structural and relational capital are the IC information that are more frequently disclosed according to the three-dimensions classification, thus suggesting that firms might be aware of the enthusiasm that secondary market investors have for such communicative information, as already discussed in the hypotheses section.

Tables 8.5 and 8.6 provide information in terms of the variables that might influence a larger IC disclosure by firms, depending on the IC classification that is used (six-dimensions in Table 8.5 and three-dimensions in Table 8.6). In particular, they show that firms belonging to IC intensive sectors (such as banks, financial sector, health care, media, software components, support service, technological equipment, and pharmaceuticals, according to Mangena et al. 2010) disclose more IC about their

Table 8.5 Average IC disclosure values for firms belonging to IC intensive vs. IC non intensive sectors and according to firm age in the six-dimensions IC

	Number	Average ICDI
IC intensive	25	0.6512
IC non intensive	49	0.3032
<10 years	21	0.2595
<25 years	23	0.3054
>25 years	30	0.6221

Firms have here been split into IC intensive sectors (banks, financial sector, health care, media, software components, support service, technological equipment e pharmaceuticals according to Mangena et al. (2010) and non-intensive sectors. They have also been categorized into young firms (less than 10 years of activity), mature firms (between 11 and 25 years of activity) and largely mature firms (More than 26 years of activity)

Table 8.6 Average IC disclosure values for firms belonging to IC intensive vs. IC non intensive sectors and according to firm age in the three-dimensions IC

	Number	Average ICDI
IC intensive	18	0.305
IC non intensive	56	0.259
<10 years	21	0.336
<25 years	21	0.347
>25 years	30	0.351

Firms have here been split into IC intensive sectors (banks, financial sector, health care, media, software components, support service, technological equipment e pharmaceuticals according to Mangena et al. 2010) and non-intensive sectors. They have also been categorized into young firms (less than 10 years of activity), mature firms (between 11 and 25 years of activity) and largely mature firms (More than 26 years of activity)

intangible assets than firms operating in IC non-intensive sectors and this supports the sectorial classification we employ.

Moreover, the disclosure of IC increases with a firm's age. This might suggest that firms that have been working in the market for more years are more inclined to inform their stakeholders about their intangible assets in order to compensate for the lower growth perspectives they can offer compared to younger firms.

4.2 IC Disclosure and Price Adjustment in the Six-Dimension and Three-Dimension Classifications

After controlling for a set of variables we find that, in model (8.4), where the six-dimensions classification proposed by Cordazzo (2007) is employed, the dimensions of IC disclosure that impacts the way the offer price is fixed is the description of the processes (ICDI_PROC) that the firm carries out during its activity and the information and technology (ICDI_IT), as shown in Table 8.7. Moving on to model (8.5), which employs the three-dimension classification of Li et al. (2008), the IC dimension that has to be considered is human capital; this dimension is significant and positively connected to the price adjustment (see Table 8.8). The positive sign of the relationships reveals that when

Table 8.7 The effects of IC disclosure on the price adjustment (PA) according to the six-dimension classification

ICDI	ICDI_STRAT	0.060					
		0.073					
	ICDI _RD		0.029				
			0.055				
	ICDI _PROC			0.115[b]			
				0.055			
	ICDI _IT				0.073[c]		
					0.039		
	ICDI _HR					0.173	
						0.108	
	ICDI _CUST						0.020
							0.056
IPO	DUMMY_YEAR	0.056[a]	0.056[b]	0.060[a]	0.056[a]	0.060[a]	0.054[b]
		0.020	0.021	0.021	0.020	0.020	0.021
	SIZE	0.000	0.000	0.000	0.000	0.000	0.000
		0.000	0.000	0.000	0.000	0.000	0.000
	UW_REP	0.210[c]	0.219[c]	0.221[b]	0.202[c]	0.225[b]	0.217[b]
		0.108	0.107	0.101	0.105	0.106	0.107
	INST_DEM	0.045	0.050	0.021	0.044	0.044	0.047
		0.041	0.043	0.045	0.044	0.043	0.042
	INT	−0.001	−0.001	−0.001	−0.001	−0.001	−0.001
		0.001	0.001	0.001	0.001	0.001	0.001
	VC	0.035	0.033	0.041[c]	0.037	0.030	0.032
		0.025	0.025	0.022	0.023	0.023	0.024
	RANGE	−0.090	−0.094	−0.121	−0.146	−0.123	−0.103
		0.169	0.162	0.176	0.169	0.163	0.166
FIRM	ROE	0.001[a]	0.001[a]	0.001[a]	0.001[a]	0.001[a]	0.001[b]
		0.000	0.000	0.000	0.000	0.000	0.000
	DEBT	−0.001[c]	−0.001[b]	−0.001[b]	−0.001[b]	−0.001[c]	−0.001[c]
		0.000	0.000	0.000	0.000	0.000	0.000
	AGE	0.000	0.000	0.000	0.000	0.000	0.000
		0.000	0.000	0.000	0.000	0.000	0.000
	IC_INT	0.015	0.022	0.020	0.005	0.017	0.021
		0.029	0.026	0.025	0.026	0.026	0.027
	TECH	0.008	0.004	0.007	0.005	0.006	0.005
		0.024	0.023	0.023	0.022	0.024	0.023
	MKTSHR	−0.091[b]	−0.093[b]	−0.088	−0.080[b]	−0.091[b]	−0.092[b]
		0.040	0.040	0.039	0.039	0.038	0.041
	Constant	−0.018	−0.011	−0.011	−0.012	−0.037	−0.005
		0.779	0.064	0.053	0.057	0.058	0.061
	n observations	70	70	70	70	70	70
	r squared	0.422	0.420	0.459	0.450	0.439	0.418

This table contains the multivariate regression results of the price adjustment models described in Eq. (8.4) (regression coefficient plus the standard error below)

[a], [b], and [c] indicate statistical significance at the 1%, 5%, and 10% levels, respectively. VIF scores are all lower than 2.0

Table 8.8 The effects of IC disclosure on the price adjustment (PA) according to the three-dimensions classification

ICDI	ICDI_HC	0.688[b]		
		0.330		
	ICDI _RC		−0.064	
			0.079	
	ICDI _SC			0.027
				0.086
IPO	DUMMY_YEAR	0.064[a]	0.052[a]	0.058[a]
		0.020	0.019	0.021
	SIZE	0.000	0.000	0.000
		0.000	0.000	0.000
	UW_REP	0.213[c]	0.220[c]	0.218[b]
		0.107	0.115	0.116
	INST_DEM	0.091[c]	0.063	0.054
		0.046	0.048	0.046
	INT	−0.001	−0.001	−0.001
		0.001	0.001	0.001
	VC	0.020	0.028	0.023
		0.023	0.023	0.024
	RANGE	−0.214	−0.136	−0.143
		0.168	0.165	0.168
FIRM	ROE	0.001[b]	0.001[b]	0.001[b]
		0.000	0.000	0.000
	DEBT	−0.001[b]	−0.001[b]	−0.001[b]
		0.000	0.000	0.000
	AGE	0.000	0.000	0.000
		0.000	0.000	0.000
	IC_INT	0.001	0.012	0.020
		0.022	0.024	0.023
	TECH	0.014	0.010	0.010
		0.021	0.021	0.021
	MKTSHR	−0.076[c]	−0.097[c]	−0.095[b]
		0.040	0.038	0.039
	Constant	−0.155	−0.011	−0.034
		0.086	0.066	0.064
	n observations	70	70	70
	r squared	0.433	0.391	0.387

This table contains the multivariate regression results of the price adjustment models described in Eq. (8.5) (regression coefficient plus standard error)

[a], [b], and [c] indicate statistical significance at the 1%, 5%, and 10% levels, respectively. VIF scores are all lower than 2.0.

institutional investors have a wide range of IC information available to them for free, they are more willing to accept a higher offer price and this, in turn, allows listing firms to raise more capital. Considering this empirical data together, we notice that the three dimensions (processes, IT, and human resources) that influence the IPO result the most all relate to the general concept of "hard (technical) information" (see Cardi and Mazzoli 2015); indeed, this makes sense because the investors taking part in the primary market (usually investment managers) particularly appreciate IC variables that describe in detail the way in which a firms operates. Nevertheless, the different results obtained from the two classifications mean that it is still unclear which of these types of information a firm should disclose in order to please primary market investors: Depending on the classification that is used, processes and IT, or human capital, play the largest role. Table 8.9 provides a comparison of the single items that are included into the processes and IT on the one hand and into the human capital on the other hand. It shows that, although the three categories can all be ascribed to "hard information" (as in Cardi and Mazzoli 2015), they include items that are very different to each other, thus generating no clear recommendation for firms about what types of information are most appreciated by primary market investors.

Regarding the control variables, in relation to the IPO characteristics, the variable DUMMY_YEAR is significant and positive for both models, suggesting that the PA tends to be higher in hot IPO periods. The reputation of the underwriter (UW_REP) also significantly and positively influences the PA, as was expected. As far as the FIRM characteristics are concerned, the return on equity (ROE) and the debt-ratio (DEBT) are shown to be the quality variables that influence the pricing process in the bookbuilding, as hypothesized. Moreover, the market share (MKTSHR) is significant and negatively linked to the price adjustment, indicating that shareholders prefer managers to restrain the disclosure of information that could be adversely used by competitors, considering that a firm's market share is a measure of its exposure to such threats (Barton and Waymire 2004).

Table 8.9 Comparison of the single items included in the dimensions: IT and processes (six-dimension classification) and human capital (three-dimension)

Six-dimension classification (Cordazzo 2007)	Three-dimension classification (Li et al. 2008)
(C) Dimension of information technology	**(III) Human capital**
46. IT investments	40. Number of employees
47. IT systems	41. Employees age
48. Software	42. Employee diversity
49. IT benefits	43. Employee equality
50. IT costs	44. Employee relationship
(D) Dimension of processes	45. Employee education
51. Internal communication system	46. Skills/know-how/expertise/ knowledge
52. Working environment system	47. Employee work-related competences
53. Online working	48. Employee work-related knowledge
54. Internal information and knowledge	49. Employee attitudes/behavior
55. External information and knowledge	50. Employee commitments
56. Measurement of internal and external risk	51. Employee motivation
57. Social programs and plans	52. Employee productivity
58. Environmental programs, plans, and certification	53. Employee training
	54. Vocational qualification
	55. Employee development
	56. Employee flexibility
	57. Entrepreneurial spirit
	58. Employee capabilities
	59. Employee teamwork
	60. Employee involvement with community
	61. Other employee features

4.3 IC Disclosure and Underpricing in the Six-Dimension and Three-Dimension Classifications

Moving on to the determinants of underpricing, the first variable to consider as worthy of attention as an explanatory variable is the price adjustment (PA). The positive and significant association of the PA on the UP indicates that any effects on the underpricing are linked to events that have already occurred during the bookbuilding. Moreover, the PA is able to explain around 70% of the underpricing that takes place in the secondary market (see the reported coefficients in Tables 8.10 and 8.11). In other words and as largely asserted in the literature, the price adjustment is a good predictor of the IPO initial return (Hanley 1993).

As far as the core variables are concerned, according to underpricing model (8.7), which employs the six-dimension classification proposed by Cordazzo (2007), the one IC disclosure dimension that significantly and positively impacts the level of underpricing is research and development (ICDI_RD) (Table 8.10). Moving on to model (8.8), which employs the three-dimension classification proposed by Li et al. (2008), the IC dimension revealed as influencing the underpricing is relational capital; this dimension is significantly and positively connected to the underpricing (see Table 8.11). Overall, these results suggest that when "soft (communicative) information" is disclosed in the prospectus, secondary market investors aggressively bid up due to their positive expectations about the firm's creation of future value (Cardi and Mazzoli 2015).

Furthermore, investors might be afraid of losing a good opportunity to buy profitable stocks. Thus, we can suggest that the fear of losing the potential value linked to the intellectual capital, should it occur, represents an additional incentive to bid the market price up. This result confirms the findings of previous studies (Amir and Lev 1996; Ballester et al. 2003; Mangena et al. 2010) and indicates that unsophisticated investors react more in response to variables that are easier to understand for share evaluation and find IC variables that are easier to understand more relevant for share evaluation. Nevertheless, as for the price adjustment models, this result does not clarify which information firms should disclose in order to please secondary market investors as, depending on which classification is used, research and development or relational capital play the largest role. Table 8.12 provides a comparison of the single items included in the research and development dimension *vs.* those included in the relational capital dimension. Similarly to Tables 8.9, 8.12 shows that although both categories can be ascribed to "soft information" (as in Cardi and Mazzoli 2015) they include items that are very different to each other, thus generating no clear recommendations for firms about which information are appreciated the most by secondary market investors.

Table 8.10 The effects of IC disclosure on the underpricing (UP) according to the six-dimension classification

ICDI	ICDI_STRAT	0.143					
		0.116					
	ICDI _RD		0.135^{c}				
			0.075				
	ICDI _PROC			−0.137			
				0.111			
	ICDI _IT				−0.033		
					0.066		
	ICDI _HR					0.040	
						0.182	
	ICDI _CUST						0.039
							0.083
IPO	PA	0.681^{a}	0.675^{a}	0.814^{a}	0.744^{a}	0.704^{a}	0.702^{a}
		0.240	0.246	0.267	0.266	0.250	0.243
	DUMMY_YEAR	0.044	0.051	0.016	0.031	0.038	0.036
		0.031	0.031	0.039	0.035	0.035	0.031
	SIZE	0.000	0.000	0.000	0.000	0.000	0.000
		0.030	0.031	0.030	0.031	0.031	0.031
	UW_REP	0.102	0.127	0.095	0.116	0.118	0.124
		0.158	0.151	0.150	0.158	0.160	0.160
	INST_DEM	0.093	0.121	0.143	0.113	0.107	0.105
		0.088	0.086	0.089	0.089	0.090	0.090
	INT	−0.008^{a}	−0.007^{a}	−0.006^{b}	−0.007^{b}	−0.007^{b}	−0.007^{a}
		0.003	0.003	0.003	0.003	0.003	0.003
	VC	0.021	0.021	0.002	0.009	0.012	0.016
		0.035	0.034	0.032	0.033	0.033	0.034
FIRM	CVEARN	0.000	0.000	0.000	0.000	0.000	0.000
		0.000	0.000	0.000	0.000	0.000	0.000
	DEBT	0.000	0.000	0.000	0.000	0.000	0.000
		0.001	0.001	0.001	0.001	0.001	0.001
	AGE	0.000	0.000	0.000	0.000	0.000	0.000
		0.001	0.001	0.001	0.001	0.001	0.001
	IC_INT	−0.028	−0.007	−0.016	−0.009	−0.014	−0.015
		0.023	0.025	0.026	0.024	0.024	0.024
	TECH	−0.014	−0.032	−0.029	−0.023	−0.024	−0.025
		0.035	0.028	0.034	0.033	0.033	0.032
	MKTSHR	−0.013	−0.025	−0.015	−0.019	−0.017	−0.013
		0.037	0.037	0.045	0.042	0.039	0.041
	Constant	0.094	0.070	0.141	0.135	0.119	0.117
		0.084	0.082	0.084	0.084	0.094	0.083
	n observations	66	66	66	66	66	66
	r squared	0.427	0.448	0.360	0.414	0.411	0.413

This table contains the multivariate regression results of the underpricing models described in Eq. (8.7) (regression coefficient plus standand error below)

^{a}, ^{b}, and ^{c} indicate statistical significance at the 1%, 5%, and 10% levels, respectively. VIF scores are all lower than 2.0

Table 8.11 The effects of IC disclosure on the underpricing (UP) according to the three-dimensions classification

ICDI	ICDI_HC	0.760		
		0.663		
	ICDI_RC		0.353[b]	
			0.137	
	ICDI_SC			0.140
				0.104
IPO	PA	0.623[a]	0.698[b]	0.677[a]
		0.231	0.217	0.238
	DUMMY_YEAR	0.055	0.073	0.053
		0.034	0.030	0.032
	SIZE	0.000	0.000	0.000
		0.000	0.000	0.000
	UW_REP	0.140	0.098	0.124
		0.163	0.144	0.156
	INST_DEM	0.143	0.067	0.095
		0.091	0.078	0.087
	INT	−0.008[a]	−0.008[a]	−0.008[a]
		0.002	0.002	0.003
	VC	0.001	−0.009	−0.003
		0.034	0.030	0.033
FIRM	CVEARN	0.000	0.000	0.000
		0.000	0.000	0.000
	DEBT	0.000	0.000	0.000
		0.000	0.001	0.001
	AGE	0.000	−0.001	0.000
		0.001	0.001	0.001
	IC_INT	−0.029	0.023	−0.007
		0.026	0.026	0.024
	TECH	−0.014	−0.021	−0.021
		0.029	0.028	0.030
	MKTSHR	−0.014	−0.012	−0.026
		0.045	0.044	0.039
	Constant	−0.032	0.033	0.086
		0.155	0.081	0.088
	n observations	66	66	66
	r squared	0.435	0.481	0.423

This table contains the multivariate regression results of the underpricing models described in Eq. (8.8) (regression coefficient plus standard error below)

[a], [b], and [c] indicates statistical significance at the 1%, 5%, and 10% levels respectively. VIF scores are all lower than 2.0

Table 8.12 Comparison of the single items included into the research and development (six-dimension classification) and relational capital (three-dimension

Six-dimension classification (Cordazzo 2007)	Three-dimension classification (Li et al. 2008)
(C) Dimension of R&D	**(II) Relational capital**
59. R&D plans, programs, strategies	19. Customers
60. R&D costs	20. Market presence
61. R&D costs on sales	21. Customer relationships
62. First stage of R&D	22. Customer acquisition
63. Development stage of R&D	23. Customer retention
64. R&D prospects	24. Customer training and education
65. Patents	25. Customer involvement
66. Numbers of patents and licenses	26. Company image/reputation
67. Outstanding patents	27. Company awards
68. Marks	28. Public relations
	29. Diffusion and networking
	30. Brands
	31. Distribution channels
	32. Relationship with suppliers
	33. Business collaborations
	34. Business agreements
	35. Favorable contracts
	36. Research collaborations
	37. Marketing
	38. Relationship with stakeholders
	39. Market leadership

As far as the control variables are concerned, only the number of days from prospectus registration to listing date (INT) is significantly related to the underpricing and, as expected, it carries a negative sign.[6]

5 Concluding Remarks

Our study contributes to the recent debate regarding the effects that IC disclosure produces in terms of IPO results. Previous studies fail to provide a consistent interpretation of such effects, possibly due to the different

[6] This evidence suggests that by adding further variables the underpricing models could be made more specific, although its r squared suggests that it was able to explain around 40 per cent of the dependent variable.

variables of Intellectual Capital being employed. This paper aims to shed light on this point by analyzing the effects that non-financial information exert on the IPO results, and whether the way in which they are classified affects these results. To do so, we make use of the six-dimension classification proposed by Cordazzo (2007) and the three-dimension classification proposed by Li et al. (2008). Our empirical evidence shows that primary market investors broadly appreciate "hard (technical) information", while secondary market investors are mostly influenced by "soft (communicative) information" (consistent with Cardi and Mazzoli 2015). Nevertheless, although this general result was consistent across the two different classifications, the single IC items are not totally comparable between the two models. In particular, in the PA models, the information that investors tend to prefer regards company processes and IT when the six-dimension classification is used, while human capital emerges as the preferred information dimension when the three-dimension classification is applied. The underpricing is mostly influenced by research and development information in the six-dimension classification and by relational capital in the three-dimension classification. As a consequence, these discrepancies effectively result in restricted operative recommendation being provided to firms in terms of the IC information that they should disclose in their prospectuses in order to please primary and secondary market investors. Nevertheless, we can propose that technical information appears to be the IC category that most influences funds, whereas communicative information appears to be of most interest to traders.

Future improvements of this research will disengage from the traditional IC classifications proposed in the literature in order to analyze in more depth the single intellectual capital items that influence the behavior of primary and secondary market investors. In particular, factor analysis will be carried out, starting with the individual IC items suggested by Cordazzo (2007) and by Li et al. (2008) in order to identify those that exert an effect on the two investor categories considered here. Indeed, as Rastogi (2003) and Swart (2006) have both pointed out, while the categorization of intangible assets is useful in many ways, we can only understand the true value of the IC items by considering the dynamic intercorrelations between such elements; factor analysis should provide a compromise in this sense.

References

AIAF. (2002). The communication of intangibles and intellectual capital: An empirical model of analysis. *Associazione Italiana Analisti Finanziari (Italian Association of Financial Analysts), Official Report 106.*

Amir, E., & Lev, B. (1996). Value-relevance of nonfinancial information: The wireless communications industry. *Journal of Accounting and Economics, 22*, 3–30.

Ballester, M., Garcia-Ayuso, M., & Livnat, J. (2003). The economic value of the R&D intangible asset. *European Accounting Review, 12*(4), 605–633.

Barsky, N. P., Jr Catanach, A. H., Rhodes-Catanach, S. C., & Thbodeau, J. C. (2003). Enron: Did the financial reporting model really fail? *Commercial Lending Review, 18*(2), 5–9.

Barton, J., & Waymire, G. (2004). Investor protection under unregulated financial reporting. *Journal of Accounting & Economics, 38*, 65–116.

Beattie, V., & Thomson, S. J. (2004, July). *A comprehensive analysis of intellectual capital categories as a precursor to empirical investigation of disclosures in annual reports.* Paper presented at the Annual Financial Reporting and Business Communication Conference, Cardiff Wales.

Beaulieu, P., Williams, S., & Wright, M. (2002). Intellectual capital disclosures in Swedish annual reports. In N. Bontis (Ed.), *World congress on intellectual capital readings* (pp. 135–56). Oxford: Butterworth-Heinemann.

Benveniste, L. M., & Spindt, P. A. (1989). How investment bankers determine the offer price and allocation of new issues. *Journal of Financial Economics, 24*, 343–361.

Boedker, C., Guthrie, J., & Cuganesan, S. (2005). The strategic significance of human capital information in annual reporting. *Journal of Human Resource Costing and Accounting, 8*(2), 7–22.

Bontis, N. (2001). Assessing knowledge assets: A review of the models used to measure intellectual capital. *International Journal of Management Reviews, 3*(1), 41–60.

Boreiko, D., & Lombardo, S. (2011). Stabilization activity in Italian IPOs. *European Business Organization Law Review, 12*(3), 437–467.

Botosan, C. A. (1997). Disclosure level and the cost of equity capital. *Accounting Review, 72*(3), 323–349.

Bozzolan, S., Favotto, F., & Ricceri, F. (2003). Italian annual intellectual capital disclosure: An empirical analysis. *Journal of Intellectual Capital, 4*(4), 543–558.

Brammer, S. J., & Pavelin, S. (2006). Corporate reputation and social performance: The importance of fit. *Journal of Management Studies, 43*(3), 435–455.

Bukh, P. N. D. (2003). Commentary: The relevance of intellectual capital disclosure: A paradox? *Accounting, Auditing and accountability Journal, 16*(1), 49–56.

Bukh, P. N. D., Larsen, H. T., Gormsen, P., & Mouritsen, J. (2001). *Disclosure of intellectual capital indicators in Danish IPO prospectus* (Working paper). Aarhus: The Aarhus School of Business.

Bukh, P. N., Nielsen, C., Gormsen, P., & Mouritsen, J. (2005). Disclosure of information on intellectual capital in Danish IPO prospectuses. *Accounting, Auditing and accountability Journal, 18*(6), 713–732.

Cardi, C., & Mazzoli, C. (2015). Intellectual capital disclosure in IPOs: Is it worth it? *Journal of Financial Markets and Institutions, 3,* 91–110.

Carter, R. B., Dark, F. H., & Singh, A. K. (1998). Underwriter reputation, initial returns, and the long run performance of IPO stocks. *Journal of Finance, 53,* 285–311.

Cerisola, S., D'Alfonso, E., Felice, G., Giannangeli, S., & Maggioni, D. (2013). Investment in intangible assets and level of sophistication: The role of Italian firms' financial structure. EFIGE country report, Italy.

Chartered Institute of Management Accountants (CIMA). (2001). *Managing the intellectual capital within Today's Knowledge-based Organisations* (Technical Briefigs). London: CIMA.

Chemmanur, T. J., & Krishnan, K. (2012). Heterogeneous beliefs, IPO valuation, and the economic role of the underwriter in IPOs. *Financial Management, 41,* 769–811.

Chiucchi, M. S. (2004). *Sistemi di misurazione e di reporting del capitale intellettuale: criticità e prospettive.* Torino: Giappicchelli Editore.

Cordazzo, M. (2007). Intangibles and Italian IPO prospectuses: A disclosure analysis. *Journal of Intellectual Capital, 8*(2), 288–305.

Dimovski, W., & Brooks, R. (2004). The importance of intangible assets in initial public offerings. *International Journal of Knowledge, Culture and Change Management, 4,* 1505–1509.

Dimovski, B., & Brooks, R. (2006). Intangible assets and the underpricing of industrial company initial public offerings. *International Journal of Knowledge, Culture and Change Management, 6*(4), 67–73.

Dye, R. A. (2001). An evaluation of "essays on disclosure" and the disclosure literature in accounting. *Journal of Accounting and Economics, 32,* 181–235.

Francis, J., & Schipper, K. (1999). Have financial statements lost their relevance? *Journal of Accounting Research, 37*(2), 319–352.

Gu, F., & Lev, B. (2004). The information content of royalty income. *Accounting Horizons, 18*(1), 1–12.

Guo, R., Lev, B., & Zhou, N. (2005). The valuation of biotech IPOs. *Journal of Accounting, Auditing & Finance, 20*(4), 4423–459.
Guthrie, J., & Petty, R. (2000). Intellectual capital: Australian annual reporting practices. *Journal of Intellectual Capital, 1*(3), 241–251.
Hanley, K. (1993). The underpricing of initial public offerings and the partial adjustment phenomenon. *Journal of Financial Economics, 34*, 231–250.
Hanley, K. W., & Hoberg, G. (2008). Strategic disclosure and the pricing of initial public offerings (Working paper). University of Maryland.
Hanley, K. W., & Hoberg, G. (2010). The information content of IPO prospectuses. *Review of Financial Studies, 23*(7), 2821–2864.
Holland, J. (2003). Intellectual capital and the capital market- organization and competence. *Accounting, Auditing and Accountability Journal, 16*(1), 39–48.
Lev, B. (2001). *Intangibles: Management, measurement and reporting*. Washington, DC: The Brookings Institution.
Lev, B., & Zambon, S. (2003). Intangibles and intellectual capital: An introduction to a special issue. *European Accounting Review, 12*(4), 597–603.
Lev, B., & Zarowin, P. (1999). The boundaries of financial reporting and how to extend them. *Journal of Accounting Research, 37*(2), 353–385.
Li, J., Pike, R., & Haniffa, R. (2008). Intellectual capital disclosure and corporate governance structure in UK firms. *Accounting and Business Research, 38*(2), 137–159.
Liu X., & Ritter, J. R. (2011). Local underwriter oligopolies and IPO underpricing. *Journal of Financial Economics, 102*, 579–601.
Lowry, M., & Murphy, K. J. (2007). Executive stock options and IPO underpricing. *Journal of Financial Economics, 85*, 39–65.
Mangena, M., Pike, R., & Li, J. (2010). *Intellectual capital disclosure practices and effects on the cost of equity capital: UK evidence*. Edinburgh: The Institute of Chartered Accountants of Scotland.
Marr, B., & Schiuma, G. (2001). Measuring and managing intellectual capital and knowledge assets in new organisations. In M. Bourne (Ed.), *Handbook of performance measurement*. London: Gee.
Meritum Project. (2002). *Guidelines for managing and reporting on intangibles*. Available at: www.pnbukh.com/site/files/pdf_filer/MERITUM_Guidelines.pdf. Accessed 25 Mar 2009.
Miller, G. S. (2002). Earnings performance and discretionary disclosure. *Journal of Accounting Research, 40*(1), 173–204.
Nunnally, J. C. (1978). *Psychometric theory* (2nd ed.). New York: McGraw-Hill.

Orens, R., Aerts, W., & Cormier, D. (2010). Web-based non-financial disclosure and cost of finance. *Journal of Business Finance & Accounting, 37*(9–10), 1057–1093.

Previati, D., & Vezzani, P. (2007). Il capitale intellettuale: misurazione, gestione e valorizzazione. Prospettive di analisi e prassi manageriali per il settore dei servizi finanziari, Bancaria Editrice.

Rastogi, P. N. (2003). The nature and role of IC—rethinking the process of value creation and sustained enterprise growth. *Journal of Intellectual Capital, 4*(2), 227–248.

Riegler, C., & Hollerschmid, C. (2006). Voluntary disclosure on project intangibles from R&D in business reporting: A principles-based approach for R&D intensive companies. *Journal of Intellectual Capital, 7*(4), 511–528.

See, K. F., & Rashid, A. A. (2011). Determinants of non-disclosure of intellectual capital information in Malaysian IPO prospectuses. *International Journal of Economics and Finance, 3*(5), 178–186.

Signori, A., Meoli, M., & Vismara, S. (2013). Short covering and price stabilization of IPOs. *Applied Economics Letters, 20*(10), 931–937.

Singh, I., & Van der Zahn, J. (2007). Does intellectual capital disclosure reduce an IPO's cost of capital? *Journal of Intellectual Capital, 8*(3), 494–516.

Stewart, T. A. (1997). *Intellectual capital: The wealth of organizations*. New York: Doubleday/Currency.

Sveiby, K. E. (1997). *The new organizational wealth*. San Francisco: Berrett-Koehler.

Swart, J. (2006). Intellectual capital: Disentangling an enigmatic concept. *Journal of Intellectual Capital, 7*(2), 136–159.

Tayles, M., Pike, R., & Sofian, S. (2007). Intellectual capital, management accounting practices and corporate performance. *Accounting, Auditing & Accountability Journal, 20*(4), 522–548.

Vismara, S., Paleari, S., & Ritter, J. R. (2012). Europe's second markets for small companies. *European Financial Management, 18*, 352–388.

Williams, S. L. M. (2001). Is intellectual capital performance and disclosure practices related? *Journal of intellectual capital, 2(3)*, 192–203.

Wyatt, A. (2014). Is there useful information in the 'use of proceeds' disclosures in IPO prospectuses? *Accounting & Finance, 54*(2), 625–667.

9

The Drivers of Dividend Policies in Europe

Giusy Chesini and Elisa Giaretta

1 Introduction

The dividend policy has been widely analyzed in the academic literature, from the pioneering irrelevance theory of Miller and Modigliani (1961) that argued the irrelevance of dividends in perfect capital markets to a number of complementary or conflicting theories that find evidence when the Modigliani and Miller's assumptions of perfect capital markets are relaxed.

Some theories have developed around the proposition that asymmetric information is present. Above them, the signaling theory states that managers' private information about the companies' current and future earnings are shared to the market through the signal of dividend payment so that investors use cash flows for valuing companies (see Bhattacharya

G. Chesini • E. Giaretta (✉)
University of Verona, Verona, Italy
e-mail: elisa.giaretta@univr.it

S. Carbó Valverde et al. (eds.), *Bank Funding, Financial Instruments and Decision-Making in the Banking Industry*, Palgrave Macmillan Studies in Banking and Financial Institutions,
DOI 10.1007/978-3-319-30701-5_9

1979; John and Williams 1985; Miller and Rock 1985; Hoberg and Prabhala 2009).

Also the pecking order theory is developed in the case of asymmetric information; it suggest that managers prefer to finance their managed companies by paying out lower amounts of dividends than to approach the debt and capital markets and dismiss investment opportunities (see Myers 1984; Myers and Majluf 1984).

Moreover, the agency cost theory is based on the assumption that dividends are used to mitigate the potential agency conflicts between shareholders and management or shareholders and bond-holders so that dividends are used as a tool to monitor the use of funding (see Lintner 1956; Jensen and Meckling 1976; Easterbrook 1984).

Furthermore the bird-in-the-hand theory (Graham and Dodd 1934; Gordon and Shapiro 1956) suggests a link between dividend payout and stock price as dividend payments are positively valued by the investors.

There are also other theories that have received some attention by academics and practitioners, such as the tax effect theory which states that investors prefer companies to retain most of their earnings because of the tax advantages of capital gains over dividends; the maturity hypothesis that affirms that mature companies presenting greater cash flows can distribute more dividends; the rent seeking theory that studies the effects of ownership on the dividend payouts asserting that controlling shareholders tend to decrease dividend payments.

The empirical findings based on the theoretical literature have been mixed when considering which factors may act as determinants of dividend policy. This conducted Black (1976) in his most cited paper to refer to this issue as the "dividend puzzle" and Fama and French (2001) to call dividend policy as an "enigma". More recently Brealey et al. (2008), in their well-known text book, listed the dividend policy among the ten unsolved problems in finance. Indeed, there is no general consensus as to what factors influence the dividend policy and how these factors interact. Although the debate between these theoretical models remains unresolved, an important observation to emerge from this literature, however, is that dividend policy is not irrelevant, but there are many possible factors that may act as a determinant of dividend policy.

The objective of the present work is to study the dividend policy of the companies listed in the main European stock exchanges, testing the leading theories from the academic literature, with the aim of finding the key characteristics of the European market in the perspective of the European Capital Markets Union (CMU).

Based on a sample of 241 European listed companies included in the main European stock market indexes, the analyses are conducted by a statistical OLS regression model in 14 years panel data (3,374 company-year observations).

The results of the analyses suggest that the pecking order theory, the signaling theory and the bird-in-the-hand theory complementarily explain dividends' payments, while the missed significance of the agency cost theory implies that debt-holders funds are expropriated through dividend payments so that more constraints in funding contracts are needed.

The contribution of this paper resides in providing a further insight into dividend policy within European listed companies.

The structure of the paper is as follows: the following section analyses the literature specific to this topic. Section 3 draws the data-collection and the research methods. Section 4 reports the results of the analyses, and Sect. 5 restates the major conclusions and discusses the implications for investors and for further research.

2 Literature Review

The term "dividend policy" refers to "*the practice that management follows in making dividend payout decisions or, in other words, the size and pattern of cash distributions over time to shareholders*" (Lease et al. 2000). Unexpectedly, dividend policy remains one of the most contested issues in finance.

The study of dividend policy has captured the attention of finance scholars since the middle of the last century. They have attempted to solve several issues pertaining to dividends and formulate theories and models to explain corporate dividend behavior, with both theoretical and empirical papers. Among the theories on dividend policy, the most important theory is the irrelevance theory (Miller and Modigliani 1961).

In their highly-cited paper, Miller and Modigliani (1961) demonstrated that dividend policy would be irrelevant under certain assumptions about perfect capital markets,[1] as it has no effect on either the price of a company's stock or its cost of capital. Basically, investors calculate the value of companies based on the capitalized value of their future earnings, and this is not affected by whether companies pay dividends; consequently all dividend policies are the same since investors can adjust their portfolios in a way that matches their preferences.[2]

The Modigliani and Miller's irrelevance theory is followed by other complementary or conflicting theories, such as the signaling theory (Bhattacharya 1979; John and Williams 1985; Miller and Rock 1985; Hoberg and Prabhala 2009), the pecking order theory (Myers 1984; Myers and Majluf 1984), the agency cost theory (Lintner 1956; Jensen and Meckling 1976; Easterbrook 1984) and the bird-in-the-hand theory (Graham and Dodd 1934; Gordon and Shapiro 1956).

The following paragraphs provide a description of the main theories about dividend policies from the academic literature and discuss of the main proxies to be used.

2.1 Agency Cost Theory

The agency cost theory is based on the assumption that agency problems arise from the potential conflict between shareholders and debt-holders. In fact, excess dividend payments to shareholders may be taken as owners wants to expropriate wealth from debt-holders (Jensen and Meckling 1976).

---

[1] The assumptions of a perfect capital market necessary for the dividend irrelevancy hypothesis can be summarized as follows: (i) no differences between taxes on dividends and capital gains; (ii) no transaction and flotation costs incurred when securities are traded; (iii) symmetrical and costless information for all market participants; (iv) no agency problem; and (v) all participants in the market are price takers. Under these assumptions the valuation of all shares would be governed by the following fundamental principle: the price of each share must be such that the rate of return (dividends plus capital gains per dollar invested) on every share will be the same throughout the market over any given interval of time. Relaxing one or more of the assumptions of perfect capital markets and introducing market imperfections dividend decision becomes relevant and interact with other decisions made by the company about investment and financing.

[2] Miller and Modigliani (1961) stated that "(…) *given a firm's investment policy, the dividend payout policy it chooses to follow will affect neither the current price of its shares nor the total returns to shareholders*".

Easterbrook (1984) argued that dividends could be used to reduce the cash in the hands of managers, so that dividend payments oblige managers to approach the capital market to raise funds. In this case, investment professionals such as bankers and financial analysts will also be able to monitor managers' behavior. Therefore, shareholders are able to monitor managers at lower cost (and minimize any agency problems). This suggests that dividend payments increase management scrutiny by outsiders and reduces the chances for managers to act in their own self-interest. However, Easterbrook claimed that increasing dividend payments might force managers to take undesirable actions like increasing company leverage, which may sometimes raise the risk-level of the company.

Furthermore, debt-holders interests may not be protected when high levels of dividend are paid out. Hence dividend restrictions can be found in debt covenants to alleviate this conflict. Rozeff (1982) suggests that ceteris paribus, companies with higher financial leverage tend to pay lower dividends to reduce the transaction costs associated with external financing. From the other side, a company with high financial leverage will be monitored by its debt-holders and will have less discretionary funds available to its managers: Hence highly leveraged companies are expected to pay lower dividends (Jensen and Meckling 1976). As a result, paying more dividends will reduce the agency costs between managers and shareholders. Von Eije and Megginson (2007) following Jensen (1986) assume that leverage may help control agency costs, as do dividends. In this view, companies might not need to pay dividends to discourage managers from pursuing their own interests, unless leverage is already high. Leverage and dividends are then substitutes for checking managers and a negative relationship between dividends and debt ratios might be expected. Alternatively, higher leverage might imply older, larger, more stable, and profitable companies that are able to afford to pay dividends more easily. In this view, leverage and paying dividends are statistically complementary and a positive relationship between cash and dividends might be expected.

Based on the foregoing considerations, we hypothesize a negative relationship between the company's dividend payments and the funding with external financing. Following the previous literature (see Rozeff 1982; Ho 2003; Al-Malkawi 2008; Patra et al. 2012), we proxy the external financing as measured by the financial leverage.

2.2 Signaling Theory

The signaling theory is based on the existence of asymmetric information between insiders (managers and directors) and outsiders (shareholders and potential investors) of the companies. Actually, managers usually possess information about the companies' current and future prospects that is not available to outsiders. Because of this informational gap between insiders and outsiders, the true intrinsic value of the company may be unavailable to the market. If so, share price may not be an accurate measure of the company's value. In an attempt to close this gap, managers need to share their knowledge with outsiders. As investors use cash flows for valuing companies, dividends act as a useful tool for managers in which to convey their private information to the market.

Many academics and financial practitioners suggest that dividends possess implicit information about companies' prospects: Dividend announcements act as a signal about the company's future earnings (signaling hypothesis). According to the signaling hypothesis, investors can infer information about a company's future earnings through the dividend announcements, both in terms of the amount and the stability of dividends. In the letter case, dividends payout act as a signal of a company's risk (Hoberg and Prabhala 2009). Specifically, companies with higher business risk are expected to pay lower dividends due to the volatility of their earnings.

In any case, for the signaling hypothesis to hold, managers should first possess private information about a company's prospects, and have incentives to share this information with the market. Second, the signal should be true: That is, a company with poor future prospects should not be able to send false signals to the market by increasing dividend payments.

The most cited dividend signaling models can be found in Bhattacharya (1979), John and Williams (1985), and Miller and Rock (1985). Referring to the literature, in this paper we adopt two different measures to test the signaling hypothesis. First, we investigate the company's earnings as measured by the return on equity (ROE), presuming a positive relationship with dividend paid that is the higher the company profitability, the higher the dividend paid. Second, we analyze the (negative) relationship between the business risk—approximated by the volatility of the share price—and the company's dividend payments—the higher the risk, the lower the dividend payment.

2.3 Pecking Order Theory

The pecking order theory assumes that, when asymmetric information is present, a company may underinvest. A tool to reduce underinvestment and consequently ex-ante loss in company value is to hold financial reserves by paying out fewer dividends. Thus, for the pecking order theory, the dividend policy may be used to manage the underinvestment problem arising from asymmetric information. Based on this reasoning, the higher the level of asymmetric information, the lower will be the dividend paid in order to mitigate the problem of underinvestment (Patra et al. 2012).

Myers and Majluf (1984) study a situation in which companies must issue common stock to raise cash to undertake valuable investment opportunities and management is assumed to know more about the companies' value than potential investors. They find explanations for several important aspects of corporate financing behavior.[3] First, companies generally prefer to issue safe securities, going to bond markets for external capital, rather than risky ones by raising equity. That is, external financing using debt is better than financing by equity. Moreover and more important is that companies whose investment opportunities outstrip operating cash flows, and which have used up their ability to issue low-risk debt, may forego good investments rather than issue risky securities to finance them. Thus, companies may restrict dividends payout when investment opportunities are relevant (Myers 1984).

Following the pecking order theory, we hypothesize a positive relationship between dividends and investment opportunities. As in the case of good investment opportunities, the market value of the company with a greater value than the book value of her assets, the literature suggests to proxy the investment opportunities as the enterprise value to book ratio.

[3] Obviously, these items depend on the specific assumptions of the model and may not follow in other contexts.

2.4 Bird-in-the-Hand Theory

In an early study about dividend policy, Graham and Dodd (1934) argued that "*the sole purpose for the existence of the corporation is to pay dividends*", so that companies paying higher dividends are able to sell their shares at higher prices.[4] Indeed, dividends increase company value as investors prefer the "bird in the hand" of cash dividends rather than the future capital gains. According to the bird-in-the-hand hypothesis, as a higher current dividend reduces uncertainty about future cash flows, that is high dividends payout may increase the share value and hence its price.

Gordon and Shapiro (1956), starting from the statement that the objective of a company is the maximization of the value of the stockholders' equity, presented a definition of the rate of profit required by the market on a share of common stock, that should theoretically be superior to the income and dividend yields because it recognizes that the revenue stream provided by a share can be expected to grow. Furthermore, its empirical characteristics are also superior to those of the income and dividend yields since its value is generally in closer agreement with common sense notions concerning the prevailing rate of profit on a share of stock and since its value fluctuates in a narrower range over time.

Studies that provide support for the bird-in-the-hand theory include Gordon (1959, 1963) and Lintner (1962). Conversely, Miller and Modigliani (1961) have criticized the bird-in-the-hand hypothesis arguing that the company's value is determined by the riskiness of its operating cash flows, not by the way it distributes its earnings.[5] Further, Bhattacharya (1979) suggested that the reasoning underlying the bird-in-the-hand hypothesis is fallacious: The company's risk affects the level of dividend not the other way around, that is, the company's cash flow influences its dividend payments, but increases in dividends will not reduce the risk of the company.

[4] Graham and Dodd (1934) argued that a dollar of dividends has, on average, four times the impact on stock prices as a dollar of retained earnings.

[5] Miller and Modigliani (1961) called this argument the "bird-in-the-hand fallacy".

We proxy stock value as measured by the price to book value (Gordon 1959, 1963). We hypothesize a positive relationship between the company's dividends and the proxy of stock value.

2.5 Other Theories and Control Variables

Other dividend policy theories have found some evidence in the literature. Among them, the maturity hypothesis links the age of the company to its dividends payout (Grullon et al. 2002; Al-Malkawi 2008; Von Eije and Megginson 2007). The hypothesis is based on the assumption that new, young companies find it difficult to raise enough capital to fund investment opportunities. It is at this stage in a company's life cycle that asymmetric-information problems are likely to be most acute, and result in the company's foregoing attractive investments. Conversely, a mature company presents cash flows that greatly exceed what can be reinvested at returns equal to or above its cost of capital: it would return greater quantities of cash to its shareholders, invest relatively less, and grow ever more slowly. Consequently, if it maximized shareholders' wealth, a mature company would make large dividend payments.

Taxes may have a significant influence on dividend policy and the value of the company. The tax-effect hypothesis (see Brennan 1970) suggests that low dividend payout lower the cost of capital and increase the stock price. In other words low dividend payout contributes to maximizing the company's value. This argument is based on the assumption that dividends are taxed at higher rates than capital gains. In addition, dividends are taxed immediately, while taxes on capital gains are deferred until the stock is actually sold. These tax advantages of capital gains over dividends tend to predispose investors, who have favorable tax treatment on capital gains, to prefer companies that retain most of their earnings rather than pay them out as dividends, and are willing to pay a premium for low-payout companies. Therefore, a low dividend payout ratio will lower the cost of equity and increases the stock price. Note that this prediction is almost the exact opposite of the bird-in-the hand hypothesis.

Also the ownership structure may affect the dividend payout. The rent-seeking theory is based on the assumption that dividend payout policy can be used as a corporate governance mechanism, acting as a monitoring and/or disciplining device. Murgia (1993) studied the effects of ownership on the dividend payouts. Disaggregating the agency costs for companies with low or high cash flows, in order to verify when the conflict of interest in dividend policy arises from the ownership structure or the presence of excess free cash flow, the author finds that in the presence of high free cash flow the average payout decreases when the control shares increases. Conversely, in the presence of modest free cash flow, the payout increases with the control share: The higher payout increases the investment appeal for minority shareholders and provides the controlling shareholder the necessary funds to increase the investment in the company or to make new investments. Mancinelli and Ozkan (2006) tested the rent extraction hypothesis by relating the companies' dividend payout ratio to various ownership variables, which measure the degree of concentration in terms of the voting rights of large shareholders. Companies make lower dividend payouts as the voting rights of the largest shareholders increase. The presence of agreements among large controller shareholders might explain the limited monitoring power of the other "strong" non-controlling shareholders.

In addition to the above mentioned theories, there may be other factors that can influence dividend payments that are not explicitly related to dividend theories. Among these, some researchers have shown that a company's size is a significant determinant of dividend policy (see Lloyd et al. 1985; Fama and French 2001; Aivazian et al. 2003; Al-Malkawi 2008; Patra et al. 2012). The lack of theoretical justification conduces to treat this proxy as a control variable. As larger companies would usually have relatively better access to capital markets and easier fundraising, they tend to pay higher dividends; consequently we hypothesize a positive relationship between the company's dividends and size. There are different measures of company size, such as employment, sales, assets, and total capitalization that have been used in the empirical research. In this paper, we proxy size as measured by the natural logarithm of companies' total assets.

Moreover, it is also expected that a company's dividend payout is linked to its liquidity position. Less liquid companies tend to pay lower dividends due to shortage of cash (Patra et al. 2002). Thus, the second control variable we use is liquidity. In this paper, we proxy the liquidity as measured by the free cash flow and we hypothesize a positive association between dividend payout and liquidity.

A synoptic table resuming the main theories related to dividend policy, the proxies used in the past empirical literature, the expected sign, and the references to the authors is in Appendix (Table 9.3).

Considering the vastness of the dividend policies theories, in this study we aim to understand the dividend policies of listed companies in the main European markets in the last 14 years. The research question that this paper wants to answer is the following: *What drives the distribution of dividends in European listed companies?*

3 Data and Methods

We study companies included at the end of 2014 in the most important stock market indexes of the main European stock exchanges, namely BEL20, CAC40, DAX, FTSE100, FTSEMIB, IBEX35, OMXS30, PSI20 and SMI.[6]

[6] The BEL20 is the main stock market index of the Belgian stock exchange Euronext Brussels. It is composed by a minimum of 10 to a maximum of 20 blue-chip companies, following the ICB.

The CAC 40 is the primary benchmark stock market index of the French stock exchange Euronext Paris. It is an Industry Classification Benchmark (ICB) index that tracks the segment of the 40 largest and most actively traded shares listed on Euronext Paris.

The DAX reflects the performance of the 30 largest and most liquid companies on the German stock exchange Deutsche Börse. Following the DGB classification standard, the DAX is diversified across sectors such as automotive, chemicals, banking and industrials and covers about 80% of the aggregated prime standard's market cap, and is thus an established indicator for the performance of the German economy as a whole.

The FTSE 100 is one of the world's most recognized stock market indexes and accounts for 7.8% of the world's equity market capitalization. It is the main stock market index of the London Stock Exchange (LSE) and represents the performance of the 100 largest UK listed blue-chip companies which meet FTSE's size and liquidity screening, providing a global measure that spans far beyond the UK economy.

The FTSE MIB is the main stock market index of the Italian stock exchange Borsa Italiana, part of the London Stock Exchange Group. The index comprises the 40 highest liquid, leading companies

In order to consider for each stock market index only companies with the same accounting policies and accounting standards, we drop companies located outside the country of the stock exchange and companies active in the sector of financial intermediation, real estate, and rental activities.

We obtained a sample of 241 European companies, as follows:

- 14 Belgian companies in BEL20;
- 31 French companies in CAC40;
- 25 German companies in DAX;
- 72 UK companies in FTSE100;
- 23 Italian companies in FTSEMIB;
- 26 Spanish companies in IBEX35;
- 21 Swedish companies in OMXS30;
- 14 Portuguese companies in PSI20;
- 15 Swiss companies in SMI.

Data is taken from Bloomberg Database for the period 2001–14 (panel data). In total we analyzed 3,374 company-year observations.

We built an OLS regression model to test the significance of the relationship between dividend payout and the above mentioned theories from the literature. The dependent variable is the dividend payout ratio of the company, while the explanatory variables represent the proxies of

in Italy, deriving from the stocks traded on the Borsa Italiana MTA and MIV markets. It follows the Global Industry Classification Standard (GICS) and seeks to replicate the broad sector weights of the Italian stock market.

The IBEX 35 is the key stock market index designed to represent real-time evolution of the most liquid stock in the Spanish Stock Exchange Bolsa y Mercados Espanoles (BME), composed by the 35 most liquid securities listed on the Spanish Stock Exchange Interconnection System market segment of the Joint Stock Exchange System for the four Spanish Stock Exchanges called Main Trading Market.

The Nasdaq Stockholm OMX 30 (OMXS 30) is the main stock market index of the Swedish stock exchange Nasdaq OMX Stockholm (Stockholmsbörsen). It is composed by 30 blue-chip companies, following the ICB.

The PSI 20 is a stock market index that reflects the performance of the maximal 20 most actively traded shares listed on Euronext Lisbon. It covers the Blue-chip tradable companies, and is the most widely used indicator of the Portuguese stock market.

The Swiss Market Index (SMI) is the main stock market index of the Swiss stock exchange Six Swiss Exchange, composed by the 20 largest and most liquid stocks. It represents about 85% of the free-float capitalization of the Swiss equity market (Federation of European Security Exchanges 2015).

different dividend policy theories calculated in the prior year—agency cost theory, signaling theory, pecking order theory, and bird-in-the-hand theory. We insert as control variables the company size and liquidity both calculated in the prior year and also dummies relative to the year of the observation, the industry of the company, and the country of incorporation of the company. The model is run separately for each dividend policy theory. Precisely, we run the following five OLS regressions:

$$\text{Agency cost theory regression}: Y_{i,t} = \beta_0 + \beta_1 \text{Leverage}_{i,t-1} + \beta_2 \text{Control}_{i,t-1} \quad (9.1)$$

$$\text{Signaling theory regression 1}: Y_{i,t} = \beta_0 + \beta_1 \text{ROE}_{i,t-1} + \beta_2 \text{Control}_{i,t-1} \quad (9.2)$$

$$\text{Signaling theory regression 2}: Y_{i,t} = \beta_0 + \beta_1 \text{Volatility}_{i,t-1} + \beta_2 \text{Control}_{i,t-1} \quad (9.3)$$

$$\text{Pecking order theory regression}: Y_{i,t} = \beta_0 + \beta_1 \text{EV / market}_{i,t-1} + \beta_2 \text{Control}_{i,t-1} \quad (9.4)$$

$$\text{Bird-in-the-hand theory regression}: Y_{i,t} = \beta_0 + \beta_1 \text{Price / book}_{i,t-1} + \beta_2 \text{Control}_{i,t-1} \quad (9.5)$$

The analyses are conducted through the use of the Stata 11 software package.

The precise constructs of the variables analyzed are in Appendix (Table 9.4).

The descriptive statistics (mean, median, standard deviation, minimum, and maximum) for variables analyzed are reported in Table 9.1. As we can see from the table, the mean dividend payout ratio is 68.0937, and it ranges from 0 to more than 5,700 euros, with a standard deviation of 187.4479. The mean value for dividend payout ratio is greater for companies in OMXS30, followed by companies included in BEL20, IBEX35, and FTSE100. We highlight that all indexes analyzed present one or more companies paying no dividend.

The mean value of the leverage for companies analyzed is 228.1515. This ratio presents a great standard deviation (4,271.8065), as it goes from 0 to 100 times the mean value. The maximum value (236,546.0741) relates to a Spanish company in IBEX35.

Table 9.1 Descriptive statistics (no. of observations, mean, median, standard deviation, minimum and maximum) for the companies analyzed

	Obs	Mean	Std. dev.	Min	Max
Dividend payout ratio	2.82	680,937	1,874,479	0.0000	5707.5412
Leverage	3.14	2,281,515	4271.8065	0.0000	236,546.0741
ROE	3.08	172,190	309,803	−4,665,820	5,940,476
Volatility	2.93	327,317	142,301	87,350	1,659,600
EV/market	3.03	15,497	18,487	0.2298	665,942
Price/book	2.97	39,605	164,269	0.0856	6,467,119
Free cash flow	3.11	1191.7214	2929.1217	−28,067.0000	23,740.0000
LN Assets	3.17	93,646	15,150	38,057	128,278

Source: Our elaboration on Bloomberg database

The value of the ROE for companies analyzed is not always positive: It goes from a minimum value of −466% (exhibited by a company in CAC40) to a maximum value of 594% (presented by a company in FTSE100). In any case, the mean value is positive (17%) and the standard deviation is around 30.

The mean value of volatility for companies in the sample is 32.7317. This value is close to the mean value of volatility calculated separately for each country analyzed. In fact, the standard deviation of volatility is slight (14.2301). The minimum value of volatility is 8.7350, while the maximum value amounts to 165.9600.

The ratio between the enterprise value and market value presents a mean of 1.5497 and a standard deviation of 1.8487. Minimum and maximum values are respectively 0.2298 and 66.5942.

The price to book value of companies in the sample is greater than their enterprise value to market ratio, with a mean value of 3.9605, strongly influenced by the high values for companies in IBEX35 and FTSE100. It ranges from a minimum value of 0.0856 and a maximum value of 646.7119, with a standard deviation of 16.4269.

As regards the first control variable, the free cash flow takes a mean of more than one thousand (precisely 1,191.7214) included between a minimum (negative) value of −28,067 and a maximum value of 23,740 (both presented by companies in IBEX35). Due to the great variability of the free cash flow for companies in the sample, its standard deviation amounts to 2,929.1217.

Finally the natural logarithm of total assets has a mean of 9.3646 and a standard deviation of 1.5150. Minimum and maximum values are respectively 3.8057 and 12.8278.

4 Results

The results of the regressions are reported in Table 9.2.

From the analyses of the results it emerges that the agency cost theory is not verified, as the variable leverage has not a significant coefficient in the regression (9.1). It means that no agency problems should arise from the conflict between shareholders and management. The monitoring of investment professionals to managers' behavior is not necessary. Contrary to the previous literature we fail to find that increasing dividend payments might force managers to increase company leverage.

We found evidence to support the signaling theory, as we found positive significant value for the variables ROE (coefficient 0.0680, p-value 0.000***) in regression (9.2) and negative significant value for the variable Volatility (coefficient -0.6593; p-value 0.000***) in regression (9.3). These results demonstrate that the dividends possess information about companies' earnings, as well as their stability. Dividend payments have a function for the market, as they convey information for shareholders.

The negative signs combined with the statistical significances of the variable EV/market in regression (9.4) confirm the pecking order theory (coefficient −1.4995, p-value 0.000***). It follows that companies with great investment opportunities confirmed by the market do not distribute dividends. Although the presence of investment opportunities should be seen positively for companies' shareholders, their detrimental effects on dividend payments create negative consequence for companies' shareholders.

The results of the regression (9.5) highlight positive significant coefficient for the variable Price/book and provide evidence of the bird-in-the-hand theory (coefficient 0.1175, p-value 0.004***). In fact, companies paying higher dividends should be able to sell their shares at higher prices.

Table 9.2 OLS regression model with robust standard errors. Period of analyses: 2001–14 (panel data)

	Agency cost theory (1)	Signaling theory1 (2)	Signaling theory2 (3)	Pecking order theory (4)	Bird-in-the-hand theory (5)
Explanatory variables					
Leverage	−0.0001 (0.826)				
ROE		0.0680 (0.000***)			
Volatility			−0.6593 (0.000***)		
EV/market				−1.4995 (0.000***)	
Price/book					0.1175 (0.004***)
Control variables					
Free cash flow	0.0004 (0.019)	0.0003 (0.051**)	0.0003 (0.084*)	0.0004 (0.032**)	0.0004 (0.033**)
Ln assets	4.5429 (0.000***)	4.6298 (0.000***)	3.1582 (0.000***)	4.5614 (0.000***)	4.4062 (0.000***)
Country dummies	Yes	Yes	Yes	Yes	Yes
Industry dummies	Yes	Yes	Yes	Yes	Yes
Year dummies	Yes	Yes	Yes	Yes	Yes
Const.	13.6313 (0.001***)	11.1210 (0.011**)	40.4851 (0.000***)	15.1651 (0.000***)	14.6290 (0.001***)
No. of obs.	2734	2697	2600	2676	2630
Prob>F	0.0000	0.0000	0.0000	0.0000	0.0000

The dependent variable is the dividend payout ratio, while the regressors are Leverage, ROE, Volatility, EV/market, Price/book calculated in the prior year. We include as control variables size and liquidity in the prior year. Country dummies, industry dummies and year dummies are also included in the model. The model is run five times for different dividend policies theories. The sample includes 241 companies included in the main European stock market indexes

Source: Our elaboration on Bloomberg database

Coefficients and p-values (p-values in brackets). Statistical significance at the 1%, 5% and 10% levels is indicated by ***, ** and *, respectively

As a higher current dividend reduces uncertainty about future cash flows, dividends payout increase the share value and hence its price.

As regards the control variables, the free cash flow is significant, with a positive sign for almost all the regressions, while the natural logarithm of total assets is significant, again with positive sign and is significant for all five regressions. It follows that the liquidity and the size of a company both have a positive effect on dividend payment.

5 Conclusions

In this study we analyzed 241 companies included in the benchmark stock market indexes of the main European stock exchanges, namely BEL20, CAC40, DAX, FTSE100, FTSEMIB, IBEX35, OMXS30, PSI20 and SMI. We ran an OLS regression model with as dependent variable the dividend payout ratio, while as independent variables the most common proxies for dividend policy theories—that is agency cost theory, signaling theory, pecking order theory, bird-in-the-hand theory—with size and liquidity as controls.

Agency cost theory suggests that there is a conflict between shareholders and debt-holders. Managers raise capital from debt-holders and shareholders and debt-holders prefer constraint on dividend payments while shareholders prefer large dividend payments. In fact, debt-holders interests may not be protected when high levels of dividend are paid out. Rozeff (1982) suggests that, other things equal, companies with higher financial leverage tend to pay lower dividends to reduce the transaction costs associated with external financing. Jensen (1986) points out that debt can be used as a substitute device for dividends in reducing the agency costs. This means that a company with financial leverage will be monitored by its debt-holders and will have less discretionary funds available to its managers. Hence, highly leveraged companies are expected to pay lower dividends.

However, our results fail to demonstrate the main statement of the agency cost theory. We found that there is no equal repartition between debt-holders and shareholders of cash generated by the company. Managers tend to repay shareholders by distributing dividends as they want to come to the capital market and raise funds in the future, and hence need to establish a reputation as a good risk in order to convince future investors to give them money (Gomes 1996). In contrast, companies may establish reputations as good borrowers by repaying their short term loans (Diamond 1989, 1991). It follows that the expropriation of company funds through dividend payments reduces the amount of resources that debt-holders are willing to put up ex ante to finance the company. The main costs are that companies may be prevented from undertaking good projects because their reputations as low-quality borrowers keep them from raising additional funds in the debt market. Consequently, some covenants and constraints in the funding contracts are needed. Hence dividend restrictions should be implemented in debt covenants to alleviate this conflict (Kalay 1982).

It is important to note that legal protection of debt-holders' interests is often more effective than that of the shareholders', since default is a reasonably straightforward violation of a debt contract that a court can verify. In fact, unlike debt-holders, individual shareholders are not promised any payments in return for their financial investment in the company, so they receive dividends *at the discretion* of the board of directors. However, the courts in Organization for Economic Cooperation and Development (OECD) countries have generally accepted the idea of managers' duty of loyalty to shareholders—that is shareholder rights are supplemented by an affirmative duty for managers to act in the shareholders' interest. This is because shareholders have fewer protections from expropriation than the other stakeholders do and to induce them to invest in the first place, they need stronger protections ex ante, such as the duty of loyalty. On the other hand, the legal protection of debt-holders—although default is a reasonably straightforward violation of a debt contract that a court can verify—when the bankruptcy procedure gives companies the right of automatic stay of the debt-holders, managers can keep debt-holders at bay even after having defaulted. Debt-holders may be too soft because they fail to terminate unprofitable projects they have invested in when continuation is preferred to liquidation. Moreover, large debt-holders often have equity in the company; small debt-holders instead have no power to interfere in the major decisions of the company.

Furthermore, when managers are paid with stock option they prefer to distribute dividends in order to enhance the value of the stock of the company.

Our results are consistent with Naceur et al. (2006) who find that financial leverage has no impact on the dividend policy. This result does not confirm the common view that a risky firm pays out lower dividends in order to decrease its dependence on external financing but it reflects the idea set out by Fama and French (2001) where debt is the residual problem. Moreover, also Dong et al. (2005) and Maditinos et al. (2007) show results that do not support the agency theory whereby a company by paying dividends would be expected to raise additional capital through financial markets, hence subjecting it to the monitoring and disciplining of these markets.

Nevertheless, results provide evidence of the influence of the signaling theory in dividend distribution. It follows that dividends are a tool for managers in which to convey their private information to the market about the company's future incomes (Bhattacharya 1979; John and Williams 1985; Miller and Rock 1985). Results demonstrate that investors may understand company's future earnings through the dividend announcements, not only in terms of profitability, but also in terms of the stability of earnings (Hoberg and Prabhala 2009). Specifically, companies with higher volatility of their earnings pay lower dividends.

Moreover, as stated by the pecking order theory, we find that companies restrict dividend payments in the case of substantial investment opportunities (Myers 1984; Myers and Majluf 1984). This happens because companies whose investment prospects outstrip operating cash flows, and which cannot issue more debt, would miss out on good investments rather than issue risky securities to finance them.

Likewise, contrary to Miller and Modigliani (1961) and Bhattacharya (1979), we find a link between dividend payout and share price. In fact, companies paying higher dividends sell their shares at higher prices as investors prefer cash dividends to future capital gains (Gordon and Shapiro 1956; Gordon 1959, 1963).

In general, there are still many factors that influence the dividend distribution of European listed companies, confirming the Black's puzzle (1976). Anyway, the expropriation of company funds through dividend payments that reduces the resources that debt-holders are willing to put in the company, results in the need for more dividend constraint in the funding contracts.

We conclude our work with the limitation and the directions for future research. The most important limitation of this work is the statistical significance of the constant in the regressions. This means that there are important factors that are not included in the models. Moreover, we can further investigate the phenomena within the use of other methodologies and by adopting other measures of dividend payout. It can also be useful to analyze this issue outside Europe, e.g. studying S&P 100, Nasdaq 100, S&P ASX 200. Furthermore, it could be interesting analyzing the dividend policy by dividing the pre-crisis and post-crisis periods.

Appendix

Table 9.3 Dividend policy theories and proxies

Theory	Proxy	Expected sign	References [Author(s), year]
Agency cost theory	Financial leverage	–	Rozeff (1982), Jensen (1986)
Signaling theory	ROE	+	Bulan et al. (2007), Hoberg and Prabhala (2009)
Signaling theory	Volatility	–	Bulan et al. (2007), Hoberg and Prabhala (2009)
Pecking order theory	EV/market	+	Lintner (1956), Easterbrook (1984), Jensen (1986), Aivazian et al. (2003), Naceur et al. (2006)
Bird-in-the-hand theory	Price/book	+	Graham and Dodd (1934), Diamond (1967), Gordon and Shapiro (1956), Gordon (1963), Lintner (1962), Walter (1963)
Control variable	Natural logarithm of Total assets	+	Aivazian et al. (2003), Al-Malkawi (2008)
Control variable	Free cash flow	+	Petra et al. (2012)

Table 9.4 Data source and definition

Variable	Definition	Source
ROE	Return on equity. It is a profitability ratio that measures the ability of a company to generate profits from its shareholders investments in the company. It is calculated as follows: Net income/shareholders' equity. Bloomberg code: RETURN_COM_EQY	Bloomberg database
Leverage	Financial leverage. Ratio between total debt and total shareholders' capital, multiplied by 100 Total shareholders' capital is calculated as follows: Preferred shares + Minority Interest + Total ordinary shares. Total ordinary shares must exist and not be zero Bloomberg code: TOT_DEBT_TO_TOT_EQY	Bloomberg database
Volatility	Annualized standard deviation of the variation of share price calculated for the previous 360 days of negotiations. It is a percentage. Bloomberg code: VOLATILITY_360D	Bloomberg database
Price/book	Price Book Value Ratio. The relationship between the stock price and the book value per share. Calculated as follows: Last Price/Book Value per Share Last price: PX_LAST Book Value per Share: BOOK_VAL_PER_SH The calculation uses the data from the last reporting period (quarterly, half-yearly or yearly) Bloomberg code: PX_TO_BOOK_RATIO	Bloomberg database
Free cash flow	Cash flow from operating activities minus total capital expenditures. Capital expenses are the amount the company spends to purchase tangible fixed assets Bloomberg code: F_FREE_CASH_FLOW	Bloomberg database
LN assets	Total assets (natural logarithm). This account is equivalent to the total assets in the annual financial statements, except for facilities of public services net of deferred income tax. Deferred taxes on income are included in the balance sheet with claims or liabilities. Total assets are the sum of net investment property, cash and cash equivalents, other investments, accounts receivable, other assets and active bound Bloomberg code: BS_TOT_ASSET (natural logarithm)	Bloomberg database

(continued)

Table 9.4 (continued)

Variable	Definition	Source
Dividend payout ratio	Dividend payout ratio. Ratio between cash flow from ordinary dividends payment and Profit before extraordinary items—minority interest—cash preferred dividends Bloomberg code: D_PAYOUT_RATIO	Bloomberg database
D2001	Dummy variable that takes the value 1 if the observation of company's payout ratio is relative to 2001 and 0 otherwise	Bloomberg database
D2002	Dummy variable that takes the value 1 if the observation of company's payout ratio is relative to 2001 and 0 otherwise	Bloomberg database
D2003	Dummy variable that takes the value 1 if the observation of company's payout ratio is relative to 2001 and 0 otherwise	Bloomberg database
D2004	Dummy variable that takes the value 1 if the observation of company's payout ratio is relative to 2001 and 0 otherwise	Bloomberg database
D2005	Dummy variable that takes the value 1 if the observation of company's payout ratio is relative to 2001 and 0 otherwise	Bloomberg database
D2006	Dummy variable that takes the value 1 if the observation of company's payout ratio is relative to 2001 and 0 otherwise	Bloomberg database
D2007	Dummy variable that takes the value 1 if the observation of company's payout ratio is relative to 2001 and 0 otherwise	Bloomberg database
D2008	Dummy variable that takes the value 1 if the observation of company's payout ratio is relative to 2001 and 0 otherwise	Bloomberg database
D2009	Dummy variable that takes the value 1 if the observation of company's payout ratio is relative to 2001 and 0 otherwise	Bloomberg database
D2010	Dummy variable that takes the value 1 if the observation of company's payout ratio is relative to 2001 and 0 otherwise	Bloomberg database
D2011	Dummy variable that takes the value 1 if the observation of company's payout ratio is relative to 2001 and 0 otherwise	Bloomberg database
D2012	Dummy variable that takes the value 1 if the observation of company's payout ratio is relative to 2001 and 0 otherwise	Bloomberg database

(*continued*)

Table 9.4 (continued)

Variable	Definition	Source
D2013	Dummy variable that takes the value 1 if the observation of company's payout ratio is relative to 2001 and 0 otherwise	Bloomberg database
D2014	Dummy variable that takes the value 1 if the observation of company's payout ratio is relative to 2014 and 0 otherwise. Omitted for perfect collinearity with D2001, D2002, D2003, D2004, D2005, D2006, D2007, D2008, D2009, D2010, D2011, D2012 and D2013 and taken as benchmark	Bloomberg database
Dagricolture	Dummy variable that takes the value 1 if the company is active in the industry of agriculture and mining activities (Bloomberg two-digits NACE codes from 1 to 9) and 0 otherwise	Bloomberg database
Dtrade	Dummy variable that takes the value 1 if the company is active in the industry of trade (Bloomberg two-digits NACE codes from 45 to 47) and 0 otherwise	Bloomberg database
Dservices	Dummy variable that takes the value 1 if the company is active in the industry of services (Bloomberg two-digits NACE codes from 48 to 99) and 0 otherwise	Bloomberg database
Dmanufactury	Dummy variable that takes the value 1 if the company is active in the industry of manufactury (Bloomberg two-digits NACE codes from 10 to 43) and 0 otherwise. Omitted for perfect collinearity with Dagricolture, Dtrade and Dservices and taken as benchmark	Bloomberg database
DBelgium	Dummy variable that takes the value 1 if the company's country of incorporation is Belgium and 0 otherwise	Bloomberg database
DFrance	Dummy variable that takes the value 1 if the company's country of incorporation is France and 0 otherwise	Bloomberg database
DGermany	Dummy variable that takes the value 1 if the company's country of incorporation is Germany and 0 otherwise	Bloomberg database
DItaly	Dummy variable that takes the value 1 if the company's country of incorporation is Italy and 0 otherwise	Bloomberg database

(*continued*)

Table 9.4 (continued)

Variable	Definition	Source
DPortugal	Dummy variable that takes the value 1 if the company's country of incorporation is Portugal and 0 otherwise	Bloomberg database
DSpain	Dummy variable that takes the value 1 if the company's country of incorporation is Spain and 0 otherwise	Bloomberg database
DSweden	Dummy variable that takes the value 1 if the company's country of incorporation is Sweden and 0 otherwise	Bloomberg database
DSwitzerland	Dummy variable that takes the value 1 if the company's country of incorporation is Switzerland and 0 otherwise	Bloomberg database
DUK	Dummy variable that takes the value 1 if the company's country of incorporation is the UK and 0 otherwise. Omitted for perfect collinearity with DBelgium, DFrance, DGermany, DItaly, DPortugal, DSpain, DSweden and DSwitzerland and taken as benchmark	Bloomberg database

References

Aivazian, V., Booth, L., & Cleary, S. (2003). Do emerging market firms follow different dividend policies from the US firms? *Journal of Financial Research, 3*, 371–387.

Al-Malkawi, H. N. (2008). Factors influencing corporate dividend decision: Evidence from Jordanian panel data. *International Journal of Business, 13*, 177–195.

Bhattacharya, S. (1979). Imperfect information, dividend policy, and the bird in the hand fallacy. *Bell Journal of Economics, 10*, 259–270.

Black, F. (1976). The dividend puzzle. *Journal of Portfolio Management, 2*(2), 5–8.

Brealey, R., Myers, S., & Allen, F. (2008). *Principles of corporate finance*. New York: McGraw-Hill/Irwin.

Brennan, M. J. (1970). Taxes, market valuation and corporate financial policy. *National Tax Journal, 23*, 417–427.

Bulan, L., Subramanian, N., & Tanlu, L. (2007). On the timing of dividend initiations. *Financial Management, 36*, 31–65.

Diamond, J. J. (1967). Earnings distribution and the valuation of shares: Some recent evidence. *Journal of Financial and Quantitative Analysis, 2*(1), 15–30.

Diamond, D. (1989). Reputation acquisition in debt markets. *Journal of Political Economy, 97*, 828–862.

Diamond, D. (1991). Debt maturity structure and liquidity risk. *Quarterly Journal of Economics, 106*, 1027–1054.

Dong, M., Robinson, C., & Veld, C. (2005). Why individual investors want dividends. *Journal of Corporate Finance, 12*, 121–158.

Easterbrook, F. H. (1984). Two agency costs explanations of dividends. *American Economic Review, 74*, 650–659.

Fama, E. F., & French, K. R. (2001). Disappearing dividends: Changing firm characteristics or lower propensity to pay? *Journal of Financial Economics, 60*(1), 3–43.

Federation of European Security Exchanges. (2015). *Index database*. Available at http://www.fese.eu/statistics-market-research/index-database/. Accessed on June 2015.

Gomes, A. (1996). *Dynamics of stock prices, manager ownership, and private benefits of control*. Manuscript, Harvard University.

Gordon, M. J. (1959). Dividends, earnings, and stock prices. *The Review of Economics and Statistics, 41*, 99–105.

Gordon, M. J. (1963). Optimal investment and financing policy. *The Journal of Finance, 18*(2), 264–272.

Gordon, M. J., & Shapiro, E. (1956). Capital equipment analysis: The required rate of profit. *Management Science, 3*(1), 102–110.

Graham, B., & Dodd, D. L. (1934). *Security analysis: Principles and technique*. New York/London: McGraw-Hill.

Grullon, G., Michaely, R., & Swaminathan, B. (2002). Are dividend changes a sign of firm maturity? *The Journal of Business, 75*(3), 387–424.

Ho, H. (2003). Dividend policies in Australia and Japan. *International Advances in Economic Research, 9*(2), 91–100.

Hoberg, G., & Prabhala, N. R. (2009). Disappearing dividends, catering and risk. *Review of Financial Studies, 22*, 79–116.

Jensen, M. C. (1986). Agency costs of free cash flow, corporate finance and takeovers. *American Economic Review, 76*, 323–329.

Jensen, M. C., & Meckling, W. H. (1976). Theory of the firm: Managerial behavior, agency costs and ownership structure. *Journal of Financial Economics, 3*, 305–360.

John, K., & Williams, J. (1985). Dividends, dilution, and taxes: A signaling equilibrium. *The Journal of Finance, 40*(4), 1053–1070.

Kalay, A. (1982). Stockholder-bondholder conflict and dividend constraints. *Journal of Financial Economics, 10*, 211–233.

Lease, R. C., Kose, J., Kalay, A., Loewenstein, U., & Sarig, O. H. (2000). *Dividend policy: Its impact on firm value*. Boston: Harvard Business School Press.

Lintner, J. (1956). Distribution of incomes of corporation among dividends, retained earnings and taxes. *American Economic Review, 46*, 97–113.

Lintner, J. (1962). Dividends, earnings, leverage, stock prices and the supply of capital to corporations. *Review of Economics and Statistics, 44*(3), 243–269.

Lloyd, W. P., Jahera, J. S., & Page, D. E. (1985). Agency costs and dividend payout ratios, *Quarterly Journal of Business and Economics, 24*(3), 19–29.

Maditinos, D. I., Sevic, Z., Theriou, N. G., & Tsinani, A. V. (2007). Individual investors' perceptions towards dividends: The case of Greece. *International Journal of Monetary Economics and Finance, 1*, 18–31.

Mancinelli, L., & Ozkan, A. (2006). Ownership structure and dividend policy: Evidence from Italian firms. *European Journal of Finance, 12*(03), 265–282.

Miller, M. H., & Modigliani, F. (1961). Dividend policy, growth, and the valuation of shares. *The Journal of Business, 34*(4), 411–433.

Miller, M. H., & Rock, K. (1985). Dividend policy under asymmetric information. *Journal of Finance, 40*, 1031–1051.

Murgia, M. (1993). Struttura della proprietà, conflitti d'interesse e politica dei dividenti delle imprese italiana. *L'industria, 14*, 109–125.

Myers, S. C. (1984). The capital structure puzzle. *Journal of Finance, 39*, 575–592.

Myers, S. C., & Majluf, N. S. (1984). Corporate financing and investment decisions when firms have information that investors do not have. *Journal of Financial Economics, 13*, 187–221.

Naceur, S. B., Goaied, M., & Belanes, A. (2006). On the determinants and dynamics of dividend policy. *International Review of Finance, 6*, 1–23.

Patra, T., Poshawake, S., & Ow-Yong, K. (2012). Determinants of corporate dividend policy in Greece. *Applied Financial Economics, 22*, 1079–1087.

Rozeff, M. (1982). Growth, beta and agency costs as determinants of dividend payout ratios. *Journal of Financial Research, 5*, 249–259.

Von Eije, H., & Megginson, W. L. (2007). Global Privatization Advisory Committee, Italian Ministry of Economics and Finance.

Walter, J. E. (1963). Dividend policy: Its influence on the value of the enterprise. *The Journal of Finance, 18*(2), 280–291.

10

Long-Range Financial Decision-Making: The Role of *Episodic Prospection*

Gianni Brighetti, Caterina Lucarelli, Nicoletta Marinelli, and Giulia Giansiracusa

1 Introduction

Humans are generally engaged in farsighted decisions that involve a mind-set involving mental time travel. The conscious awareness of subjective time is summarized by the concept of chronesthesia (Tulving 1983, 2002) and refers to the ability to be aware of one's past and future, although mental time travel is particularly related to planning for the future. Projection towards the future, in neuroscience, is referred to as

G. Brighetti • G. Giansiracusa
University of Bologna, Bologna, Italy

C. Lucarelli (✉)
Università Politecnica delle Marche, Ancona, Italy
e-mail: c.lucarelli@univpm.it

N. Marinelli
University of Macerata, Macerata, Italy

S. Carbó Valverde et al. (eds.), *Bank Funding, Financial Instruments and Decision-Making in the Banking Industry*, Palgrave Macmillan Studies in Banking and Financial Institutions,
DOI 10.1007/978-3-319-30701-5_10

the faculty of *prospection*, that can take two different forms: On the one hand, *episodic prospection* "refers to the capacity to mentally project oneself into the future to pre-experience a spatiotemporally specific event"; on the other hand, *semantic prospection* "refers to the capacity to imagine facts and general conceptual knowledge free of context and personal significance" (Race et al. 2013, p. 268; Suddendorf and Corballis 2007).

Within the realms of economics and finance, future projection frequently relates to consumption decisions. The stability of life-long consumption has been frequently related to the human ability to undertake long-range decision-making, which includes attitudes towards saving and the ability to plan retirement protection schemes. Nevertheless, surveys have revealed strong evidence that a significant proportion of people fail to take care of their long-range well-being via adequate saving or participation in voluntary retirement schemes; a phenomenon that has persisted over time and across countries.

Such evidence casts some doubts on the functioning of human prospection as well as on the issue of "rationality" in long-range decision-making. The term "rational" takes on various meanings in different disciplines, but in economics it refers to a condition of compliance to a normative model and its axioms (Kalenscher and Pennartz 2008).

In this field, preference over time has been modelled by the Discounted Utility Theory (DUT), as the normative model for intertemporal decision-making (Samuelson 1937). Empirical observation of intertemporal choices of both humans and animals consistently reveals violations of several DUT's assumptions, giving rise to debates within psychological literature (see, for example: Loewenstein 1988, 1992; Prelec and Loewenstein 1991). Time-inconsistent preferences generally emerge when observing the devaluation of outcomes over time (temporal discounting) that do not follow a constant discounting function, but rather hyperbolic discounting (see, for example: Ainslie 1992; Ainslie and Haslam 1992; Laibson 1997; Strotz 1956; Thaler 1981).

In this paper, we argue that time-inconsistent preferences are sensitive to the type of prospection involved. Given that episodic prospection increases the subjective importance of a future reward (Benoit et al. 2011), we investigate if and how it can effectively attenuate human biases of temporal discounting.

We devised an experimental task that required a sample of young individuals to make farsighted decisions (N = 77; 40 Germans and 33 Italians; average age 22 years, range 18–30). Decisions referred to future scenarios and required individuals to engage their episodic prospection that is the vivid and concrete imagining of delayed rewards. We offered future scenarios associated to three distinct domains, characterized as: First priority (job), secondary priority (saving for a treat), and entertainment (travelling). Existing literature indicates the role of episodic prospection in attenuating temporal discounting (Benoit et al. 2011). We further the debate by hypothesizing that this human faculty, and its engagement in imagining future events, is able to reduce hyperbolic discounting bias. Moreover, we explore whether certain personality traits correlate with the tendency to care about the future, and whether cultural and environmental conditions, such as belonging to a different "nation" (in this case, Germany *vs.* Italy) may influence the role of episodic prospection, thus affecting the ability to undertake sound long-range decisions.

2 Conceptual Framework: Exponential Versus Hyperbolic Discounting

Several theoretical and experimental studies have identified certain difficulties that people experience when making decisions involving future benefits, for example, when comparing immediate versus delayed rewards or two delayed rewards of different value. These are referred to as time-inconsistent preferences, and suggest the occurrence of "irrational" intertemporal decision-making since a number of the DUT assumptions are violated. First of all, the stationarity axiom is violated, since individuals prefer a small short-delayed reward over a large long-delayed reward; but when the delays to both rewards are shifted in the future by the same time interval, their preference is reversed away from the small towards the large reward (Prelec and Loewenstein 1991; Frederick et al. 2002). Preference reversals implicate the violation of a further DUT assumption in terms of constant discounting. A "rational" individual, according to the DUT axiom, should hold a neutral attitude towards time delay, as implicated, for example, by exponential discounting:

$$V = \frac{A}{(1+k)^D} = A(1+k)^{-D} \approx Ae^{k'D}, k' = ln(1+k) \tag{10.1}$$

where V is the temporally discounted reward value (utility); A is the amount of expected reward; D is the delay between response and reward, k and k' are different discount rates in discrete and continuous time, respectively.

Preference reversals, as discussed above, cannot be explained by a constant discounting function, such as the exponential discounting of (10.1), because they imply a different impact of delay depending on when it occurs. This structure of preference is related to a hyperbolic discounting of values along time. Since the seminal work of Ainslie (1975), and the later theoretical and empirical work by Mazur (Mazur 2007; Mazur and Biondi 2009) and others (Thaler 1981)—to quote just a small selection of the vast literature on the topic—inter-temporal behaviors in humans, but also in animals, are now described by a hyperbolic model:

$$V = \frac{A}{1+kD} \tag{10.2}$$

Although some disagreement exists regarding which discounting function (hyperbolic or exponential) best describes the effect of delayed rewards (Mazur and Biondi 2009), recent general theory from behavioral neuroscience on intertemporal decision-making predicts it to be hyperbolic (Namboodiri et al. 2014).

In this paper, we investigate whether the perception of oneself, stimulated by means of episodic prospection, is able to influence the ability to undertake human farsighted decisions, and to improve its"rationality". Existing literature (Benoit et al. 2011) indicates that when chronesthesia exploits the episodic prospection, it is able to attenuate temporal discounting, that is the propensity to devalue rewards that are only delivered following a delay. Our research furthers the discourse by asking whether a context involving episodic prospection induces individuals to show exponential rather than hyperbolic discounting processes, thus stimulating sound long-term decision-making.

3 Methods

Our experiment was designed to investigate the role of episodic prospection in intertemporal choices, and required participants to vividly imagine future rewards. The role of personality traits, mutually influenced by the subjects' environmental conditions, was also considered.

We addressed our experimental task towards a sample population of young people (aged 18–30 years), since subjects in this relatively early stage of life tend to exhibit a greater capacity for mental time travel. The same experimental protocol was performed using two subsamples of young individuals, belonging to two different European countries characterized by noticeably different economic conditions, especially in terms of youth employability perception: Germany and Italy. The experiment was conducted in the summer/autumn period of 2014.

3.1 Sample

The recruitment criteria for the task are strictly compliant with the goals of the research. The two experimental groups are based on a difference in "nationality", and it was held that individuals comprising each group had been exposed to: A common culture, a common language, common social conditions, and common juridical conditions (that is German *vs.* Italian citizens). Participants were excluded if they did not meet the following demographic conditions:

- Condition 1: born and raised in the country in question (that is in Germany or Italy);
- Condition 2: German or Italian mother-tongue;
- Condition 3: both parents also consistent with conditions 1 and 2;
- Condition 4: aged between 18 and 30 years;
- Condition 5: living out of the family context (for example students living in a different city from that of their families; young workers that have left the family home, and so on)

Recruitment involved the University of Heidelberg in Germany and the University of Bologna in Italy, and involved the posting of advertizements on student notice boards and the web (social networks). We recruited 40 German subjects and 33 Italian subjects. The average age for the sample was 22 years. The experimental task was run in July 2014 in Germany and in October 2014 in Italy.

In Germany, enrolled students were rewarded with extra credits for participation in research activities or with money (7.50 Euros, provided by the University of Heidelberg); while in Italy individuals were compensated in the form of an additional grade for a curricular exam.

3.2 Experimental Task

The task was organized into two phases: The experimental assignment; and the assessment of personality traits.

The experimental assignment is based on an interactive decision-making process, where each interviewee is asked to make a set of choices regarding delayed future rewards across monthly periods (t); the choices are made by negotiating with the experimenter and recorded into a Matlab interface. Episodic prospection is employed to imagine future scenarios that simulate real-life situations that the interviewees, for their age, are expected to be familiar with. We deliberately selected individuals with no specialized knowledge, experience, or skills in relation to economics or finance in order to detect evidence of spontaneous discounting that is not distorted by any technical framing.

We compared three alternative domains, defined by descending priority levels: (i) a first priority domain (job), described by the scenario—*Loan to the interviewee's employer*; (ii) a secondary priority domain, solicited in the scenario—*Saving for a treat;* and (iii) an entertainment domain, depicted in the scenario—*Travelling*. The choice of these domains also influenced the selection of the two European countries considered (Germany and Italy) as observation areas; young people from these countries are shaped by different economic perspectives, thus offering two valid experimental fields within which to investigate reactions to different domains, especially those related to the first priority.

Before answering, each participant was asked, and continuously reminded by the experimenter, to consider the situation as if it were real, and not a simulation. Appendix A provides a detailed description of the experimental assignment.

At the end of this phase, the interviewee was asked to fill out three questionnaires in order to gather information about the individual's personal traits: the Ruminative Response Scale (RRS), the Zimbardo Time Perspective Inventory (STPI) and the Worry Domain Questionnaire (WDQ).

The Rumination Response Scale includes 22 items "...describing responses to depressed mood that are self-focused ... symptom-focused ... and focused on the possible consequences and causes of the mood..." (Nolen-Houseman et al. 1999, p. 1064). Respondents rate each questionnaire item on a scale from one (almost never) to four (almost always).[1] Although rumination in considered a form of thinking found in different pathologies and largely present in humans, it is most often related to depressive mood (Nolen-Hoeksema 1991; Watkins and Nolen-Hoeksema 2014) and has consistently been linked to negative effects. Here, we consider depressive rumination as a particular response style that interferes with a problem solving mind-set, and that tends to enhance pessimism and perseverative cognitions. Therefore, we expect that the higher the rumination, the lower the attitude to plan and self-project into the future.

The Zimbardo Time Perspective Inventory (STPI) provides an easy way to measure multiple time perspectives as individual temporal profiles (D'Alessio et al. 2003; Orkibi 2015). It is built on a theoretical basis considering social, cognitive, and motivational emotional processes that are assumed to mutually influence time perspectives. Not very distant from the concept of chronesthesia, here the concrete representation of the present lies between the abstract psychological constructions of prior past and anticipated future events. The STPI offers

[1] Interviewers read the following instructions to participants: '*People think and do many different things when they feel sad, blue or depressed. I'm going to read a list of possibilities. Turn to the next scale in your book and please tell me if you never, sometimes, often, or always think or do each one when you feel down, sad or depressed. Please indicate what you generally do, and not what you think you should do.*'

a standard measure of the individual time perspective. This subjective temporal orientation is deduced by scores of five different specific scales: positive past, negative past, hedonistic present, fatalistic present, and future. We mainly focused on the last scale. We expect those revealing a high score for the future scale to exhibit a greater propensity to self-project into the future.

Finally, the Worry Domain Questionnaire is an instrument that measures the level of worry (Tallis et al. 1992). The WDQ is designed to assess different facets of worry and consists of 25 items referring to worries regarding relationships, lack of confidence, aimless future, work incompetence, and finances. Items are scored on a five-point scale, with total scores ranging from zero to 100 (Tallis et al. 1992). We expected that higher worry scores would correlate with lower abilities to self-project into the future.

3.3 Experimental Values

For each scenario, the interviewee was asked to make a decision, choosing between two reward formats: one is small, one-off, and immediately available; the other one is bigger than the immediate one, but available only in the future, the deferral time of which could vary. We also set an indifference condition where values of the two reinforces are equal:

$$V = A_t \tag{10.3}$$

V stands for the standard alternative, that is the amount of money available *now*, and A_t refers to the adjusting alternative at time t. The specific framing of our task does not require interviewees to decide a present value (discounted value), but rather the alternative set of monetary rewards *delayed* by t (A_t) that make them indifferent between the two reinforces. The time t can range from one (one month) to 19 periods (rescaled time: 19 periods = 10 years).

Consequently, our experimental values reveal evidence of a capitalization process, rather than a discounting process. Hence, formulas (10.1) and (10.2) need to be reverted, using the corresponding exponential (10.4) or linear capitalization function (10.5):

$$A_t = Ve^{k't} \tag{10.4}$$

$$A_t = V(1 + kt) \tag{10.5}$$

where V is the amount of money available now; A_t are the competing future rewards, declared by interviewees to be indifferent respect to V after time periods t, k and k' representing individually different capitalization interest rates. Precisely, V = 900 Euros in the scenario "Loan to the interviewee's employer"; V = 300 in the scenario "Travelling"; and V = 50 in the scenario "Saving for a treat". The set of A_t for the three scenarios are the experimental values collected from individuals. Considering these values, we tested the presence of an exponential, rather than hyperbolic, discounting process by checking whether the distribution of the experimental values along time was best fitted by (10.4) or by (10.5).

Figure 10.1 offers two examples of capitalization functions underlying experimental values collected from two interviewees (Subject x and Subject y) for two of the three scenarios. The R-square of each capitalization function (linear *vs.* exponential) applied to experimental choices indicates which is the prevailing discounting process "implicit" in the interviewee's responses. As discussed above, a linear capitalization function implies a reverse hyperbolic discounting process, while an exponential capitalization function indicates an exponential discounting process. These R-square values will be used as evidence to answer the paper's research questions described in the following section.

Subject y: scenario "Loan to your employer"	Subject x: scenario "Travelling"
$A_s = 900\text{euros}$	$A_s = 300\text{euros}$
Fig. 10.1a	Fig. 10.1b

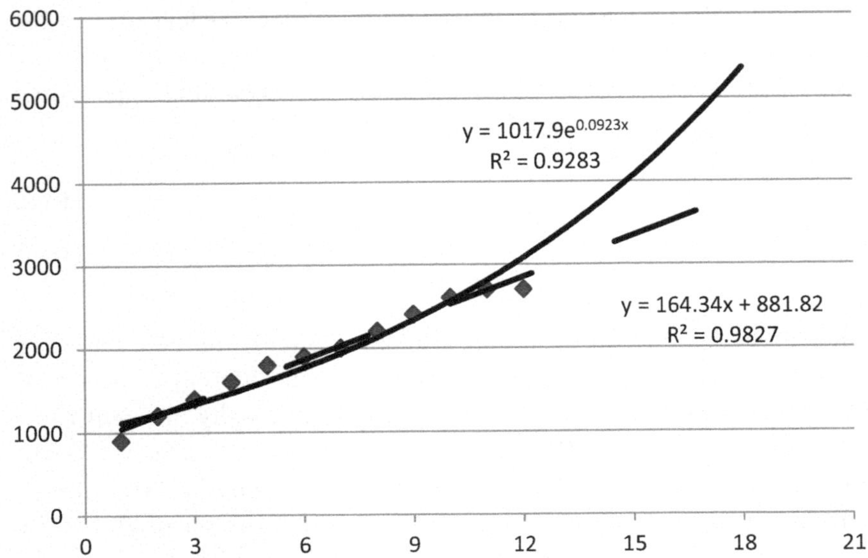

Fig. 10.1a Capitalization functions fitting to experimental choices (*Note:* The *red line* plots the trend of experimental values using a linear capitalization function, thus revealing the fit to 'implicit' (reverse) hyperbolic discounting; the *blue line* makes use of an exponential capitalization function for the same purpose, thus revealing the fit to 'implicit' exponential discounting)

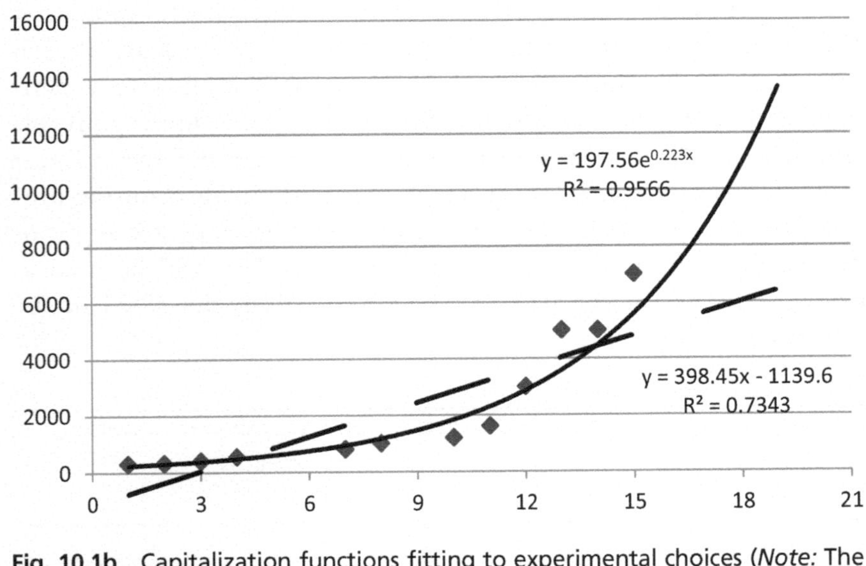

Fig. 10.1b Capitalization functions fitting to experimental choices (*Note:* The *red line* plots the trend of experimental values using a linear capitalization function, thus revealing the fit to 'implicit' (reverse) hyperbolic discounting; the *blue line* makes use of an exponential capitalization function for the same purpose, thus revealing the fit to 'implicit' exponential discounting)

3.4 Research Hypotheses

Our paper investigates whether and to what extent episodic prospection is able to render long-range decision-making more "rational". We expect to find a non-negligible presence of exponential discounting processes that is "rational" farsighted decision-making, among participants performing our experimental task, where episodic prospection is employed as the choice framework. Nonetheless, the role of episodic prospection may vary according to the solicited domain and the relative level of priority. A higher level of urgency related to the need involved should intensify the participants' attention towards the task, thus catalyzing the role of episodic prospection in rendering the expected future vivid and real. As a consequence, our first hypothesis is as follows:

H1

we expect a larger dominance of exponential discounting (rational) respect to hyperbolic discounting (not compliant with rationality) when considering first priority domains, respect to the alternatives.

Data on the socio-economic conditions of the two countries analyzed (Germany *vs.* Italy) might offer further insight in favour, or against, H1. From the EUROSTAT Labour Force on-line survey database (EUROSTAT 2014), we could derive that unemployment rates in people aged 15–24 years stand at 7.9 per cent in Germany and 40.0 per cent in Italy; in people aged 15–39 years, unemployment rates are 6.3 per cent in Germany and 18.6 per cent in Italy. Moreover, the 2013 Global Entrepreneurship Monitor (GEM 2013), concerning entrepreneurial attitudes and perceptions, reports that perceived opportunities refer to 31.3 per cent of the population (18–64 years) in Germany, and 17.3 per cent of the population (18–64 ages) in Italy; fear of (entrepreneurial) failure affects 38.6 per cent of the population in Germany, and 48.6 per cent of the population in Italy. This data allow us to set a specification of H1:

H1.A

when considering a first priority domain, we expect to observe a larger dominance of exponential discounting (rational) respect to hyperbolic discounting (not compliant with rationality) in the national environment in which the relative need is perceived more severely.

Additionally, we investigated whether some personal traits relate to an individual's personal predisposition to care about the future. Thus, we set the following three hypotheses considering the outstanding literature described in the previous section.

We expect to observe a larger dominance of exponential discounting (rational) respect to hyperbolic discounting (not compliant with rationality):

H2.A

the greater the future scale in the individual's temporal profile, as higher scores on this scale indicate a strong inclination to take action, not for their own immediate sake, but with more far-sighted vision.

H2.B

the lower the rumination, as rumination may work as an "anchor" to the present.

H2.C

the lower the individual's level of worry, as worry may couple with rumination in the overestimation of the present.

4 Results

4.1 Episodic Prospection: Efficacy

We ran a descriptive data analysis in order to investigate whether episodic prospection helps to reduce long-range choice inefficiencies, when in the form of a hyperbolic (not compliant with rationality) discounting function.

First, we compared the explanatory power (R-squared- *R2*) of an exponential capitalization function when fitting individual choice patterns with the corresponding explanatory power of a linear function. It is important to remember that both capitalization processes (exponential *vs.* linear) correspond to an exponential discounting form rather than a hyperbolic one. Hence, hereinafter we discuss our findings in terms of discounting, rather than capitalization, in order to be consistent with the theoretical background.

The results, reported in Table 10.1, show that the number of individuals, for whom an exponential discounting function fits the choice pattern

Table 10.1 Explanatory power of exponential vs. hyperbolic discounting function

	First priority		Secondary priority		Entertainment
	Scenario		Scenario		Scenario
	'Loan to employer'		'Saving for a treat'		'Travelling'
Number of individuals (valid cases)	67		52		
Individuals with R2-exp > R2-hyp	45		28		
(%)	*–67%*		–54%		
	Mean	**Std. Dev.**	**Mean**	**Std. Dev.**	
R2 exponential discount. function	0.869	0.134	0.887	0.182	
R2 hyperbolic discount. function	0.853	0.134	0.863	0.197	

Note: The sample population involved n = 73 individuals. However, the first row indicates the number of 'valid' cases considered, that is cases where individuals provided a series of At long enough to estimate discounting functions. The second row shows the number of valid cases whose choice patterns, in terms of series of At, are best described by an exponential rather than a hyperbolic discounting function. The third row shows the percentage of valid cases where R2-exp > R-hyp. Finally, the basic statistics (mean and standard deviation) for the R2 values are shown for the exponential and hyperbolic discounting functions

better than the hyperbolic one, is non-negligible for all three domains. The explanatory power of the exponential discounting function (*R2-exp*) is, on average, greater than that of the alternative function (*R2-hyp*), suggesting that hyperbolic discounting, when used to interpolate data, returns a poorer representation of the pattern of choices. The highest percentage of individuals showing a *R2-exp* higher than *R2-hyp* refers to the *first priority domain (job)*, calculated as 67 per cent of respondents.

This evidence is in support of H1.

Our analysis also addresses the potential influence of social and economic environments on intertemporal choices. Hence, the percentages of cases that are best fitted by an exponential function were also calculated according to nationality (German vs. Italian). The expected result is defined by H1.A.

In contrast to our expectations, we can see that the percentage of Italians whose responses are best described by exponential discounting, in relation to the *first priority domain (job)*, is lower (64 per cent) than

Table 10.2 Explanatory power of exponential vs. hyperbolic discounting function by nationality

	First priority		Secondary priority		Entertainment	
	Scenario 'Loan to employer		Scenario 'Saving for a treat'		Scenario 'Travelling'	
	German	Italian	German	Italian	German	Italian
Number of individuals (valid cases)	34	33	37	15	38	32
Individuals with R2-exp > R2-hyp	24	21	20	8	19	10
(%)	71%	64%	54%	53%	50%	31%

Note: Results refer to 40 individuals from Germany and 33 individuals from Italy. The first row indicates the number of 'valid' cases, that is cases where individuals provided a series of At long enough to estimate discounting functions. The second row shows the number of valid cases hose choice patterns, in terms of series of At, are best described by an exponential rather than a hyperbolic discounting function. The third row shows the percentage of valid cases where R2-exp > R2-hyp

the corresponding percentage for German interviewees (71 per cent). Consequently, H1.A is rejected.

Nevertheless, note that the dominance of German over Italian individuals, concerning the variable "Individuals with R2-exp > R2-hyp" (Table 10.2), is persistent in all three domains, suggesting a greater tendency of Germans to exhibit "compliant with rationality" behavior compared with Italians (Henrich et al. 2002).

The second set of hypotheses tested examined the influence of certain personality traits on the ability to exploit the power of prospection in making "rational" intertemporal choices. Hence, for each personality trait (future orientation, rumination or worry), we divided the individuals according to whether their values were above or below the sample median, generating two subsamples (that is future orientated *vs.* not future orientated; high *vs.* low rumination; and high *vs.* low worry); then, we assessed the percentage of cases in each subsample that were best predicted by an exponential discounting function rather than by a hyperbolic discounting function. The results are reported in Table 10.3.

The hypothesis relative to the future orientation of individuals (H2.A) is largely confirmed: for the tasks "Loan to your employer" and "Saving for a

Table 10.3 Exponential discounting and individual features

		First priorities Scenario 'Loan to employer'	Secondary priorities Scenario 'Saving for a treat'	Entertainment Scenario 'Travelling'
Future oriented	N. individuals (valid cases)	**32**	**25**	**34**
	Individuals with R2-exp>R2-hyp	24	14	13
	(%)	–75%	–56%	–38%
Not future oriented	N. individuals (valid cases)	**35**	**27**	**36**
	Individuals with R2-exp>R2-hyp	21	14	16
	(%)	–60%	–52%	–44%
High rumination	N. individuals (valid cases)	**29**	**24**	**30**
	Individuals with R2-exp>R2-hyp	19	12	15
	(%)	–66%	–50%	–50%
Low rumination	N. individuals (valid cases)	**38**	**28**	**40**
	Individuals with R2-exp>R2-hyp	26	16	14
	(%)	–68%	–57%	–35%
High worry	N. individuals (valid cases)	**34**	**20**	**34**
	Individuals with R2-exp>R2-hyp	23	12	13
	(%)	–68%	–60%	–38%
Low worry	N. individuals (valid cases)	**33**	**32**	**36**
	Individuals with R2-exp>R2-hyp	22	16	16
	(%)	–67%	–50%	–44%
Whole sample	N. individuals (valid cases)	**67**	**52**	**70**
	Individuals with R2-exp>R2-hyp	45	28	29
	(%)	–67%	–54%	–41%

Note: This Tables reports percentage of individuals whose choice patterns are best described by an exponential discounting function rather than a hyperbolic

(*continued*)

Table 10.3 (continued)

discounting function for each population subsample. Precisely, for each psychological test we compared pair-wise subsamples: in the Zimbardo Time Perspective Inventory, we considered the subsamples of 'Future oriented' and 'Not future oriented' individuals, which correspond to subjects with a test score 'higher' and 'lower' than the sample median, respectively. In the Zimbardo Time Perspective Inventory, we considered the subsamples of 'High rumination' and 'Low rumination' individuals, corresponding to people with a level of rumination 'higher' and 'lower' than the sample median, respectively. Finally, in the Worry Domain Questionnaire, we analysed the subsamples of 'High worry' and 'Low worry' individuals, defined as subjects with test scores 'higher' and 'lower' than the sample median, respectively

treat", we observe that the percentages of cases best fitted by an exponential function were higher among people with future orientation behavioral traits (75 per cent and 56 per cent, respectively), compared to those defined as "Not future orientated" (60 per cent and 52 per cent, respectively). The reverse is true for the task "Travelling", for which the higher percentage is observed for the subsample of subjects "Not future oriented" (44 per cent). The same trend holds for the second personality trait (rumination): In the tasks "Loan to your employer" and "Saving for a treat", the percentage of cases best fitted by an exponential function was higher for people with choice patterns characterized by levels of mental rumination that were below the median (68 per cent and 57 per cent respectively), as we expected (H2.B). Conversely, for the task "Travelling" we observed the opposite trend (50 per cent for mental rumination above the median score, compared with 35 per cent for mental rumination below the median score). More contradictory results were obtained for the third personality trait (worry): Only for the task "Travelling" do we observe a higher percentage of cases that are best fitted by an exponential function among people with a levels of worry below the sample median, thus supporting our hypothesis (H2.C.); the evidence relating to the other two tasks, on the other hand, are not in line with our expectations.

4.2 Episodic Prospection: Limits

An interesting aspect of our experiment is related to its specific framing, which allowed interviewees to either exploit the maximum future time span available (19 periods corresponding to 10 years), or to interrupt their choices, after a given time frame. This feature of the experiment explores the willingness of individuals to embrace long time frames when self-projecting into the future. Paradoxically, the use of *episodic* (concrete) *prospection*, rather than *semantic* (vague, not individually-specific) *prospection,* may exacerbate the inability of a subject to self-project in the "distant" future.

For each scenario, we calculated the "number of periods" an individual was able to cope with, in absolute terms and relative to the overall "number of periods" proposed (Table 10.4). We observed that people projected themselves an average of only seven, five and eight steps forward in the three scenarios, respectively, corresponding to a projection of eight, five and 12 months, respectively. In relative terms, this means that, on average, individuals were unwilling to accept a number of delays that exceeded half the maximum projection proposed, especially for the task "Saving for a treat", where the percentage

Table 10.4 Inability to self-project into the 'distant' future

Variable	Obs.	Mean	Std. Dev.	Min	Max
'Loan to your employer'					
Accepted periods (n. of steps)	73	7.75	4.41	0	17
Accepted periods (% total steps)	73	40.81	0.23	0	89.47
N. cases with no projection into the future	6 *(−11%)*				
'Saving for a treat'					
Accepted periods (n. of steps)	73	5.14	4.24	0	14
Accepted periods (% total steps)	73	27.04	0.22	0	73.68
N. cases with no projection into the future	21 *(−31%)*				
'Travelling'					
Accepted periods (n. of steps)	73	8.95	3.61	0	18
Accepted periods (% total steps)	73	47.08	0.19	0	94.74
N. cases with no projection into the future	3 *(−6.7%)*				

Note: This Table reports the descriptive statistics for the number of periods individuals were able to accept in relation to self-projection into the future. The maximum number of periods proposed was 19. For each scenario, the first row describes the number of periods accepted by interviewees in terms of number of steps forward. The second row summarises the same information in percentage terms, as a ratio between the number of periods accepted and the total number of steps proposed. Finally, the third row reports the number of individuals that do not accept any delay beyond today, thus revealing an inability to self-project into the future; the relative percentage is specified below in parentheses

Table 10.5 Inability to self-project into the 'distant' future: A comparison of Germany vs. Italy

	First priorities		Secondary priorities		Entertainment	
	Scenario		Scenario		Scenario	
	'Loan to employer'		'Saving for a treat'		'Travelling'	
	Deutsche	Italian	Deutsche	Italian	Deutsche	Italian
N. cases with no projection into the future	6	0	3	18	2	1
(%)	15%	0%	7.50%	54.55%	5%	3%

Note: Results refer to 40 individuals from Germany and 33 individuals from Italy

of accepted periods was only 27 per cent of the maximum. For the sake of completeness, we also report the number of individuals that were unwilling to project themselves into the future, that is unable to express any preference beyond today: the maximum number of cases with no projection into the future was again observed for the task "Saving for a treat" (31 per cent).

Table 10.5 presents the data for individuals with no projection into the future according to nationality. We note that *none* of the Italians interviewed were unable to self-project into the future, demonstrating their commitment to the task in hand and particular sensitivity towards personal involvement in the job market.

5 Discussion and Concluding Remarks

The results obtained from experimental analysis are mixed, confirming our research hypotheses in a selective way. Overall, our experimental setting reveals an undoubted role of episodic prospection in human decision-making, which induces a more "rational" attitude towards decision-making: in two of the three scenarios considered, the majority of participants show choice patterns that fitted better to an exponential (rational) discounting function than a hyperbolic (not-compliant-with-rationality) discounting function. *This was particularly true if the solicited scenario referred to a primary need (that is a first priority).* These results imply that the vivid representation of future events could be used as a *"nudge" or stimulate sound long-term decision-making, with clear implications for both policy makers and the financial industry.*

Nevertheless, caution is necessary, because we also provide evidence showing that this "nudging" effect may be enhanced or weakened according to specific personality traits and environmental conditioning; it may also change in relation to the kind of domain being projected into the future (that is first priority, secondary priority, or entertainment).

Finally, as an ancillary result, we found that the more vivid the self-projection in terms of real-life situations, the more likely individuals were to refuse concrete forms of self-projection into the future. This suggests that the sample population tended to feel *uncomfortable* thinking about themselves realistically in the "distant" future, or are at least less *willing* to do so. Thus, under certain conditions, episodic prospection could reverse its role and constrain far-sighted decision-making.

Acknowledgements We thank Graziella Pacelli, Luca Guerrini, Alberto Niccoli for helpful suggestions and comments.

Appendix A: Task-Instructions

Introduction presented by the experimenter:

> *"During the following scenarios, we are going to simulate some real-life situations—that most people your age will face at some point: you will be asked to make decisions in relation to the three scenarios, which regard the following fields: Work, consumption goods, and travel.*
>
> *In each scenario, your task is to make a decision. You have to choose between two rewards: One is small and immediately available, and the other one is bigger and only available in the future.*
>
> *Remember, you must consider every scenario as if it were real and not a simulation. So before you answer, try to imagine that the situation is occurring right now and real-life decisions are being taken.*
>
> *Is everything clear? Ok, let's start!"*

Scenario 1[2]: "Travelling" (Negotiation With the Experimenter, Who Plays the Role of Website Manager)

"For months you have been writing your opinions on a website, in which users are invited to post their opinions about the services they have used. Specifically, you have posted your opinions about the hotels, restaurants and clubs you visited during your recent trips. Now, the company owning this website wants to reward you because of the "usefulness" and the "high quality" of the opinions you posted. The prize is a sum of 300 Euros, offered by the online company in order for you to book another trip with them. However, the website offers you a choice: You can accept the 300 Euros now, and spend them immediately (within the next week), or you can decline the prize, but keep on writing your opinions and accumulate additional points in order to negotiate an even bigger future prize.

Here's an example: If the website offers you 300 Euros now, but you choose to decline it in preference of waiting another month, for example, for an even bigger prize, you have to tell the website how much money would you like to receive after the additional month of posting your opinions. Remember, you're making a deal with the website; that means that the website will only accept your counter-offer if it is reasonable and fair.

The amount that you request must be reasonable: Try to imagine that the situation is really happening (for example, requesting 5000 Euros after a month is not reasonable! In such a case, the proposal will be refused and you will lose all opportunity to win the monetary credit to spend on travelling because you have already refused the initial 300 Euros offer)."

Note: The entire amount of money awarded must be spent on a single holiday (that includes all of the following: Transport, food, accommodation, souvenirs, entertainment, and so on. For example, if you have for example a friend who lives in London and can host you, it does not qualify and you will not receive money in relation to accommodation).

[2] This is the actual order in which scenarios were presented during the task; it does not depend on further economic interpretation.

Every time you make a choice, please think about how you will spend the money realistically (ask yourself, for example: Where do I want to travel? By train, bus, plane…? How many days? Alone or with another person? Where could I sleep and eat?). Remember that the situation is supposed to be real, so your planned holiday is not hypothetical but real!

Is everything clear? Ok, let's start.'

The interviewer receives the Matlab interface, negotiates his/her choices, and then inserts them into the computer, as shown in Fig. 10.2.

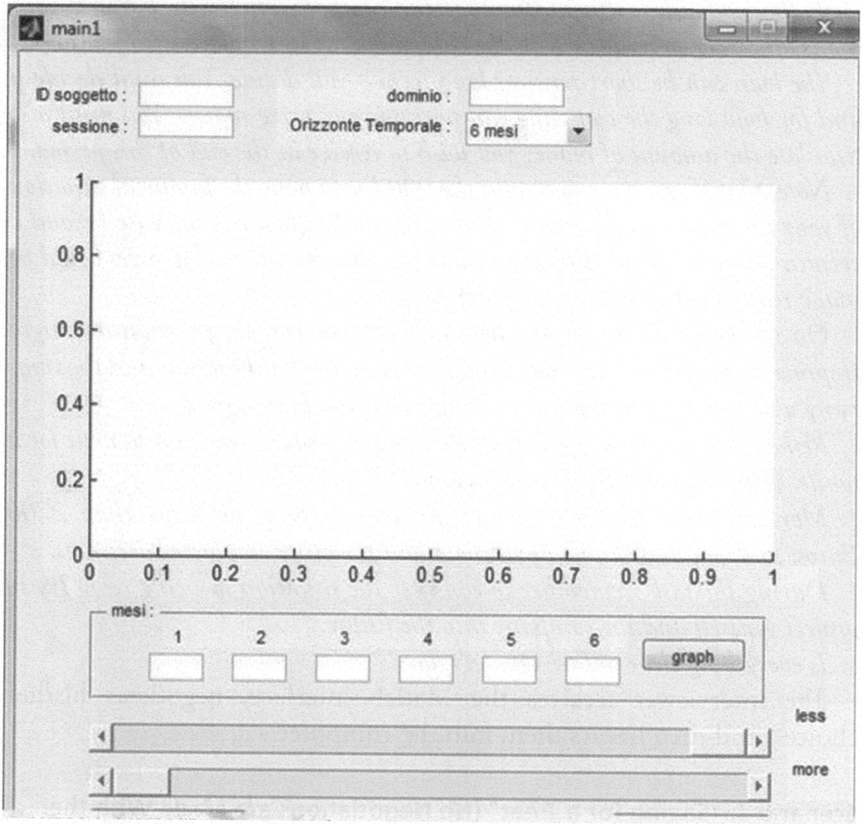

Fig. 10.2 Matlab interface (*Source:* Authors elaboration)

Scenario 2: "Loan to Your Company' (Negotiation With the Experimenter, Who Plays the Role of Company Director)"

"Imagine that you are an employee working in my company, so I'm your boss.

During the last months, you and other employees proved to be very proficient at your work, and you all won a prize as the best employees of the year. The prize that each employee is offered is 900 Euros. The company has chosen to offer you this prize, despite its present financial difficulties.

This is your boss's offer: You can accept 900 Euros immediately and spend it whenever and however you want, or you can choose to "leave it for a while" with the company—this means that the company effectively borrows your money in order to reinvest it in the company and its employees (so you too).

The loan can be short-term or long-term—you decide. You must decide if and for how long the company can borrow your prize money. You must also stipulate the amount of money you wish to receive at the end of this period.

Note, that if you chose to receive the 900 Euros now, the financial situation of your company could worsen; if the financial difficulties increase beyond a certain point, the possibility exists that you and the other employees could be made redundant in a few months' time.

On the other hand, if you chose to wait, the company's situation might improve in the future and that would, in part, be thanks to you and the company will pay you the amount of money that you have agreed.

Remember, if you choose to lend the company your prize and to wait for a while, your counter-offer must be reasonable and fair.

Moreover, note that you cannot ask the company for more than 2700 Euros, and you don't know anything about the other employees' decisions.

During the task, remember to consider the situation as being real. Try to project yourself and the company into the future.

Is everything clear so far? Ok, let's start!"

The interviewer receives the Matlab interface, negotiates his/her choices, and then inserts them into the computer.

Scenario 3: "Saving for a Treat" (No Negotiations are Made With the Experimenter: Autonomous Decision-Making)

"Over recent months you've worked hard and managed to save 50 Euros. You're up to date with payments (rent, food, taxes… everything that concerns your personal maintenance), so you're thinking about giving yourself a treat.

You also consider another alternative: You could wait a while longer, for example, one month more, keep on saving money end give yourself a later, but bigger treat. What would you prefer?

When you make your decision, please think realistically about what you would like to buy (for example: do you want to treat yourself to a new pair of shoes, sunglasses, shirt or dress, and so on). You can also choose to spend your savings on a present for another person.

If you choose to save money for an additional six months, for example, please consider carefully how much money you would realistically be able to save in that time: That means that you have to consider your monthly income and all of your future payments.

nIs everything clear so far? Ok, let's start!"

The interviewer receives the Matlab interface, makes his/her choices, and then inserts them into the computer.

References

Ainslie, G. (1975). Specious reward: A behavioral theory of impulsiveness and impulse control. *Psychological Bulletin, 82*(4), 463–496.

Ainslie, G. (1992). *Picoeconomics: The strategic interaction of successive motivational states*. Cambridge: Cambridge University Press.

Ainslie, G., & Haslam, N. (1992). Self-control. In G. Loewenstein & J. Elster (Eds.), *Choice over time*. New York: Russell Sage.

Benoit, R. G., Gilbert, S. J., & Burgess, P. W. (2011). A neural mechanism mediating the impact of episodic prospection on farsighted decisions. *Journal of Neuroscience, 31*(18), 6771–6779.

D'Alessio, M., Guarino, A., De Pascalis, V., & Zimbardo, P. G. (2003). Testing Zimbardo's Stanford Time Perspective Inventory (STPI)–Short form: An Italian study. *Time and Society, 12*(2–3), 333–347.

EUROSTAT. (2014). *European Union labour force survey*. Available at: http://ec.europa.eu/eurostat/web/microdata/european-union-labour-force-survey.

Frederick, S., Loewenstein, G. F., & O'Donoghue, T. (2002). Time discounting and time preference: A critical review. *Journal of Economic Literature, 40*(2), 351–401.

GEM. (2013). *Global entrepreneurship monitor*. Available at: http://www.gemconsortium.org/docs/3106/gem-2013-global-report.

Henrich, J., Albers, W., Boyd, R., Gigerenzer, G., McCabe, K. A., Ockenfels, A., et al. (2002). Group report: What is the role of culture in bounded rationality? In G. Gigerenzer & R. Selten (Eds.), *Bounded rationality. The adapriove toolbox*. Cambridge, MA: MIT Press.

Kalenscher, T., & Pennartz, C. M. A. (2008). Is a bird in the hand worth two in the future? The neuroeconomics of intertemporal decision-making. *Progress in Neurobiology, 84*(3), 284–315.

Laibson, D. (1997). Golden eggs and hyperbolic discounting. *The Quarterly Journal of Economics, 112*(2), 443–478.

Loewenstein, G. F. (1988). Frames of mind in intertemporal choice. *Management Science, 34*(1), 200–214.

Loewenstein, G. F. (1992). The fall and rise of psychological explanations in the economics of intertemporal choice. In G. Loewenstein & J. Elster (Eds.), *Choice over time*. New York: Russell Sage.

Mazur, J. E. (2007). Choice in a successive-encounters procedure and hyperbolic decay of reinforcement. *Journal of the Experimental Analysis of Behavior, 88*(1), 73–85.

Mazur, J. E., & Biondi, D. R. (2009). Delay-amount trade offs in choices by pigeons and rats: Hyperbolic versus exponential discounting. *Journal of the Experimental Analysis of Behavior, 91*(2), 197–211.

Namboodiri, V. M. Y., Mihalas, S., Marton, T. M., & Shuler, M. G. H. (2014). A general theory of interpemporal decision-making and the perception of time. *Frontiers in Behavioral Neuroscience, 8*(61), 1–18.

Nolen-Hoeksema, S. (1991). Responses to depression and their effects on the duration of depressive episodes. *Journal of Abnormal Psychology, 100*(4), 569–582.

Nolen-Hoeksema, S., Larson, J., & Grayson, C. (1999). Explaining the gender difference in depressive symptoms. *Journal of Personality and Social Psychology, 77*(5), 1061–1072.

Orkibi, H. (2015). Psychometric properties of the Hebrew short version of the Zimbardo Time Perspective Inventory. *Evaluation & the Health Professions, 38*(2), 219–245.

Prelec, D., & Loewenstein, G. F. (1991). Decision making over time and under uncertainty: A common approach. *Management Science, 37*(7), 770–786.

Race, E., Keane, M. M., & Verfaellie, M. (2013). Losing sight of the future: Impaired semantic prospection following medial temporal lobe lesions. *Hippocampus, 23*(4), 268–277.

Samuelson, P. A. (1937). A note on measurement of utility. *Review of Economic Studies, 4*(2), 155–161.
Strotz, R. H. (1956). Myopia and inconsistency in dynamic utility maximization. *The Review of Economic Studies, 23*(3), 165–180.
Suddendorf, T., & Corballis, M. C. (2007). The evolution of foresight: What is mental time travel, and is it unique to humans? *Behavioral and Brain Sciences, 30*(3), 299–313.
Tallis, F., Eysenck, M., & Mathews, A. (1992). A questionnaire for the measurement of nonpathological worry. *Personality and Individual Differences, 13*(2), 16–168.
Thaler, R. (1981). Some empirical evidence on dynamic inconsistency. *Economic Letters, 8*(3), 201–207.
Tulving, E. (1983). *Elements of episodic memory*. New York: Oxford University Press.
Tulving, E. (2002). Chronesthesia: Awareness of subjective time. In D. T. Stuss & R. C. Knight (Eds.), *Principles of frontal lobe function*. New York: Oxford University Press.
Watkins, E. R., & Nolen-Hoeksema, S. (2014). A habit-goal framework of depressive rumination. *Journal of Abnormal Psychology, 123*(1), 24–34.

Index

S. Carbó Valverde et al. (eds.), *Bank Funding, Financial Instruments and Decision-Making in the Banking Industry*, Palgrave Macmillan Studies in Banking and Financial Institutions,
DOI 10.1007/978-3-319-30701-5

The manufacturer's authorised representative in the EU is Springer Nature Customer Service Centre GmbH, Europaplatz 3, 69115 Heidelberg, Germany. If you have any concerns regarding our products, please contact ProductSafety@springernature.com

Printed and bound by CPI Group (UK) Ltd, Croydon, CR0 4YY
25/09/2026
02222849-0007